IMPERIALISM
AND
DEPENDENCY

IMPERIALISM AND DEPENDENCY

Obstacles to African Development

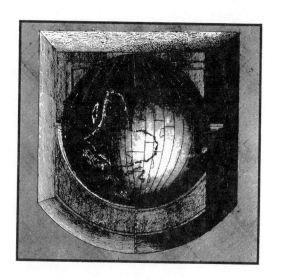

DANIEL A. OFFIONG

HOWARD UNIVERSITY PRESS
WASHINGTON, D.C. 1982

Copyright © 1982 by Daniel A. Offiong. First published in the United States in 1982 by Howard University Press. Published in 1980 by Fourth Dimension Press.

Printed in the United States of America.

Library of Congress Cataloging in Publication Data

Offiong, Daniel A.
  Imperialism and dependency.

  Includes index.
  1. Africa—Foreign economic relations.   2. Africa—
Dependency on foreign countries.   3. Africa—Colonial
influence.   4. Underdeveloped areas.   5. Imperialism.
  I. Title
HF1611.O35 1982   338.96   82-15833 1982
ISBN 0-88258-126-0
ISBN 0-88258-127-9 (pbk.)

For

Asukwo
Essen
Akon
and Aniefiok

CONTENTS

LIST OF TABLES

PREFACE

This book is an attempt to contribute to the debate on the problems of Third World development. In rejecting the bourgeois sociologists' explanation of Third World underdevelopment, I have turned to the dependency model for my explanation. Despite the subtitle of the book, I have freely drawn from Third World countries outside Africa.

I have given a great deal of attention to the analysis of the methods and techniques used by the monopoly capitalists to impoverish the Third World. My position is that if something is to be done to ameliorate our present conditions of underdevelopment, the methods and techniques used to accomplish our exploitation must be fully comprehended. I have also given appropriate space to the analysis of those whom Frantz Fanon has referred to as "phantom bourgeoisie" because it is emphasised that without these internal collaborators or compradors our exploitation would not have reached its present level.

The problems of underdevelopment discussed in this book are colossal and herculean but this does not mean that underdeveloped countries are condemned to eternal damnation. But by the same token the solution to these problems requires great dynamism, foresight, courage, and sometimes risks.

I am thankful to the editorial staff of Fourth Dimension Publishing Co. for their encouragement. I am grateful to their very articulate anonymous reader for his review of the draft manuscript. His comments and criticisms have helped in improving the quality of this book. But all errors in judgment and facts are entirely mine.

Finally, my thanks also go to my typists, particularly Mr. Samuel A. Edu, Mr. O. Iwok, and Mrs. Grace Anwana, my student, and my other office staff who helped in some ways. I want to thank my wife, Bassey, and our children for their patience and understanding during the long days and nights I spent working on this book.

INTRODUCTION

The United Nations General Assembly resolution 1710 (XVI) designated the 1960s as the United Nations Development Decade. The objective of the First Development Decade was to

> accelerate progress towards self-sustaining growth of the economy of the individual nations and their social advancement so as to attain in each underdeveloped country a substantial increase in the rate of growth, with each country setting its own target, taking as the objective a minimum rate of growth of aggregate national income, of 5 per cent at the end of the decade.[1]

Much of the ideological warfare (cold war) which reached its climax in the 1960s was fought over development, that is, to determine whether the so-called "Free World Model" (capitalism) or the "Communist Model" (communism) would be adopted by the developing nations.

At the time the Secretary-General (SG) wrote his reports, the estimate of the growth rate of national incomes of all developing countries, together, was about 3 1/2 per cent a year. The "immediate task," apparently by the developing countries, was to raise the figure by about 1 1/2 per cent within a few years and by another 1 1/ 2 per cent to get it over 6 per cent per annum at the end of the decade. The SG stated rather emphatically that almost "all the underdeveloped countries have in their physical and human resources the potential means for achieving decent standards of living for their people." "The problem," according to him "is to mobilize these latent physical and human resources and get them into production."[2] He further stated that the United Nations (U.N.) knew for a fact that "careful development planning" could be "a potent means of mobilizing these latent resources by a rational solution of the problems involved."[3]

In order for the objective of the Development Decade to be achieved, the SG enumerated six "tasks" which had to be accomplished. These were:

1. The more systematic survey, development and utilization of physical and human resources in the underdeveloped countries;
2. The formulation of true development plans providing for maximum mobilization of domestic resources and the effective utilization of external assistance;
3. An improvement in the machinary of administration, in institutions and in production incentives in order to meet the new and increased demands arising from these development plans;
4. A redirection of science and technology to increase the attention given to specific problems of low-income countries;
5. An increase, and subsequent more vigorous growth, of the export earnings of underdeveloped countries;
6. An increased and a more assured flow of capital on suitable terms to the underdeveloped countries, to be further added to if the declaration adopted in General Assembly resolution 724 (VIII) is put into effect.[4]

According to the economists of the First Development Decade, a developing society was one in which its per capita

2

income and gross national product were advancing. If a country whose per capita was ₦75 should embark on policies that would increase that per capita income to, say, ₦100 within four years or so, that country was developing. By the same token, if the gross national product, that is, the sum total of goods and services exchanged within a society, should increase, that also was a measure of development. By these criteria the annual growth of the developing countries taken together passed the margin mark of 5 per cent and their per capita income rose appreciably, at least in some countries; for example, Mexico had its per capita income raised from $488 in 1960 to $717 a year in 1972. The GNP of the same country grew by 9 per cent per year. On the basis of the prevailing theories of the Development Decade, countries that demonstrated such economic growth had reached the so-called "take-off" stage in development. Their increasing levels of economic activity, it was hoped, would propel them into the twentieth century and that their abject penury would become a thing of the past.

In all this, however, it should be pointed out that while growth of total product and income per head had been quite impressive in the First Development Decade in many developing countries, Africa had lagged behind. As noted earlier, growth in all developing countries in this period had passed the 5 per cent mark and growth per head was 2.4 per cent. The least developing countries in Europe realised the highest growth rates of 7.1 total, 5.6 per head.

At the same time our continent which harbours many of the least developed countries, recorded the lowest growth rates of 3.1 total and 0.9 per head. Between 1965 and 1968 total GDP grew annually by 3.3 per cent and GDP per head grew by a dismal 0.5 per cent. It was reported that income per head in some African countries actually declined over this period. Libya, Nigeria and Liberia were the only three African countries that featured among those developing or underdeveloped countries with growth records of 6 per cent or better per annum.[5] Nigeria registered a growth rate of 12 per cent. It should be added that it has been established that it is largely those countries in which income levels are relatively high which have higher growth rates, while the least developed countries have been recording the lowest growth rates. Africa has 21 of the 27 countries with lowest GDP per head. Of about 40 developing countries in Africa, 21 of them are among those with lowest national income per head in the world.[6]

That total African growth in the First Development Decade lagged behind those of other developing areas does not mean that African growth was stagnant. But the one important lesson that was learned in the First Development Decade was that despite significant economic growth in a few developing countries it had become crystal clear that the gap between rich and poor countries was widening. The disparity of growth rates within the developing countries implied that gaps in income per head was also widening between very poor and not terribly poor countries. Various studies by the U.N. and other international bodies confirmed the persistence of global poverty. It became common knowledge that, to between 40 percent and 60 percent of the world's population, the First Development Decade did not bring them job opportunities and better purchasing power. In a World Bank survey of income-distribution patterns in poor countries around the world, Adelman and Morries[7] established that development along the lines of the First Development Decade showed a "striking" increase in incomes, in both absolute and relative terms, of the richest 5 per cent while the share of the poorest 40 per cent actually shrank. While such gross economic indicators as GNP showed that the countries were really developing, millions that made up the bottom 40 per cent of the population did not have enough to eat, had less to wear, and also lived in worse housing than their parents had. Even though Libya and Liberia were doing very well in terms of their economic growth, most people in these countries were not doing well at all. For example, in Liberia, significant economic growth merely means much better living standard for a handful of Americo-Liberians whereas those they insultingly refer to as tribal peoples or natives continue to languish in abject poverty.

It is paramountly important to note that while the underdeveloped countries fulfilled their 5 per cent growth target during the First Development Decade, the rich and powerful countries did not fulfill the 1 per cent of GNP target for financing development in the underdeveloped countries. Despite the fact that the flow of governmental aid and private funds nearly doubled, increasing from $8.6 billion in 1960-62 to $14.7 billion in 1970, their GNP increased at a faster rate, so that the proportion of GNP transferred fell from 0.95 per cent in 1970. Furthermore, governmental aid declined from 0.52 to 0.34 per cent of GNP, and promises to "unite" aid were not fulfilled. Up to 1969 United States aid accounted for 50 per cent of the total supplied by the 16 member countries of the Organization for Economic Cooperation and Development (OECD) although this amounted to a declining proportion of its GNP. In 1970 the U.S. proportion declined to 40 per cent and this trend has been constant.[8]

On the basis of this disappointing performance and also on the basis of the World Bank's Pearson Report, the General Assembly of the U.N. adopted by acclamation, in October, 1970, a Development Strategy for the Second Development Decade, which set new targets for growth by the underdeveloped countries and for aid from the rich countries.

The underdeveloped countries are asked to achieve an overall growth rate of 6 per cent, and a per capita rate of 3.5 per cent. This time the U.N. takes into consideration the population explosion, a 2.5 per cent growth rate having been assumed. It is assumed that a 3.5 per cent growth rate would "represent a doubling of average income per head in the course of two decades." The underdeveloped countries are expected to expand expenditure on research and development to 0.5 per cent of their GNP by 1980.

On the other hand, the rich countries were asked to transfer a minimum of 1 per cent of their GNP by 1972 but not later than 1975 to increase the component of governmental aid to 0.7 per cent of the 1 per cent by 1975, to "unite" bilateral aid, to "soften" the terms of loans and to see to it that debt crises do not result in the underdeveloped countries' repayments of loans.[9] The rich countries were further asked to increase "to the fullest extent possible" the volume of aid given through multilateral channels. By this statement, the U.N. evaded the Pearson Report's recommendation that such aids be increased from 10 to 20 per cent. The rich countries have also been asked to substantially increase their aid for the direct support of science and technology in the underdeveloped countries during this Second Decade of Development. The underdeveloped countries attach a great importance to this particular measure because they believe it to be a means through which they would begin to liberate themselves from "technological colonialism." At this moment only one miserable per cent of all the research and development in the world has to do with the problems of the underdeveloped countries, while 50 per cent is concentrated on military and space matters.[10] What the U.N. document did was to outline a global development strategy in which the rich and powerful and the poor and underdeveloped countries would work together as partners in promoting integrated and comprehensive development. The document also proposed certain objectives with regard to education, health, nutrition, reform of land tenure, housing and employment, and affirmed that growth must be accompanied by social justice, in order that its benefits may be enjoyed by all concerned.

The poor countries interpreted the U.N. document as a sort of "moral and political commitment." The rich countries also accepted this interpretation. The document was interpreted by the group of 77 (the non-aligned nations) as "the best possible reflection of the present stage of the collective conscience of mankind in one of the most crucial areas of organising human society."[11]

Sadly enough, there is no indication that the rich countries have shown any serious intention of implementing their "moral and political commitment." By 1971, the total level of governmental aid given by the OECD countries increased from 0.34 per cent of their GNP in 1970 to 0.35 per cent. In his comment on this bastardly performance by the rich countries, Mr. McNamara, President of the World Bank, said:

> The collective GNP of the developed countries in 1970 totaled roughly $2,000 billion. In constant prices, it is projected to grow to at least $3,000 billion by 1980... in order to raise the current (OECD) flows of 0.35 per cent to the targeted 0.7 per cent, the developed countries would need to devote only about 1.5 per cent of the amount by which they themselves will grow richer during the decade. The remaining 98.5 per cent will provide them with sufficient funds to meet their domestic priorities ... Are we to say seriously that these wealthy countries cannot reach the ... target of 0.7 per cent of their combined GNPs? It is manifestly not a case of their not being able to afford it.[12]

In 1970 world expenditure on armaments passed $200 billion mark. In 1971 a U.N. report had observed thus:

> It would take only a 5 per cent shift of current expenditure on arms to development to make it possible to approach the official targets for aid. A more substantial curtailment of the arms race would permit for the first time the kind of massive transfer of resources which could make a fundamental change in the

prospects for social and economic development. The volume of fixed investment in the developing countries is estimated to have been around $ 65 billion in 1969. A shift of 10 per cent from world military expenditure to investment would provide enough resources to raise the figure by almost one third.[13]

That the rich countries had begun to harden their attitude towards their "moral commitment" became apparent at the third meeting of UNCTAD, which was held at Santiago, Chile in April-May, 1972. Previously in 1964 and 1968, the rich countries had expressed their willingness to make some concessions. But in 1972 in Santiago their attitude became very defensive. They either rejected or evaded demands from the underdeveloped countries for more agreements to stabilize the prices of primary products; for further reduction of tariffs or non-tariff trade barriers, for assistance to enable them to diversify their exports; for some kind of debt relief; for an international code to regulate shipping charges which would take their interest into consideration — the underdeveloped countries own only 7.4 per cent of the world's shipping but provide 41 per cent of the world's total cargoes; for the reform of the international monetary system that would take interest of the underdeveloped countries into account; for the untying of aid, and for a promise to meet the aid targets of the Second Development Decade.

The evasiveness of the rich countries continued during the fourth UNCTAD meeting held in Nairobi, Kenya in May, 1976. Apparently alluding to threats of oil and other raw material boycotts as well as to the demands for better international economic order from the underdeveloped countries, the U.S. Secretary of State, Henry A. Kissinger, boasted, "The United States, better than almost any other nation, could survive a period of economic warfare. We can resist confrontation and rhetorical attacks if other nations choose that path. And we can ignore unrealistic proposals and preemptory demands."[14] Although Kissinger talked about "a collective moral responsibility" to assist the underdeveloped countries by increasing resource flows, by improving their terms, by enhancing their quality, by giving aids softer terms since "the poorest countries are by definition unable to service debts except on a highly concessional basis,"[15] these goals have remained a vision yet to be realized.

What could be said to be the achievement of the UNCTAD meeting in Nairobi was the near absence of confrontation between the rich and the underdeveloped countries. Despite the sometimes threatening tone of Kissinger's speech, his was a key event. Although he did not give up the American assumption that development or sustained economic growth was the ultimate answer to the problem of world poverty, he did admit that the disparity between rich and poor was a serious issue for international politics and he did offer to meet some of the demands made by UNCTAD. On behalf of the U.S., Kissinger proposed assistance in the area of technology, such as stopping the "brain drain" and sharing new technology for exploiting the deep sea bed. But as already stated, these promises are yet to be matched by performance.

The rich nations have tended to stall on trade liberalization and monetary reform because they want these matters dealt with in General Agreement on Tariffs and Trade (GATT) and International Monetary Fund (IMF), both bodies strongly under their control. They are yet to agree on an UNCTAD scheme for "Market Sharing" whereupon they would allocate a proportion of their markets to the underdeveloped countries by reducing their own protected production. The Director General of the United Nations Food and Agriculture Organization had estimated that if the rich nations were willing to cut down their self-sufficiency in temperate agricultural products by 2 per cent, this would make available to the underdeveloped world a share in their market totaling $4 billion dollars a year. In reaction to this the rich countries have said that this arrangement would be against the working of the free-enterprise system.

The Pearson Report had assumed that an expanded amount of aid would help in bridging the gap between the rich and the underdeveloped countries. The Report further assumed that such aid would bring the underdeveloped countries within two or three more decades to the so-called take-off point of development.

But the rich countries despite their platitudes, have not really committed themselves. In the words of Waterlow,

> There is a general disillusion with aid. The substantial achievements — the useful capital projects which have sprouted all over the poor countries; the valuable surveys of most major problems; the vital research which has, for example, produced the Green Revolution — are overshadowed in the public and often in the official mind by the glaring failures: the unrepaired tractors rusting in the fields; the unneeded prestige projects; the waste and incompetence and corruption. Critics in the rich countries overlook the fact that they themselves are partly responsible for those failures by giving their aid in uncoordinated and partisan ways, by not relating it fully to the developing countries' real needs, which in many countries are now more clearly identifiable as planning techniques improve.[16]

But fundamentally, the disillusionment lies in the fact that a great part of aid has been counterproductive or "imperialistic," in relation to the actual goals of development, because the tendency is to supply it to regimes which anxiously want to promote quantitative economic growth through some rapid industrialization, which tends to benefit the internal elite and their international allies, than to carry out social reforms which benefit the masses. Once a government that dedicates itself to social justice emerges, this is likely to involve the replacement of a feudal or conservative middle-class regime (allied with international capitalists) by a socialistic one, sometimes by force. Such socialistic regimes often expropriate the private companies of the rich countries. The fear that socialistic regimes would expropriate their companies, the fear that "communism" will infiltrate and that Russian and/or Chinese economic and political aid might infiltrate, tend to encourage Western aid-giving countries to bolster up reactionary regimes.

> The twenty billion dollars in aid offered to Latin American countries by the United States under the Alliance for Progress of 1961 was, for example, made conditional upon the carrying out of land tenure, taxation, health and educational reforms. But regimes such as those of Chile and Peru, which have been seriously undertaking such reforms, have disqualified themselves for American aid by their expropriation policies, while rightwing dictatorships such as those of Brazil, South Korea and the Philippines, which have pushed up economic growth at the expense of social progress, have received substantial aid. Even international capital-aid organizations such as the World Bank and the International Monetary Fund ... whose objectives are strictly nonpolitical, are affected by this attitude, since they raise their funds through and operate within the free-enterprise economy. They are thus naturally inclined to help governments which concentrate on financial stability and economic growth — which may involve neglecting social policies.[17]

These words were written in 1974 but the U.S. foreign policy has not changed. For many years the U.S. aided and abetted the repressive regime of Emperor Haile Selassie of Ethiopia. The U.S. was solidly behind Portugal in her colonial wars in Africa and when the defeat of Portugal was

11

imminent, the U.S. created and backed a reactionary leader who would protect U.S. imperial interests in Angola. Zaire offers an excellent example of how the U.S. has gone out of its way to support a repressive regime since this encourages the exploitation of the people. In South Africa, the U.S. is solidly behind what happens there. The case of Chile which is given some attention here is a good example of how the U.S. can topple a constitutionally elected government to set up a dictatorship in order to enhance its imperialistic interests.

Russian and East European aid policies can be styled "imperialistic" in a different way. Their aid policies attempt to tie the recipient country's economy to their own by demanding that payment must be in locally produced goods, such as Egyptian and Sudanese cotton, which they buy at cheap prices and then sell on the world markets at higher prices. The underdeveloped countries are thus deprived of their ability to earn hard currency, and at the same time may be compelled to buy their goods at inflated prices. But we should hasten to add that this work does not concern itself with this brand of Soviet imperialism. The West colonized Africa and also commands dominant control over these supposedly independent states. The analysis of this book therefore is on the relationship between primarily Africa and generally the underdeveloped world on one hand and the West on another.

Returning again to the problem of aid, it is not an exaggeration to say that aid rather than solving the problems of the underdeveloped world instead exacerbates them. As Madeira Keita of Mali had noted:

> If we agree that there must be investment in
> Africa — since Africa has not had the time to build
> up capital — if we want to construct the country, we
> need not only technical resources but also financial
> resources. If on the international (institution) plane, we

can find the minimum external aid we need, we shall accept it. If other public capital is ready to help us we shall accept it, too. But I think it is logical to ask on what conditions we accept investment and what is the programme to be implemented as a condition upon which investment is contingent. I think that, so far as we are masters of our programme and our legislation, the concessions we can make to public or private capital are concessions freely made by us.[18]

This pretty much expresses the wish of all African leaders although their emphases may differ. All leaders feel that foreign skills and technical assistance are useful and in some cases very necessary. But there are problems in securing funds and personnel and in getting them without strings which distort their investment programmes, tax policies and even basic sociopolitical options for development. In the words of a Ugandan parliamentarian, Shaban Nkutu, "all aid comes with strings or ties like tails. But there are different kinds of tails. Some are like a lizard's, and if one pulls they break off. Some are like a cow's, and pulling affects both parties. But some are like the tails of crocodiles, and when we try to pull free we are badly lashed and beaten by them. The important thing is to see what kind of a tail each aid proposal has."[19]

Not surprisingly, therefore, the theme of this work seeks to provide an answer to the question as to why the Third World is poor, why they remain underdeveloped relative to their counterparts in Western Europe and North America. In trying to answer this all-important question, I draw data freely from Africa and other Third World societies.

Theories of Development and Underdevelopment

There are two broad competing paradigms or models of theoretical understanding that seek to explain why some countries are poor and others are wealthy. These are theory of modernization and theory of imperialism. Each paradigm has its own "clue concepts" or "key explanatory categories." Those who espouse the theory of modernization can be identified by their almost tenacious addiction to the concept "modern" and its permutations and by categories such as "institutional differentiation," "development," "nation-building," "economic growth," "advanced industrial societies," "Westernised," "backward," "primitive," "tribal," "detribalised," and many more. Those who employ the theory of imperialism have as their clue concepts such terms as "dependency," "neocolonialism," "liberation," "exploitation," "late capitalist societies," or "societies in the stage of monopoly capitalism."[20]

The instrumentarium of the theory of modernization has been derived from a convergence of sources in the social sciences in the Western societies over a long period of time. The most contributions have come from economists who have provided descriptions and explanations of the great transformations that first initiated the industrial revolution in the West. Similar contributions have been made by sociologists who have meticulously described and explained the enormous transformations that occurred in the non-economic institutions of these societies. What modernization theorists most often end up with is in eventuating ethnocentric practical recipes which admonish the poor societies to imitate them all the way and they would acquire a sudden leap into the 20th century. In other words, join the Calvinistic cult and you will experience a sudden leap into modernity.

The theory of imperialism, on the other hand, derives its concepts from Marxist sources. In a nutshell, the wealth and poverty of nations result from the global process of exploitation. This is the situation that Andre Gunder Frank refers to as "the development of underdevelopment." The problem of the poor countries is not the lack of technological know-how, cultural traits conducive to development, or modern institutions, but that they have been subjected to the exploitation of the international capitalist system and its special imperialists agents, both domestic and alien. The infiltration of Western capital into the poor countries has resulted in situations characterised by economists as "growth without development," as in the particular cases of Liberia and Ivory Coast.

The concept of "dependency" coined by Brazilian sociologist Fernando Henrique Cardoso, helps to link both economic and political analysis; that is, it links those who are the beneficiaries of development with those who make the decisions. Dependency simply states that crucial economic decisions are made not by the countries that are being "developed" but by foreigners whose interests are carefully safeguarded. Foreigners use their economic power to buy political power in the countries that they penetrate. This could mean political pressure by the imperialist metropolis or even military intervention. This collusion between alien economic and political power distorts both the economy and the policy of the dependent countries. Out of this situation emerge political alliances between the domestic and foreign bourgeoisie. The process is now complete because just as the metropolis exploits the colonies, so does the domestic colonial bourgeois class exploit the rest of the population.[21]

The fundamental conceptual instrumentarium of the critique of imperialism is provided in Lenin's theory of imperialism, *Imperialism: The Highest Stage of Capitalism* (1916). The basic proposition in the book seems to be that the evils associated with foreign capitalist penetration of the poor countries are the necessary concomitants of capitalism in its present stage. The development of England, for example, was assisted by the exploitation of India and Africa. The imperialists still need to exploit colonies for raw materials and to also expand their capital in the developing coun-

15

tries. The "internal contradictions" of capitalist societies about which Marx had written, force capitalist societies to immerse themselves ever so deeply in imperialist adventures in other countries.

The Marxist understanding of capitalism in general and the Lenist theory of imperialism have been violently attacked by modernization theorists who have denied the validity of these theories. The argument goes like this: If England, for example, achieved economic development as the result of its plundering of India, why did not Spain and Portugal do the same by their sustained plundering of the Americas? The answer to this question is that they invested the "surplus" value they extracted from their colonies in unenterprising luxury and both countries, but particularly Portugal, were both British colonies. But it is impossible for the apologists for imperialism, those who style themselves academic sociologists, to deny that such exploitation was very fundamental in the economic development of Europe, England in particular.

It has been argued by the modernization theorists that the theory of imperialism has no superficial credibility in the case of the U.S. for what they refer to as the original period of "take-off." It is unfortunate that these social scientists should ignore the role of enslaved Africans in the development of the United States. It is difficult to appreciate their ignorance of their exploitation of the various Indian nations within what is today the United States. It is sad enough that they have never found it fit to even acknowledge that it was not whites but the Indians who first "discovered" America. In order for whites to establish their capitalism, they had to exploit the Indians even to the point of a concerted effort to exterminate them. Or they have already forgotten that their leaders distributed small-pox-laden blankets to the Indians, that Presidents of United States, Ulysses S. Grant, for example, sent out military expeditions to search and annihilate Indians in order to facilitate the stealing of their lands.

Or did not white Anglo-Saxons coax, coerce and deceive Indians, just as they did Africans and other colonised peoples, into signing treaties that ended up enslaving them?

The current exploiter-exploited relationship between Latin America and the U.S. dates back to the 19th century. The U.S. had prevented further European encroachment in Latin America through the invocation of the famous Monroe Doctrine enunciated by President Monroe in 1823. This Doctrine stated that the U.S. would not accept any new colonisation in the Americas, no European interference in American nations. This followed the revolt of Latin American states against Spain. Latin American countries were tied to the U.S. through tariff concessions, trade benefits, the exploitation of natural resources through the use of U.S. capital, and the threat of intervention if the host country did not dance to the tune of the U.S. An excellent example of such intervention was the invasion of Cuba by the U.S. marines in 1917 after a Cuban revolt. Among the six demands placed upon any new Cuban government was "amenability to suggestions which might be made to (the Cuban president) by the American Legation," and "a thorough acquaintance with the desires of the United States government."[22]

In the case of U.S. penetration of Asia, the U.S. initially followed a nonmilitaristic policy as better summarized by Jones:

> The Secretary of State in 1899 issued a demand for equal access and fair treatment for U.S. economic power in China. A further note asserted America's direct interest in maintaining the territorial and administrative integrity of that country. These Open Door notes were America's characteristic contribution to the practice of imperialism. It was not akin to British imperial policy in the period. London's version of the policy acknowledged spheres of interest whereas the

U.S. demanded absolute equality of treatment. Convinced of the necessity to expand and yet wanting to avoid the pitfalls of a normal colonial empire (with the consequent necessity of war against rivals), the USA employed the strategy of the Open Door to exploit its growing economic power.[23]

Modernisation theorists have also argued that the present affluence of the West is not the result of their exploitation of the Third World countries. They state that this particular argument gives the poor societies "a moral legitimacy" to demand aid or trade concessions, sort of "reparations" from their alleged exploiters. The modernization school agrees that the rich nations depend on the poor ones for certain raw materials but that this dependence is declining; that a great decline in this dependence is expected in view of technological innovations and search for alternative resources nearer home. They violently reject the Leninist theory that the Third World countries are an expanding market for capital investment, that instead such expansion occurs within the advanced industrial countries themselves.

No one disputes the fact that internal investment among the advanced industrialised societies far exceeds that in the Third World countries. But the fact remains that the fattest profits come from their overseas investments.[24] It is not correct to say that the industrial nations will decrease their dependence of raw materials on the Third World nations. Modernity theorists know this; they know that the U.S. and NATO global policy is designed to protect the sources of their crucial raw materials and markets (no matter how small) for their finished products.

It is true that bourgeois social scientists in the West (the U.S. being the headquarters) and even in the Third World countries have gone out of their way to discredit the Marxist-Leninist theory. But the empirically accessible effects of capitalist penetration of the poor countries is based on evidence. Capitalism has resulted in high social and political costs to the poor countries. We find within each Third World country polarization between the relatively affluent people and those living in massive misery and the tendency for the misery to increase; there is an increasing economic dependency of poor countries upon the rich ones as can be attested to by the growing debts, deteriorating terms of trade and balance of payment, and vulnerability to decisions made by governments and nongovernmental bodies in the rich and powerful nations. Undoubtedly, any objective social scientist will agree that the above are empirical facts and not the invention of Marxist ideologists.

The ideology of development has it that benefits will eventually but assuredly (in the Aristotelian fashion) extend to all sectors of society. This is what is known as the "trickle-down effect," but more optimistically called the "spread effect." The existence of poverty and affluence is necessary for development. This makes it necessary for capital to be accumulated for what they call the "take-off." Once the accumulated capital has reached a certain level the development process will necessitate the distribution of the benefits in a more equitable way. The cases of North America and Western Europe are cited as examples. But the modernity theorists have not been able to tell us how soon the "spread-effect" will take place; all that they have said is "in the long run." The implication here is that millions will continue to live and die in abject poverty while we continue to wait for "the long run."

But as for now, what we in the poor countries seem to notice is what Brazilian economist Celso Furtado has characterised as "growth without development." By this is meant that a satellite country's growth becomes quite pronounced both in the product it exports and in its productive capacity but, fails to generate or even permit the structural transformation essential for development of underdevelopment. In terms of traditional economic indicators the growth appears quite real, but it has succeeded in establishing a relatively well-off and dynamic sector and a sector of stagnant and ever deepening misery. Thus, development ends up establishing two nations within a nation and the relationship between these two groups, the bourgeois and proletariat-lumpenproletariat, will determine the course of events in these countries.

Growth without development is quite noticeable in times of raw material export booms engendered by metropolitan demand. The West was the first to develop and it now dominates the international scene, with keen interest in the underdevelopment of the Third World countries. Thus one has to appreciate the critique of "developmentalism" in the Third World which has as its basic proposition that underdevelopment can be understood only if one understands the basic facts of dependency. In this work we review both modernity theories and the dependency model and present data to support the latter model.

Before closing this introductory chapter let us attempt the definitions of a few concepts that have been employed here without being defined. *Modernisation* as defined by their arch priests, like Wilbert Moore, refers to the process whereby societies or social institutions change or move from traditional or less-developed ones to those that characterise the developed ones. By this definition, modernisation theorists view modernity and tradition as polar opposites. Thus, they conclude that in order to modernise, the Third World societies must overcome their traditionalisms. Berger defines modernisation as "the institutional and cultural accompaniment of growth."[25] Berger then defines development as "*good* growth and desirable modernization."[26] Thus, as far as Berger is concerned, modernisation and development are an intertwined process, one reinforcing the other. As this writer sees it, modernisation involves a complex of changes in institutions or societies for the betterment of the citizens, without necessarily involving treating modernity and tradition as polar opposites.

20

With respect to development, Rogers defines it as "a type of social change in which new ideas are introduced into a social system in order to produce higher per capita incomes and levels of living through more modern production methods and improved social organization."[27] But in this work development is defined as "the coincidence of structural change and liberation of men from exploitation and oppression" perpetrated by international capitalist bourgeoisie and their internal colaborators.[28] Following this definition, therefore, "Real *development* involves a structural transformation of the economy, society, polity and culture of the satellite that permits the self-generating and self-perpetuating use and development of the people's potential."[29] Development results from a people's frontal attack on the oppression, poverty, and exploitation that are meted out to them by the dominant classes and their system.

Thus, before African countries can know growth and development in their territories, there must be a profound analysis of Africa's position in the global economy and stratification of power, as well as an appreciation on the growing complexity of Africa's class structure. Underdevelopment is not absence of development but it makes sense only as a way of comparing levels of development. Underdevelopment "is very much tied to the fact that human social development has been uneven and from a strictly economic viewpoint some human groups have advanced further by producing more and becoming more wealthy."[30] We now proceed to review some of the modernisation theories.

REFERENCES

[1] United Nations, Department of Economic and Social Affairs, *The United Nations Development Decade. Proposals for Action.* Report of the Secretary-General, New York, 1962.

[2] *Ibid.*

[3] *Ibid.*

[4] *Ibid.*

[5] S. J. Umoh, *Daily Times*, (June 6, 1978); and *Survey of Economic Conditions in Africa*, 1969.

[6] Paul Streeten, *Aid to Africa* (New York: Praeger Publishers, 1972), p. 149.

[7] Cynthia Taft Morris and Irma Adelman, "An Anatomy of Income Distribution Patterns in Developing Nations: A Summary of Findings, "*Economic Staff Paper*, No. 116, IBRD, (September, 1971).

[8] Charlotte Waterlow, *Superpowers and Victims* (Englewood Cliffs: Prentice-Hall. 1974), p. 120.

[9] *Ibid.*, p. 121.

[10] *Ibid.*

[11] Quoted by *Ibid.*

[12] Quoted by *Ibid.*, pp. 121-122.

[13] Quoted by *Ibid.*, p. 122.

[14] Henry A. Kissinger. "UNCTAD IV, Expanding Cooperation for Global Economic Development," a speech delivered in Nairobi, Kenya, on May 6, 1976, p. 2.

[15] *Ibid.*

[16] Waterlow, *Superpowers and Victims*, p. 123.

[17] *Ibid.*, p. 124.

[18] "The Single Party State in Africa," *Presence Africaine* (1960), p. 42. Also cited by Reginald G. Green and Ann Seidman, *Unity or Poverty* (Baltimore, Maryland, Penguin Books, 1968).

[19] Quoted by Green and Seidman, *Unity or Poverty*, p. 312.

[20] Peter L. Berger, *Pyramids of Sacrifice* (New York: Anchor Books, 1976), pp. 11-13.

[21] Andre Gunder Frank, *Latin America: Underdevelopment or Revolution* (New York: Monthly Review, 1969).

[22] Gareth Stedman Jones, "The Specificity of U.S. Imperialism," *New Left Review*, Vol. 60 (March-April, 1970), p. 79.

[23] *Ibid.*, p. 81.

[24] Green and Seidman, *Unity or Poverty*, p. 101. Also Charles H. Anderson, *The Sociology of Survival* (Homewood, Ill.: The Dorsey Press, 1976), p. 256, has noted that "Profits from Third World investments are markedly higher than those made in the developed economies. Labor costs are much lower, tax holidays and concessions are numerous, and raw material extraction yields higher gains than manufacturing."

[25] Berger, *Pyramids of Sacrifice*, p. 35.

[26] *Ibid.*

[27] Everett M. Rogers, *Modernization and Peasants* (New York: Holt, Rinehart and Winston, Inc; 1969), pp. 8-9.

[28] James D. Cockroft, Andre Gunder Frank, and Dale L. Johnson, *Dependence and Underdevelopment* (New York: Anchor Books, 1972).

[29] *Ibid.*, p. xvi.

[30] Walter Rodney, *How Europe Underdeveloped Africa* (Washington, D.C.: Howard University Press, 1974), p. 13.

A CRITIQUE OF MODERNIZATION

There is a tendency among European-American social scientists to treat African societies as self-contained units, whose political, social or economic systems can be analyzed in themselves; they constantly argue (or assume) that colonial and neocolonial imperialism (the sources of African dependency) have been such as to stimulate development in Africa. The problem with these approaches is twofold: First, they treat Africa as if it were a "closed system" and thus ignore the international system in which the rich and powerful countries dominate. Second, they erroneously assume (or maintain) that there has been a "net inflow" of capital from the rich or developed societies into Africa (through foreign investment and aid) and that the continent has been the beneficiary of that inflow.

By viewing societies as such these social scientists have concluded that underdevelopment is an original state with the concomitant characteristics of "backwardness" or "traditionalism," and that abandoning these characteristics and embracing those of the developed countries (particularly the U.S.) constitute the alpha and omega of economic development and cultural change. Thus, Wilbert Moore, one of the arch priests of American functionalism and of this particular brand of sociology of development, sees modernization as a "total transformation" of "traditional or premodern" societies into the types of technologies and associated social organization that characterise the advanced,

23

economically prosperous, and politically stable nations of the Western world.[1]

This type of sociology has led to the characterisation of Third World countries as "dual societies."[2] What this view does is to divide each nonindustrialised society into a small, industrialised, Westernised "modern" population living in cities; and a large, rural agrarian nonindustrialised, tradition-bound society.[3] This characterisation is not an error but it ignores the blunt fact that the underdeveloped sectors of the nonindustrialised societies maintain the elite and also enable them to live in the style of their peers in the industrialised societies. "This situation," observes Chambliss, "allows the industrialised societies to maintain their exploitative relationship with the nonindustrialised."[4] The egregious errors of the current sociology of development have culminated in both the blurring of the fundamental relationship between industrialized and nonindustrialised societies, and in the development of theories which enhance Western ethnocentrism. In this chapter we present and criticise a few modernisation theories of development.

Modernisation Theories

By ignoring the relationship between the industrialised and nonindustrialised countries, particularly of Western Europe and North America, theorists of development have tended to look within the individual psyches of the population for what differentiates industrialised and nonindustrilised societies. David McClelland's theory of achievement motivation is a good example.

McClelland and Need for Achievement

McClelland claims to have discovered a motivational syndrome or drive previously overlooked by Freudians which he labels "need for achievement" (n-Achievement). The discovery resulted from laboratory testing, and more evidence was advanced in his book, *The Achieving Society*.[5] The major hypothesis of McClelland's work is that a nation "with a generally high level of n-Achievement will produce more energetic entrepreneurs who, in turn, produce rapid economic development."[6] The basis of this theory is the assumption that "it is values, not motives or psychological forces that determine ultimately the rate of economic and social development.[7]

Need for achievement is one of a number of needs which characterises man and determines much of human behaviour; like other motives it is created through a person's childhood experiences, and the result is the link between individual and society. McClelland states further that social characteristics — class and religion, and historical occurrences — "affect motivational levels primarily as they affect the family, or more specifically the values and child-rearing practices of the parents."[8] After analysing the child-rearing practices of the parents in various countries, McClelland concluded that major sources of n-Achievement are parents who teach their children to be independent early in childhood, who are interested in their children and their activities, and who expect much of them.

The basic experiment consisted of giving intelligence tests to two groups of students. The test group had been informed that the tests were designed to measure intelligence and leadership which McClelland claimed to have aroused their achievement motive. The control group took the test without any information whatsoever. In other words, the control group took the tests dead "cold." Difference between the test and control groups were attributed to the achievement motive. Each group was then asked to write stories which were stimulated by showing them a series of pictures — Thematic Apperception Test, otherwise known as TAT. Again, differences in the frequency of "standards of excellence" in them were attributed to the same increase in frequency over their "cold" fellow students. The frequency count of achievement oriented ideas in stories written under normal conditions has been used as a measure of need for achievement.

McClelland found in his tests that scores varied from one individual to another, but in general it was clear that the middle class students in the U.S. had higher scores than the "upper" and "lower" classes. The high scorers were seen as the entrepreneurial types. They are those fed with certain beliefs and childrearing practices within the family. In order to supplement his contemporary data, McClelland calculated scores from the fairy tales of ancient Greece, England (1400-1900), and pre-Inca Peru. Variations in the total n-Achievement in these societies were found to be positively correlated to subsequent economic development. It is quite necessary for us to bear in mind that the presence of a large number of entrepreneurs is given as the only mediating factor between psychological measure and economic development.

The analytical problems aside, this theory raises serious questions. It is interesting to note that structural causes of the need to achieve, such as kinship, religion, and class are embedded in his conceptual scheme, yet McClelland maintains that the need to achieve is a personality variable, independent of the social structure. He thus erroneously concludes that his thesis is a refutation of structural determinism. McClelland asserts, "it is men, and in particular their deepest concerns, that shape history."[9]

Another assumption implicit in McClelland's thesis is that pre-industrial or underdeveloped societies suffer from a low achievement-orientation. But Stanley R. Barrett has shown that this assumption is "invalid," having demonstrated that "a high n-Achievement value exists in the traditional structure of Igbo society, and was there prior to Western contact."[10] In another study, after testing dream accounts of

Igbo, Hausa, and Yoruba schoolboys, LeVine tells us that Nigerians are after all not traditional:

> We might accurately regard them as pragmatic frontiersmen with a persistent history of migration, settlement and resettlement of new lands and of responding to the challenges of intertribal wars and the slave-trade.[11]

We can presume from this quotation that Nigerians have entrepreneural types, even though the Nigerian economy and growth rates are low. Nigerian n-Achievement scores were not significantly different from those recorded in developed societies. The tribal differences were not significant either, even though the Igbo as a group were found to be most "commercial." I trust that similar tests all over Africa would reveal the presence of high n-Achievement among various groups in the continent. From the perspective of McClelland's theory, it was achievement motivation that made some African groups slaves while others were slave traders. The existence of a high n-Achievement value in traditional African structure renders meaningless McClelland's solution to economic development which consists of "introducing" n-Achievement into a society. In fact, factors other than high n-Achievement scores must be identified that can explain economic growth and levels.

Kamarck, a former Director of the Economics Department of the International Bank for Reconstruction and Development, has observed that Africans

> show exceptional willingness to adapt or change their institutions to the requirements of economic development. Indeed, the African openness to innovation is comparable to or even perhaps greater than, that of the Japanese and American in the past.... Unlike some other developing areas which depended or depend on a socially or ethnically marginal group for innovation, the

African "elite" itself, like the American and Japanese, is open to innovation....

African willingness to learn has shown itself from the continent's very first contacts with the rest of the world. For example, cassava and maize spread rapidly through much of Africa as basic food crops after they were introduced by early slave traders when contact was limited and travel difficult. Many other basic African foods (yams, bananas, plantains, domestic forest goats and fowl) are also not indigenous but were acquired in the course of limited contacts with South Asia.[12]

Emphasis on economic development is not at all in conflict with the traditional African view of the world; in fact it coincides with our *Weltanschauung*. There has never been in the continent any religion that scorned or despised materialism or which claimed the body to be an impediment to reaching perfection of the soul. As Fallers has observed "there is a certain tendency for traditional African religions to make the health, fertility, and prosperity of the living individual and living community matters of central importance. A great deal of the ritual communication which takes place between living persons and the spirit world has as its object the maintenance or re-establishment of individual or group well being in a quite material, biological sense."[13]

McClelland further assumes that n-Achievement is evident primarily in entrepreneural roles.[14] Those who have a great need to achieve are likely to take to business rather than arts or teaching.[15] This assumption is not peculiar to the U.S., or to industrialized societies in general. It is supposedly a universal phenomenon.

McClelland's theory implicitly denies that five centuries of Western domination of Africa is a crucial factor in African underdevelopment. Thus the enslavement of Africans, their colonization and the concomitant upheavals; the ability of the developed countries to "destabilize," manipulate, pressurize, threaten, and even finance coups and wars against the underdeveloped countries are irrelevant to their underdevelopment. Their underdevelopment, according to McClelland, is caused by their lack of proper amount of "achievement motivation."

The theory further implies that the African continent has always been underdeveloped since it has never been fortunate to have individuals with n-Achievement. Nothing could be further from the truth. The nonindustrialised societies were at one time developed and some of them wielded much influence over large areas. Egypt was once a highly developed society. During the period that Western historians call the "Dark Ages," there were kingdoms and empires at every point of the compass in the continent of Africa. Medical practice at the University of Sankore in Timbuktu "was much advanced, and doctors performed some operations that were not known in Europe for another 250 years."[16] In 1324 the Mali Empire was so wealthy that the foreign aid (in gold) given to Egypt, according to the eyewitness account of al-Omari, a Cairo administrative official, "ruined the value of money" in Egypt.[17] High need for achievement has always been present in Africa and as already stated, one must look elsewhere for factors responsible for African underdevelopment. But for now we turn to the analysis of another psychological theory of development.

Everett E. Hagan and Status Withdrawal

Like McClelland, Hagen searches for innovators. He is a disappointed and frustrated economist who has turned to social and psychological factors to explain growth.[18] Improved technology, availability of abundant capital, the diffusion of cultural factors, adequate markets, easily exploitable natural resources, and a host of other factors are not as important for the beginning of economic growth as are individuals who take leadership in innovation. Social structure shapes parental behaviour which in turn determines the childrearing patterns adopted by adults and the "childhood environment" that moulds the personalities of the young. It is the innovative personality that impels growth. Those "subordinated groups" who have experienced status withdrawal or downward mobility lose their traditional values while still striving fanatically to recapture their lost prestige by resorting to different means to achieve them.

Hagen tells us that "in the transition to economic growth" these leaders of innovation

> were neither randomly distributed throughout the population nor drawn from the group that was most elite or had the greatest wealth or greatest opportunity for access to foreign knowledge and capital. Instead, they came disproportionately from some one or more less elite groups whose members had traditionally had a secure place in the social order but had lost the status they felt a right to expect were now disparaged by the leading social group.[19]

Authoritarianism and noninnovating personalities are both the characteristics of traditional societies. Not surprisingly, therefore, the social and economic organization of these societies is characterized by great stability. There could be a complete absence of social change in such societies for many, .many years, since "the interrelationships between personality and social structure are such as to make it clear that social change will not occur without change in personalities."[20] And as Kunkel has noted, "the process of personality formation in children produces new character types when alterations in the social organization of a society change the values and needs of certain adults."[21] As Hagen states, "the basic cause" of these changes "is the perception on the part of the members of some social group that their purposes and values in life are not respected by

30

groups in the society whom they respect and whose esteem they value,"[22] Such "withdrawal of status respect" results in retreatism among those who suffer a loss of status.

Fortunately, however, "retreatism is not a dead end. As retreatism deepens in successive generations, it creates circumstances of home life and social environment that are conducive to the development of innovational personality. The historical sequence seems to be: authoritarianism, withdrawal of status respect, retreatism, creativity."[23] This ushers in economic growth. But those Hagen calls "subordinated groups," Wilbert Moore prefers to call "marginal" groups. Among them are Chinese households, men in some African matriarchal societies, the Indian caste untouchables, the younger sons in a system of male primogenitor, merchants "unclassifiable" in feudal Japan, dispossessed landlords subsequent to a land reform, foreign enterprises and the indigenous natives and landless poor everywhere.

As in the case of McClelland, there is a serious problem with the causal chain. The question is about what causes "social structure" to change, and what are the linkages between "personality" and economic development? Like McClelland, Hagen offers innovators as the link. But Hagen claims that innovative personalities are not formed by "traditional" societies. On the basis of this theory one would have to withdraw status from parts of the population and then wait for some decades for them to innovate. The implications of Hagen's theory are not too practical.

Hagen's theory seems to neglect or disregard "Africa because it assumes that all traditional societies are stratified, ascriptive, and organized hierarchically."[24] Hagen's theory may have relevance to highly stratified, "history-conscious," and "tradition-bound" cultures of Asia and Latin America. Africans generally do not glorify tradition as much as one finds in many other developing countries. As Spiro has noted:

Africans in general are the most present-minded people on earth... Without significant exceptions, all African leaders... share the passionate desire to acquire all the good things which western civilization has produced in the two millenia of its history. They want especially to get the technological blessings of American civilization, and to do so as quickly as possible... They are not encumbered by written traditions, or by the visible and tangible physical presence of the ruins of their own "civilized" past — as most Asians have been. Therefore, they do not have to reconcile every innovation with the different practices of their past.[25]

Thus, even though Hagen, like McClelland, generalises about all developing countries, his theory appears to have no relevance to Africa. While one can appreciate the importance of a general value system of a society, Africa, indeed the underdeveloped world, is not in short supply of commercial talents and a great reservoir of entrepreneural talent. Even Wilbert Moore, a functionalist intractably committed to the modernization approach, has warned against the acceptance of the McClelland-Hagen argument, because it is

exclusively preoccupied with character formation in early socialization. Since that in turn is mainly the responsibility of parents and particularly of mothers, how do mothers come by their orientation to achievement? We are led, willy-nilly, back to the conclusion that adults must be capable of change as well as children. The other warning is practical. Within a given country, the circumstance that innovation is perpetrated by marginal groups may precisely inhibit general acceptance. The real or imagined benefits must sooner or later have a wider appeal if development is to continue.[26]

Since Hagen believes character structure is formed early in childhood socialization, he concludes that several or perhaps many generations will have to pass by in the under-developed and backward world before there will emerge the general conditions necessary to change the character types of these societies and produce the much needed innovators. But this writer contends that the problem of underdevelopment in Africa is not due to lack of entrepreneural talents. Al-though I concede that certain economic and noneconomic factors may contribute to our economic underdevelopment and backwardness, our primary and most crucial problem is Africa's position in the world economy and stratification of power.

Bert F. Hoselitz and Assignment and Reward

Hoselitz's claim is different from those of McClelland and Hagen. For McClelland, the historical development of the phenomenon called capitalism analyzed by Max Weber, may be comprehended, in its psychological aspects, by what he has labeled n-Achievement. On the other hand, Hagen claims that economic development must be understood in terms of creative personality. But unlike these two psychological theorists, Hoselitz has argued that the assign-ment of and reward in social roles based on achievement is the *sine qua non* to economic development. Hoselitz derived his theory of development from the pattern variables of Tal-cott Parsons.[27] Pattern variables, according to the *Dictionary of Sociology*, are:

> types of choices open to purposive human beings; they are dichotomies... each representing polar extremes. *Universalism* and *particularism* are the names of one. In other words, any individual in a situation requiring choice in his relationships with others must ask himself if he is going to act in terms of a universally accepted precept or one particular to the situation in which he finds himself. Is he going to act according to rule or in terms of particular qualities of the person towards

whom he is orienting his action. Another set is termed *achievement* and *ascription* (sometimes referred to as *performance* and *quality*) and here a person in deciding how to act focuses his attention on either the achieved aspects of the other person, e.g., his professional qualifications, or else his ascribed qualities, e.g. sex, age, social class... Yet another set is known as *specificity* and *diffuseness*, and here, the choice takes into account limited and specific factors, e.g., the contrast between a contract entered into, and wider diffuse obligations such as family loyalty... The point of this scheme of pattern variables is to enable the sociologist to identify the typical choices made, especially of an institutionalized kind... Pattern variable analysis may be used to identify similarities and differences between cultures, or it may be restricted in use to refer to aspects of society, to sub-systems...[28]

The other two pattern variables are affectivity-affective neutrality, and self-orientation-collectivity orientation. Affectivity-affective neutrality refers to the amount of feeling accepted as appropriate to a relationship while affectivity stands for "emotional expressiveness." Self-orientation-collectivity orientation refers to the nature of one's commitment to collectivity. Self-oriented behaviour is designed to promote one's interest, whereas collectivity-oriented activity is conducted primarily to advance the goals of the whole group.

On the basis of these pattern variables, Hoselitz contends that industrialized societies exhibit the characteristics of universalism, achievement, specificity, affective-neutrality and self-orientation while the nonindustrialized ones exhibit their opposites — particularism, ascription, diffuseness, affectivity, and collective orientation. It is not necessary to analyze all these variables and their theoretical utility since they have been analyzed elsewhere and found wanting;[29] only two pairs are considered here.

What the first pair tells us is that in Africa the criteria of achievement are particularistic. In plain language, what this means is that people become rich or poor, are hired or fired, successful or unsuccessful not because they earn or deserve it but because they are selected for personal reasons by their kinsmen or tribesmen. Success in Africa depends on "who you know" in contrast to that of the industrialized societies which depends on meritability. Western societies industrialized because of their emphasis on merit (a universalistic principle) in contrast to a particularistic principle such as kinship ties. But empirical facts in both the industrialized and nonindustrialized societies belie the presumed "meritocracy" and particularistic criteria.

The industrialization of Japan is believed to have been aided by particularistic principles. Japanese factories try to employ entire families rather than individuals — that is, kinship ties influence one's employability or unemployability at a particular plant or factory.[30] Employers try to make the factory look like a family unit.

The United States and Europe are fraught with particularistic criteria.[31] In industrialized societies children from wealthy families still inherit wealth and power regardless of their ability. Nonwhites do not attend inferior schools by choice, it is the direct result of white discrimination which takes various forms — planned school districts that insure that blacks are kept out, forcing them to live in ghettoes, and gerrymandering. In the same societies children of wealthy parentage are assured of the most expensive and quality education irrespective of their intelligence — a universalistic criterion. Power and wealth have a tendency to perpetuate themselves in both industrialized and nonindustrialized societies, which means that all societies are particularistic to a considerable degree. If the U.S. is to be characterized as universalistic, how do we explain all the court case decisions in favour of minorities — including women — who have been cheated for too long? Various commission reports have confirmed that minorities have been denied jobs and promotions, and also have been underpaid solely because of their ascriptive characteristics.

Particularism has been and continues to be a feature of American society. American trade unions, for example, continue to use informal means to exclude blacks and other minorities from apprenticeship training programs for skilled trade.[32] Using data from the 1960 Census and having adjusted for differences between whites and nonwhites in education, occupational categories, and region of residence, Paul Siegel found that "with the single exception of nonwhite farmers in the North, the figures show that at every educational level in every occupational group, and in the North as well as the South, minorities have earnings less than most whites."[33] He then estimated the differential in income at most occupational and educational levels between whites and nonwhites to be $1,000 with the largest difference being in the South.[33]

The same 1960 Census was further used by the Council of Economic Advisors in 1965 to estimate the cost of white discrimination to the national economy. It was their estimate that the personal income of the nation would rise to $12.8 billion greater if blacks having education equal to whites were given equal pay: that the GNP would rise by 3.7 per cent; and that the entire economy would significantly benefit by granting better education to blacks and by abolishing job discrimination.[34] I may add here that South Africa whose apartheid policy is worse than discrimination against blacks in the U.S. is industrializing.

In the particular case of Great Britain, the British sociologist Michael Young wrote a novel containing a description of a perfect open class system, which he called "meritocracy."[35] This was a situation in which everybody could succeed solely on the basis of merit, and nothing else. This novel contends that there were quite a few things that Britain would have to do to reach that stage. Among these were destroying the titles and estates of nobility, confiscating and prohibiting all inherited wealth, and prohibiting families from giving special help to their children. The school system would have to be revamped in order to give special attention to the culturally deprived or disadvantaged children in order to ensure them equality of opportunity. The seniority system would have to be eliminated. In the end Young appears to conclude that a true meritocracy is quite impossible.

Turning again to the U.S. a study consisting of 234 individuals with all their positions in government during 1944-1960, "Comprising the lesser posts if an individual attained the highest executive level," showed that "these key leaders held 678 posts and nearly all of them were high level and policy-making in nature."[36] The study revealed

> that foreign policy decision-makers are in reality a highly mobile sector of the American corporate structure, a group of men who frequently assume and define high level policy tasks in government, rather than routinely administer it, and then return to business. Their firms and connections are large enough to afford them the time to straighten out or formulate government policy while maintaining their vital ties with giant corporate law, banking, or industry. The conclusion is that a small number of men fill the large majority of key foreign policy posts. Their many diverse posts make this group a kind of committee government entrusted to handle numerous and varied national security and international functions at the policy level. Even if not initially connected with the corporate sector, career government officials relate in some tangible manner with the private worlds predominantly of big law, big finance, and big business.[37]

Most of these appointments are the result of the patronage system and political affiliation, not achievement. To continue to argue that nonindustrialized societies are more particularistic than industrialized societies is to indulge in scientific myth. It is common knowledge that the use of friends, relatives, classmates, club members and the like, is commonplace in America.

Roosevelt's and Kennedy's brain trusts co-opted all sorts of American social scientists. Harvard historian Arthur Schlesinger, Jr.'s aid to the development of underdeveloped countries has so far consisted of writing the now famous White Paper on Cuba which was intended to justify the coming invasion of that country at the Bay of Pigs. He later admitted lying about the invasion in the "national interest." Stanford economist Eugene Staley wrote *The Future of Underdeveloped Countries* and then planned it in the renowned Staley-(General Maxwell) Taylor Plan to put 15 million Vietnamese in the concentration camps they euphemically christened "strategic hamlets." Since the failure of that effort at development planning, M.I.T. economic historian Walt Whitman Rostow has escalated the effort by writing *The Stages of Economic Development: A Non-Communist Manifesto.* He wrote of these stages at the CIA-financed Center for International Studies on the Charles River and has been operationalizing them on the Potomac as President Kennedy's Director of Policy and Planning in the State Department and President Johnson's chief adviser on Vietnam. It is on behalf of Vietnam economic growth that Rostow has become the principal architect of escalation, napalming the South to bombing the North, and beyond.

Then, doubtless due to universalist particularism and achieved ascription, Eugene Rostow moves from professing international law at Yale University to practicing it at his brother's side in Washington. Meanwhile, after performing his role as Dean of Humanities at Harvard University, McGeorge Bundy becomes W.W. Rostow's superior in Washington and goes on television to explain to the misguided and incredulous why this economic development theory and policy is humanitarian (after which he goes on to direct the Ford Foundation and its influence on education and research). In the light of the manifest and institutionalized role-summation and diffuseness of these deans of humane scholarship and professors of applied social science, the clandestine of Project Camelot by Department of Defense and the financing of the United States National Student Association by the CIA pale into shadows.[38]

Still very dramatic is the finding by Floyd Hunter in his study of "Ivydale" that some of the most influential men in the community were a group of college classmates who had from their college days worked to put one another into positions of power. When eventually one of the clique members became president of the university he appointed others to posts of leadership.[39] Ethnicity may be the criterion in Nigeria and other African countries while that of the U.S. may be friendship, but Africans cannot be said to be more particularistic!

Walt Whitman Rostow and Stages of Economic Development

Of the many names associated with recent contributions to development theory, very few, if any, are better known than Rostow. Such familiar development terms as "the preconditions for take-off," "the take-off" and "self-sustained growth" were enunciated by him. I doubt there is any political leader in the underdeveloped world who is not familiar with the above cliches. Rostow's major work, *The Stages of Economic Growth* carries the subtitle *A Non-Communist Manifesto*, and was presented to political leaders and scholars in the poor and rich nations as an alternate theory to the self-defeating pattern of capitalist growth written about by Karl Marx. In recent U.S. Senate hearings on the Central

Intelligence Agency (CIA) and the press, it was confirmed that the CIA had infiltrated the publishing business, paying university lecturers and professors to write and publish books and articles for the CIA; such publications are propagandistic and they are said to number in the thousands. Rostow's *The Stage of Economic Growth* is one of such books, financed by and published for the CIA. It must be noted that Rostow played a highly visible role in the Kennedy Administration; he was Chairman of the Department of State Planning Council. According to Rostow:

> It is possible to identify all societies, in their economic dimensions, as lying within five categories: the traditional society, the preconditions of take-off, the take-off, the drive to maturity, and the age of mass-consumption. First the traditional society. A traditional society is one whose structure is developed within limited production functions, based on pre-Newtonian science and technology, and pre-Newtonian attitudes towards the physical world.... The second stage of growth embraces societies in the process of transition; that is, the period when the preconditions for take-off are developed; for it takes time to transform a traditional society in the ways necessary for it to exploit the fruits of modern sciences, to fend off diminishing returns, and thus to enjoy the blessing and choice opened up by the march of compound interest... the stage of precondition arise(s) not endogenously but from some external intrusion by more advanced societies... We come now to the great watershed in the life of modern societies; the third stage in this sequence, the take-off. The take-off is the interval when the old blocks and resistances to steady growth are finally overcome. The forces making for economic progress, which yielded limited bursts and enclaves of modern activity, expand and come to dominate the society. Growth becomes its normal condition. Compound interest becomes built, as it were, into its habits

and institutional structure.... The take-off is defined as requiring all three of the following related conditions: (1) a rise in the rate of productive investment from, say, 5 percent or less to over 10 percent of national income (or net national product NNP); (2) the development of one or more substantial manufacturing sectors, with a high rate of growth; (3) the existence or quick emergence of a political, social and institutional framework which exploits the impulses to expansion.[40]

Rostow's description of the traditional society is quite similar to Hagens' low-level equilibrium economy. Like Hagen, Rostow's traditional society is peasant-based, lacking in significant economic growth, custom-bound, hierarchical, unproductive, and characterized by authoritarian personality, long-run fatalism, and a low ceiling of attainable output per head because of the primitive nature of its technology. Rostow adds that its production capabilities are characterized by pre-Newtonian science and technology and pre-Newtonian attitudes towards the physical world.

In the second stage of growth the so-called preconditions for take-off are developed, and this is the period of significant economic changes. The noneconomic aspect of this change is the appearance of a new elite who consider economic modernization as being both possible and desirable. This group consists of men who are willing to mobilize savings and carry out innovational risks. There could be a rise of political risorgimento in reaction to incursion from the wealthy nations. A case in point, according to Rostow, is Commodore Perry's visit to Japan in the 1850's. The economic aspects of these changes involve a rise in the rate of capital accumulation above the rate of population growth, capitalising on current innovational opportunities while creating new ones, and the training of labour for specialized, large scale production.

At the third stage, the resistance to steady growth is

41

vanquished and growth now becomes an integral part of the society. In the preconditions stage significant economic progress occurs, but the society is still dominated by traditional attitudes and productive techniques. But the growth process becomes institutionalized in the take-off stage. After naming the three changes contained in the above quotation, and using the historical experience of industrialized countries such as great Britain, Japan, the U.S. and Russia, Rostow comes to the conclusion that the take-off period lasts about 20 years. After this comes the "drive to maturity" which takes about 20 years. This is the stage at which, according to Rostow, "an economy demonstrates that it has the technological and entrepreneural will to produce not everything, but anything it chooses to produce."

After this comes "the age of high mass-consumption," a stage in which the leading sectors shift towards the production of durable consumer's goods and services. At this stage incomes have climbed to levels where clothing, basic food and shelter are no longer the main consumption concerns of workers. Television sets, refrigerators, automobiles, phonographs, radiograms, and a host of other items, begin to interest consumers. At this stage also many resources are allocated to social welfare and security; this is brought about by the political process. According to Rostow, the U.S., most of the nations of Western Europe, and Japan are in this stage, while he thinks that Russia is ready for it.

Rostow's stages-analysis is just one of many such attempts to arrive at a stages theory. In his dialectical approach Marx felt he had discerned from social systems that had already passed through the cycle — primitive communism, the ancient slave trade, feudalism, and capitalism.

The German historical school also used this method. Those who espouse this approach tend to view development as taking place in such stages as "the household economy, the town economy, and the national economy; barter, the money economy, and the credit economy and savagery, the pastoral life, agriculture, and manufactures; and finally agriculture, manufacturing and trade."[41]

One can easily find historical experience that appears to support these various sequences. "But, as the multiplicity of stage theories suggests, there does not appear to be any one stage sequence that applies in any meaningful way to a broad sweep of development experience."[42] One can quite easily see the significant development differences between India and the U.S. But the crux of a stages theory is that development has to proceed in a particular sequence of clearly definable steps. Furthermore, the analytical relationships of any particular stage to the preceding and subsequent stage must be so clearly specified that all can come to a consensus when these connections have taken place.

Most economists feel that Rostow has not fulfilled these requirements for a valid stages theory. His concepts are regarded as mere impressionistic interpretation of a number of historical experiences rather than a rigorous, scientific analysis. As Baldwin has noted:

> From Rostow's theory we get the impression that a country should turn to vigorous industrial development efforts only after agriculture has been modernized and the stock of social overhead capital greatly increased. Yet, postwar growth experience in the developing countries has convinced more and more development economists that the agricultural and industrial sectors must expand side by side if growth is to be more than the establishment of a few flashy industries or the creation of an agricultural surplus that soon disappears into a larger rural population.[43]

One of the sharpest critics of Rostow's theory is Andre Gunder Frank.[44] He says that Rostow's stages are incorrect because they fail to correspond to the past and present conditions of the underdeveloped countries. Rostow claims that underdevelopment is an original state; he attributes history to the developed countries while denying the same thing to the underdeveloped ones. None of the underdeveloped societies today resembles what it was even fifty years ago. The whirlwind of Western imperialism has forced them to change. Rostow's stages have been analyzed and found to be wanting. The first two stages are "fictional" while the last two are "utopian." If the underdeveloped countries were to find themselves in the fourth stage of drive toward maturity or in the fifth stage, one of high mass consumption, they would not be called underdeveloped, and this would deny Rostow the opportunity to enunciate his stages. Furthermore,

> While in Rostow's rendition of reality his utopian last two stages are the mere mechanical summation of the fictitious first two stages plus third, in the unfortunate reality of the underdeveloped countries it is precisely the structure of their under-development — in which Rostow whitewashes with traditionalism and externally created pre-conditions — and their structural relations with the developed countries, which Rostow fails to mention at all, that have for so long prevented the realization of the last two stages.[45]

Piero Gheddo and the Four Revolutions

A rather interesting explanation for the development of the rich Western (North America included) nations and the poor Third World countries of Africa, Asia, and Latin America is that authored by Gheddo, a priest in the PIME Missionary Society. His book, *Why is the Third World Poor?*[46] won the Campine d'Halia Prize in Journalism in 1972. Gheddo raised the question, "Why have some people started to move forward while others remain motionless, static?"[47] His answer is that the West has undergone four crucial revolutions while the Third World countries have not.

(1) The first revolution is on the plane of ideas. This is the revolution that ignited the concepts of the equality of all

men and the dignity of each individual person. This revolutionary idea exerted a great impact on the stratificational
system which placed the slave on "the level of a domestic
animal without rights or personality." The West was radically
transformed by the Judaeo-Christian religion which taught
man that he was created in the image of God; that man was
the king of creation, and with an end superior to that of any
other creature; and that man was free to determine and
shape his own destiny. Gheddo says that all these are basic
ideas derived from biblical revelation, on which Western
civilisation rests.

> Christianity, offering the example of God-made-man,
> has suggested the possibility of man's limitless ascent
> enabling him to share in the life of God by means of
> grace. This is the initial step-recognition of the dignity
> of each single human person toward man's progress
> and that of society. In other words, in the West, man
> at the centre of creation, thinking and acting, became
> the essential nucleus around which everything else is
> organized. When this idea, slowly maturing over the
> centuries, was accepted, it put an end to the immo-
> bility of society and of mentality, and started the
> movement toward liberty, democracy, socialism, and
> social justice.[48]

But in the underdeveloped countries the idea that man
is centre of creation is not accepted or known. In these
societies "man is only one of the many elements of nature
without any particular superior dignity. It is clear that start-
ing from such a basic idea, man could not progress but
remained stationary and closed in the recurring cycles of
nature."[49]

(2) The second revolution is that of the idea of progress. If man is the king of creation, if man is made in the
image of God, then he ought to dominate nature and make
it serve his needs. The West developed because it at a cer-

tain point in time discovered "the sovereign dignity of man over all creation, the fundamental equality of all men, and the messianic vision of a better world to be constructed with his own hands and the help of others. This idea of progress has given Western culture an ideal, has broken down psychological barriers, and created a dynamic tension towards the future."[50]

Christianity, "the spirit of Western culture" gave it an eschatological and complete hope but one which was also viewed in human and earthly terms as man's course towards his great destiny. The Christian or Christianised man makes a total commitment to progress, because having been made in the image of God his potentialities for further development are limitless.

But for the non-Christian or pre-Christian culture, "history is a continued return to the past, a closed circle that repeats itself like the seasons, like the mythical serpent devouring its own tail."[51] What keeps the Third World underdeveloped or "static," according to Gheddo, is because they lack the "progressive mentality" that characterises the Western man.

(3) The third revolution is that of population growth. Man created in the image of God became the centre of experimentation to improve the conditions of, and to prolong, his life. Medicine assured man better health and in addition upset the economic balance of mere subsistence which characterised the traditional society. In Western societies population increased in situations conducive to efforts towards a better organisation of its productive forces, thus unleashing a series of powerful causes and effects in the area of economics and it is this process that has brought about material progress to their society. But in the Third World, population growth has not led to productivity or greater social justice, and the reason for this is that these men are unaware of their dignity and equality.

(4) The fourth and final revolution concerns science and

technology which have made possible Western economic development. Like in the development of medical science and all other sciences focusing on man, the fourth revolution derived its impetus from the first two revolutions. In the West science and technology are fairly recent phenomena whose occurrence was planned but both were "the product of a whole culture that was headed in that direction." According to Gheddo, the transplantation of technology and science in the underdeveloped countries cannot succeed because of the differences in culture. As Gheddo states:

> One of the fundamental differences between the Western world and the third world is precisely this: On one side are societies that have had a long cultural preparation, culminating in modern progress; on the other side are those who are unprepared for the break with the whole cultural past that would result from the introduction of new revolutionary ideas and new technology.[52]

Technical and scientific discoveries have been important in Western advancement economically in agricultural and industrial production, but there had to exist a bourgeois class to capitalize on these discoveries. The rise of the bourgeois class in the West did not happen fortuitously but through the development of the whole society that gradually broke loose from the rigid pattern of the past: the sharp demarcation between rich and poor, nobles and plebeians, freemen and slaves. The result was the intermingling of classes, with the bourgeois being the life wire of Western society.

But in the Third World, society has not yet evolved; there has not yet occurred the birth of new classes with a more progressive spirit. Until their meeting with the West, the rigid tribal patterns, the castes, the rulers remained just as they were. Gheddo then quotes one Lacoste to support his argument:

An historical fact of great importance characterizes all lands that are now underdeveloped: the absence of a bourgeoisie. Whatever be the level of civilization that may have been reached... the factors of the formation and development of a bourgeoise have not appeared... The absence of a dynamic social class, eager to overthrow to its own advantage the established order, has made the realization of an economic revolution impossible.[53]

Many of the criticisms levelled against previous theories apply to Gheddo's explanation of the underdevelopment of Africa, indeed the Third World. It is not correct, as E. B. Idowu[54] has pointed out, that the African does not recognize the Supreme Being. Gheddo, like previous theorists, believes that the underdeveloped countries are traditional, hierarchical, rigid in their class structure, and the like. Gheddo is a Reverend Father, a Catholic and it is quite interesting to note that he stresses the importance of Christianity as opposed to Protestantism. In fact Gheddo does not really say much about Western development that had not been said by previous writers. For example, Robert Merton believes that the development of science as a massive and powerful institution in the West as a way of viewing the world, was a direct result of culturally established attitudes which were somehow conducive to its development. Merton claims that science is an outgrowth of world views embodied in early Protestantism. Weber saw capitalism emerging from Protestantism; and Merton sees science as yet another contribution of the Protestant Ethic. Merton writes:

It is the thesis of this study that the Puritan ethic, as an ideal-typical expression of the value-attitudes basic to ascetic Protestantism generally so canalised the interests of seventeenth-century Englishman as to constitute one important *element* in the enhanced cultivation of science. The deeprooted religious *interests* of the day demanded in their forceful implications the systematic, rational, and empirical study of Nature for the glorification of God in his works and for the control of the corrupt world.[55]

But Gheddo does not tell us why Angola, for example, which was under the control of Portugal for centuries never experienced the liberating revolution. Those that Hagen and McClelland refer to as the entrepreneural elites, Gheddo calls them "bourgeoisie class." As we have already pointed out, Africa is not in lack of enterprising entrepreneures. It is ridiculous that Gheddo should be so ignorant as to state that there does not exist in Africa (the Third World) "a dynamic social class, eager to overthrow to its own advantage the established order." It is rather surprising that Gheddo did not know anything about what the Congolese people wanted to do in 1960 but the NATO powers ganged up, murdered Patrice Lumumba, leader of the revolution. Since then, NATO has set up the puppet government of Mobutu. On two occasions NATO had to intervene to save their marionette. Apparently in order to develop, Gheddo would recommend that all Third World countries pass through the four revolutions that the West has already undergone. Unfortunately, however, Japan, a non-Christian nation which never passed through the four revolutions, is an industrialized power to be reckoned with. And Japan is very traditional in many respects.

This brief analysis of the sociology of development inevitably leads to the conclusion that the current European-American sociology of development does not explain African underdevelopment. The works of S. N. Eisenstadt, Reinhard Bendix, Wilbert Moore, Marion Levy, David Apter, to mention just a few, do not explain African underdevelopment, because they all belong in the mainstream of European American sociology which has carefully avoided the issue of dependency and colonial imperialism as crucial factors in African underdevelopment.

Indeed, the economic and political expansionism of Europe since the fifteenth century has come to incorporate the now underdeveloped countries into a single stream of world history, which has given rise simultaneously to the present development of some countries and the present underdevelopment of others... Underdevelopment, far from being due to any supposed 'isolation' of the majority of the world's people from the modern capitalist expansion, or even to any continued feudal relations and ways, is the result of the integral incorporation of these people into the fully integrated but contradictory capitalist system which has long since embraced them all.[56]

In other words, underdevelopment, far from being an original or "natural" condition of the poor societies, is a condition imposed by the international expansion of capitalism and its inalienable partner, imperialism. In order to place African underdevelopment in its proper perspective, we must turn to the "Dependency Model."

REFERENCES

[1] Wilbert E. Moore, *Social Change* (Englewood Cliffs, N.J.: Prentice-Hall, 1963), p. 89. For an excellent critique of Moore's works, see Irving L. Horowitz, *Three Worlds of Development* (New York: Oxford University Press, 1966), p. 19.

[2] For example see Gerald M. Meir, *Leading Issues in Economic Development* (New York: Oxford University Press, 1970).

[3] William J. Chambliss, ed. *Sociological Readings in the Conflict Perspective* (Reading, Mass.: Addison Wesley, 1973), p. 16.

[4] *Ibid*. For this line of argument see also Horowitz, *Three Worlds of Development*. Horowitz takes John Galbraith's, Rostow's and Wilbert Moore's theories of development to task.

[5] David McClelland, *The Achieving Society* (New York: Van Nostrand Reinhard, 1961).

[6] *Ibid*, p. 205

[7] David McClelland, "Motivational Patterns in Southeast Asia with Special Reference to the Chinese Case," *Journal of Social Issues* XXIX/1 (January, 1963). p. 17.

[8] McClelland, *The Achieving Society,* p. 387.

[9] *Ibid.,* p. 437.

[10] Stanley R. Barrett, "The Achievement Factor in Igbo Receptivity to Industrialization, *"The Canadian Review of Sociology and Anthropology*, Vol. 5-6, (1968-69), p. 69.

[11] R.A. LeVine, *Dreams and Deeds* (Chicago: University of Chicago Press, 1966), p. 3.

[12] Andrew M. Kamarck, *Economics of African Development* (New York: Frederick A. Praeger, 1967), p. 48-49.

[13] L. A. Fallers, "Social Stratification and Economic Process," in M. J. Herskovits and M. Harwitz, eds., *Economic Transition in Africa* (Evanston Illinois: Northwestern University Press, 1964).

[14] McClelland, *The Achieving Society*, p. 55-56.

[15] David McClelland, "Some Social Consequences of Achievement Motivation," in M. R. Jones, ed, *Nebraska Symposium on Motivation 1955* (Lincoln, Nebraska, 1955), pp. 41-65.

[16] Immanuel Wallerstein, *Africa: The Politics of Independence* (New York: Vintage Books, 1961), p. 18.

[17] E. Jefferson Murphy, *History of African Civilization* (New York: Dell Publishing Company, 1974), p. 120.

[18] Everett E. Hagen, *On the Theory of Social Change* (Homewood, Illinois: Dorsey Press, 1962); Hagen "How Economic Growth Begins: A Theory of Social Change," *Journal of Social Issues*, Vol. 19, (January, 1963), pp. 20-34.

[19] Hagen, *On the Theory of Social Change*, p. 30.

[20] *Ibid.*, p. 86.

[21] John H. Kunkell, *Society and Economic Growth* (New York: Oxford University Press, 1970), p. 85.

[22] Hagen, *On the Theory of Social Change,* p. 185.

[23] *Ibid.*, p. 217.

[24] David R. Smock "Cultural and Attitudinal Factors Affecting Agricultural Development in Eastern Nigeria," *Economic Development and Cultural Change*, Vol. 18 No. 1, 1969.

[25] H. J. Spiro, *Politics in Africa* (Englewood Cliffs, N. J.: Prentice-Hall, 1962), pp. 5-6.

[26] Wilbert Moore, *Impact of Industry* (Englewood Cliffs, N. J.: Prentice-Hall, Inc., 1965), p. 42.

[27] For the evaluation of Hoselitz' theory, I draw from Andre Gunder Frank, *Latin America: Underdevelopment or Revolution* (New York: Monthly Review, 1969), Ch. 2. This chapter is reprinted in James D. Cockcroft et al, *Dependence and Underdevelopment: Latin America's Political Economy* (New York: Anchor Books, 1972), Ch. 12.

[28] Jeffrey D. Mitchell, *Dictionary of Sociology* (London: Routledge and Kegan Paul, 1967), pp. 130-31.

[29] Frank, *Latin America,* pp. 24-39.

[30] Class lecture (1969) by Bernard Karsh, the Institute of Labour and Industrial Relations, University of Illinois, Urbana-Champaign; James C. Abegglen, *The Japanese Factory* (Glencoe, Illinois: The Free Press, 1958).

[31] David Granick, *The European Executive* (Garden City, New York: Doubleday, 1962); Ferdinand Zweig, *The British Worker* (London: Penguin Books, 1962); Ferdinand Zweig, *The Worker in an Affluent Society* (London: Heinemann 1962); Raymond Williams, *Culture and Society* (London: Penguin Books, 1961); Charles Perrow, *Complex Organizations* (Glenview, Illinois: Scott, Foresman and Co., 1972).

[32] John Kain, ed. *Race and Poverty* (Englewood Cliffs, N.J.: Prentice-Hall, 1969), p. 20.

[33] *Ibid.*, pp. 61-62.

[34] *Ibid.*, p. 59.

[35] Michael Young, *The Rise of Meritocracy, 1890-2033* (Baltimore: Penguin Books, 1961).

[36] Gabriel Kolko, *The Roots of American Foreign Policy* (Boston: Beacon Press, 1969), p. 17.

[37] *Ibid.*

[38] Frank, *Latin America*, pp. 28-29.

[39] Floyd Hunter, *The Big Rich and the Little Rich,* (New York: Doubleday, 1965), pp. 31-44.

[40] Walt Whiteman Rostow, *The Stages of Economic Development: A Non-Communist Manifesto* (Cambridge: Cambridge University Press, 1960), pp. 4, 6, 7, 39.

[41] Robert E. Baldwin, *Economic Development and Growth* (New York: John Wiley & Sons, Inc; 1972), p. 29.

[42] *Ibid.*

[43] *Ibid.*, p. 80.

[44] Frank, *Latin America.*

[45] Cockcroft et al, *Dependence and Underdevelopment*, p. 351.

[46] Peiro Gheddo, *Why is the Third World Poor?*, translated by Kathryn Sullivan (New York: Orbis Books, 1973).

[47] *Ibid.*, p. 31.

[48] *Ibid.*, pp. 31-32.

[49] *Ibid.*, p. 32.

[50] *Ibid.*

[51] *Ibid.*

[52] *Ibid.*, p. 35.

[53] *Ibid.*

[54] E. Bolaji Idowu, *African Traditional Religion: A Definition* (New York: Orbis Books, 1973).

[55] Robert K Merton, *Social Theory and Social Structure* (New York: The Free Press, 1968), pp. 628-629.

[56] Frank, *Latin America*, pp. 224.

3

IMPERIALISM AND DEPENDENCY

In the last chapter we concluded after a review of some of the traditional modernisation theories that none of them completely explains African, indeed Third World, underdevelopment. It was stated that the explanation for African underdevelopment lies elsewhere. That is to say, African underdevelopment is the result of economic imperialism and the consequent dependency. This chapter briefly examines these two concepts and their relationship to underdevelopment.

Apologists for imperialism have claimed that such a phenomenon does not exist and have even refused to recognize the concept in the social science lexicon. They are willing to talk about World War I, II, and III since these numbers do not place the blame on imperialism. They are happy to be called "super powers" and they are willing to talk about "anti-Americanism," and the like, as long as one does not equate it with anti-imperialism.

The crimes committed by imperialism are endless. Within this century 60 million people have been killed in wars generated by imperialism. As many as 110 million people have been crippled, tens of additional millions have died from disease and epidemics, all generated by wars of imperialism. Some 11 million men, women and children have been slaughtered in gas chambers, shot or hanged. Not less than 3 million have been killed by air raids, by napalm bombs. Since 1870 the imperialists have conducted 121 wars and military operations against the people of Africa, and the result has been the staggering casualties of 5,300,000 Africans.[1] What, then is this imperialism?

Economic Imperialism

The phenomena associated with imperialism include monopolistic privileges and preferences, plunder of raw materials, seizure of territory, enslavement of the indigenous population, nationalism, racism, and militarism. There is a general agreement in associating imperialism with economic, political, cultural and territorial expansion. However, there is much controversy about the meaning of economic imperialism. Patcher, for example, has strongly attacked Lenin for propounding the theory of imperialism. As he puts it, "this kind of economic determinism is ... no longer tenable."[2] George Lichteim has screamed that the radical left has dumped together both old forms of colonialism with "the transfer of surplus value from poor countries through trade relationships which, in practice, discriminate against underdeveloped economies."[3] This dumping together has succeeded in achieving "startling rhetorical effect" but produces no theory of imperialism. If the contention is that "U.S. corporate investments will siphon out more than they put in, the answer is that nothing but purely political consideration forbids nationalistic regimes in Latin America from stopping this reverse flow, or even from seizing major U.S. assets, as in some cases they have already done with complete impunity."[4] No one familiar with what happened to Salvador Allende and Cuba's Fidel Castro will believe Lichteim that the poor, underdeveloped countries can nationalise U.S. corporations' assets with impunity.

There are other apologists who claim that American involvement in the domestic affairs of other countries the world over results from the benign sentiments of the American people. They then express anger as to why people should misunderstand American "Welfare imperialism" for earlier forms of rapacious imperialism which was characteristic of that practiced by its European allies. Thus, Ronald Stelle writes:

> In many of the new states we performed the tasks of an imperialist power without enjoying the economic or territorial advantages of empire. We chose politicians, paid and trained armies, built soccer stadium and airports, and where possible, instructed the new nations in the proper principles of foreign policy. We did this with good intentions, because we really did believe in self-determination for everybody as a guiding moral principle, and because we thought it was our obligation to help the less fortunate "modernize" their societies by making them more like ours. This was our welfare imperialism, and it found its roots in our most basic and generous national instincts.[5]

But despite the controversy and confusion, James O'Conner has discerned three general doctrines.[6] We proceed to summarize them.

(1) The first doctrine argues that there is no relationship between capitalism and imperialism. This school is led by Joseph Schumpeter who has contended that imperialism is "a heritage of the autocratic state ... the outcome of precapitalist forces which the autocratic state has reorganized and would never have been evolved by the inner logic of capitalism."[7] The "inner logic" of capitalism consists of free trade and "where free trade prevails no class has an interest in forcible expansion as such... citizens and goods of every nation can move in foreign countries as freely as though those countries were politically their own."[8]

According to Schumpeter, only the "expert monopolist interests" profit from imperialism. In other words, monopolies in the metropolitan countries which indulge in the habit of dumping surplus commodities behind protective

tariff walls, benefit from imperialism. Schumpeter was sup-
remely confident that these interests would fall prey to the
"inner logic" of capitalism. The basis of this super confidence was the "rationality of capitalism which he felt over-
rode any other features. This confidence was misplaced because the economic policies of the rich societies constitute
what Joan Robinson has labeled the New Mercantilism.

Schumpeter's analysis has found wide support from
bourgeois economists. Their disassociation of capitalism from
imperialism is based on three reasons: because (a) they use
political and not economic criteria to distinguish and identify
colonial and imperial relationships; (b) they have refused to
recognize capitalism as an exploitive system; (c) and finally
"because imperialism historically has contained certain features identified with the theme of expansionism which have
been uniquely associated with any given economic and social
system. Thus bourgeois writers have concluded not only that
imperialism predates capitalism but also that imperialism is
essentially an anachronistic system."[9]

But these bourgeois writers are not correct. In precapitalist societies, economic expansion is not regular, systematic, and not integral to normal economic activity. In
capitalist societies, foreign trade and investment have become
what economists refer to as the "engines of growth." In precapitalist societies, the economic gains resulting from expansion "windfall gains" was constantly in the form of "sporadic
plunder." In capitalist societies, profits resulting from overseas trade and investment have become an integral part of
national income. Whereas plunders in precapitalist societies
were consumed usually by those in the field, in capitalist
societies, exploited territories are dismembered and integrated into the structure of the metropolitan economy. The
debates in precapitalist societies centre around whether or
not to expand whereas in capitalist societies the question
among the ruling elite is "the best way to expand." In precapitalist societies, colonialism was the only means of control

which the metropolitan power could effectively exercise over the conquered territory, but in capitalist societies imperialists have developed better alternative, indirect, and more complex means of control.[10]

(2) The second doctrine states that monopoly capitalism, imperialism and colonialism are fundamentally the same phenomena. This view is sometimes referred to as "neo-Marxist" because Marx did not leave behind any comprehensive theory on this topic and moreover, it was therefore left for future Marxists to filter out empirical truths generally presaged by or contained within Marxist economics.

The first to attempt a theory of imperialism was John A. Hobson who authored *Imperialism*, published in 1902. Hobson conceived of "colonialism as the reflection of the unfulfilled promise of liberal democracy." Inequalities in wealth and income distribution in Britain had weakened the consumption power of the British working classes, and this in turn rendered it impossible for producers to utilize fully their industrial capacity. Lacking in domestic investment outlets, British capitalists turned their attention to the economically under-exploited regions of the world. Britain then established colonies as archives for their surplus capital. Imperialism and its conquests would end only when the British working classes gained more economic and political power through unionism and parliamentary representation, which would forge a redistribution of income and hence the development of a domestic economy in which the volume of consumption would correspond more closely to the volume of production.[11]

But the best read book on the theory of imperialism is Lenin's *Imperialism: The Highest Stage of Capitalism*. Like Hobson, Lenin stated that the primary cause of capital exports was the immense increase in the supply of capital in the metropolitan countries, especially Britain; he also played down the role of the demand for capital in the underdeveloped societies and he saw foreign investments as being the cause of acquisition of colonies. The special feature of Lenin's theory has to do with the cause of the surplus capital.

To Lenin, imperialism was a stage of capitalist development, and not just one possible set of foreign policy options out of many. The basic element is the formation of local and international monopolies backed by high tariff barriers in the metropolitan societies. Monopolistic organizations develop "precisely out of free competition" in four ways. First, the concentration of capital results in the centralization of capital; second, monopoly capital expands and vitalizes itself by confiscating or seizing of indispensable raw materials; third, the investment banks "impose an infinite number of financial ties of dependence upon all the economic and political institutions of contemporary capitalist society, including non-financial capital; fourth, monopoly has resulted from colonial policy. The capitalist financier has added to the previous motives those of struggling for sources of raw materials, exploring of capital and for "spheres of influence ... economic territory in general."[12]

The tendency of the rate of profit to fall has resulted in the surplus of capital and capital exportation, and monopolistic industry. The rise of trade unions, social democracy, inability to recruit labour from the countryside at the going real wage, and labour saving innovations which increase the organic composition of capital, drive down the rate of profit in the metropolitan countries. The formation of monopoly, therefore, is in part to protect profit margins. Simultaneously, economies of large-scale production (internal expansion) and mergers during periods of economic crises (external expansion) vitalize pre-existing tendencies toward monopolistic organization.

But in the economically under-exploited areas, the rate of return earned by capitals is quite high. The composition of capital is lower, labour is plentiful and therefore cheap, and colonial imperialists establish the preconditions for monopolistic privileges. Large amounts of capital are exported to the underdeveloped regions in order to make possible the exploitation of their mineral wealth, so much needed by the metropolitan countries. Thus, the tendency for profits in the imperialist domestic economy to fall is redeemed by high profit margins in the colonies; but at the same time the exportation of capital results in creating the industrial reserve army of the unemployed making it easier for the working class to be more exploited. As O'Connor has stated:

> Pushing this thesis one step forward, the precondition for a truly "favourable" investment climate is indirect or direct control of internal politics in the backward regions. Economic penetration therefore leads to the establishment of spheres of influence, protectorates, annexation.[13]

Through this technique of exploitation and domination the imperialists have been able, to use the words of Paul Sweezy, "to put off the day of reckoning."

But the theories of imperialism propounded by Hobson and Lenin have been criticized. Lenin was anxious to interpret the partition of Africa and the Pacific as a qualitatively different phenomenon and therefore ignored the theme of continuity in European expansionism. Lenin, however, recognized the continuity in European expansionism but felt that the development of monopoly capitalism had broken the continuity. But it has been argued that in the most powerful imperialist country of the time, Great Britain, there were few trusts or cartels of any significance in 1900, and that British economy failed to qualify for the monopoly stage until the early 1930's.

The second criticism challenges the thesis of Hobson and Lenin that the enormous amount of capital from the number one imperialist power, Great Britain, flowed into the colonies. By far the largest amount of British overseas investments went to India, the U.S., Canada, Australia, Argentina and South Africa. The reason for this is that these areas had the basic commodities, basically agricultural goods, which were needed in Britain and, in turn, there was need to pump in capital to finance the construction of roads and railroads to facilitate the exploitation of these resources.

Finally, although internal or home investment far exceeded foreign investment, the exporting of capital did not completely stop after the political independence of British colonies. Probably colonialism, that is, direct political control in this case, was not necessary to provide lucrative investment outlets. As a counter to this criticism, it has been argued that Britain experienced economic stagnation immediately after World War II and this could be attributed to the fall in repatriated earnings from foreign investments, and therefore a fall in the rate of profit, in turn, a result of the removal of British economic interests from their monopoly over trade, banking, agriculture, and other areas of politically independent former colonies.

These criticisms have not demolished the theories of Lenin and Hobson but merely catalogue historical facts which are not fully consistent with former theories. Lenin's description of the chief characteristics of the new colonial era, namely, foreign investments, seizure of territories, monopolistic preferences was largely accurate.

(3) The third and final doctrine, the neo-imperialism characterized by control without colonialism, is what is sometimes referred to as the neo-Leninist, or contemporary Marxist theory of imperialism. Lenin's analysis had implied that the postponed revolution that Marx had earlier predicted would come after the colonies had become independent. But after independence (pseudo-political independence) the new nations found out to their detriment that very little had changed and that they were still being dominated and controlled economically and even politically by their former

metropoles, now being headed by the most superior NATO ally, the U.S.

It was this experience that prompted Kwame Nkrumah, former president of Ghana to write his book, *Neo-Colonialism: The Last Stage of Imperialism*, published in 1965, a year before he was disstooled from office. In that book he concluded that the underdeveloped countries would not make a forward march towards economic independence until neo-colonialism or neo-imperialism was vanquished.

The dominance of the United States and its allies in the world capitalist economy and the inability of the former colonies to achieve any sustained economic and social development forced Marxist economists to rework original doctrines which have resulted in a new theory of neo-colonialism. In this new theory there is a great distinction between colonialism and imperialism, but the original Leninist identity between monopoly capitalism and imperialism is retained. Adopting this view, monopoly capitalism is a very aggressively expansionist political-economic system, while colonialism is viewed as a form of imperialist domination, and often not quite effective.

In the 1950's African and Asian leaders began to denounce what they considered to be "economic control, intellectual control, and actual physical control by a small but alien community, within a nation." The Third All-African People's Conference held in Cairo in 1961 listed some of the basic manifestations of neocolonialism:

This conference considers that Neo-Colonialism, which is the survival of the colonial system in spite of formal recognition of political independence in emerging countries, which become the victims of an indirect and subtle form of domination by political, economic, social, military or technical, forces, is the greatest threat to African countries that have newly won their independence or those approaching this status...

This conference denounces the following manifestations of Neo-Colonialism in Africa:

(a) Puppet governments represented by stooges, and based on some chiefs, reactionary elements, antipopular politicians, big bourgeois *compradors* or corrupted civil or military functionaries.

(b) Regrouping of states, before or after independence, by an imperial power in federation or communities linked to that imperial power.

(c) Balkanization as a deliberate political fragmentation of states by creation of artificial entities, such as, for example, the case of Katanga, Mauritania, Buganda, etc.

(d) The economic entrenchment of the colonial power before independence and the continuity of economic dependence after recognition of national sovereignty.

(e) Integration into colonial economic blocs which maintain the underdeveloped character of African economy.

(f) Economic infiltration by a foreign power after independence, through capital investments, loans and monetary aids or technical experts, of unequal concessions, particularly those extending for long periods.

(g) Direct monetary dependence as in those emergent independent states whose finances remain in the hands of and directly controlled by colonial powers.

(h) Military bases sometimes introduced as scientific research stations or training schools introduced either before independence or as a condition for independence.[14]

In their essay on the political economy of nineteenth century British imperialism, John Gallagher and Ronald Robinson defined imperialism thus:

Imperialism, perhaps, may be defined as a sufficient

function of this process of integrating new regions into expanding economy; its character is largely decided by the various and changing relationships between the political and economic elements of expansion in any particular region and time. Two qualifications must be made. First, imperialism may be only indirectly connected with economic integration in that it sometimes extends beyond areas of economic development but acts for their strategic protection. Secondly, although imperialism is a function of economic expansion, it is not a necessary function. Whether imperialist phenomena show themselves or not is determined not only by the factors of economic expansion, but equally by the political and social organization of the regions brought into the orbit of the expansive society, and also by the world situation in general.

It is only when the politics of these new regions fail to provide satisfactory conditions for commercial or strategic integration and when their relative weakness allows, that power is used imperialistically to adjust those conditions. Economic expansion, it is true, will tend to flow into the regions of maximum opportunity, but maximum opportunity depends as much upon political considerations of security as upon questions of profit. Consequently in any particular region, if economic opportunity seems large but political security small, then full absorption into the extending economy tends to be frustrated until power is exerted upon the state in question. Conversely, in proportion as satisfactory political frameworks are brought into being in this way, the frequency of imperialist intervention lessens and imperialist control is correspondingly relaxed. It may be suggested that this willingness to limit the use of paramount power to establishing security for trade is the distinctive feature of the British imperialism of free trade in the nineteenth century, in contrast to the mercantilist use of power to obtain commercial supremacy and monopoly through political possession.[15]

This particular definition of nineteenth century British imperialism parallels the nature of today's imperialism, especially with respect to the U.S. practice after the end of World War II. In contemporary context, political and strategic intervention constitute "rational overhead charge" for their present and future freedom to expand and act. The difference between European and American imperialism is that the former has been willing to abandon colonies when the cost is much too high, as France abandoned Algeria and Vietnam, for example. But American imperialism, until its recent defeat and forceful expulsion from Vietnam and Cambodia, never bothered about the cost. Even then, specific American economic interests in a country or region have often defined their national interest on the assumption that the nation can identify its welfare with the profits of some of its citizens. The costs to the nation as a whole are less important than the desires and profits of a specific class strata and their need to operate in all four corners of the globe in a manner, collectively, results in enormous prosperity to the U.S. and its ruling elite.

Taking the chief manifestations as spelt out by the Third All-African People's Conference and the definition of imperialism by Gallagher and Robinson, we can say that contemporary imperialism cannot function well without the active involvement of the state in international economic relationship; that there has to be a state capitalism before neo-colonialist policies can be implemented. Furthermore, contemporary imperialism works hard to prevent the newly independent states from consolidating their political independence and thus makes it possible to keep them economically dependent. In the particular case of neo-colonialism, "the allocation of economic resources, investment effort, legal and ideological structures, and other features of the old society remain unchanged"[16] except for the substitution of "internal colonialism" for formal colonialism; in other words, power is now transferred to the domestic ruling classes, those the French so revealingly refer to as *interlocuteurs valables* — "negotiators worth talking to." These are the local marionettes who are sure not to rock the colonial boat. It is this sort of situation that Green and Seidman refer to as arising out of "false decolonization."[17] This sort of independence has ignored the basic needs of such societies, promotes disunity within such societies, and in practice prevents them from attaining real sovereignty. As I have already stated, it was such conditions that prompted Kwame Nkrumah to write his *Africa Must Unite*, and *Neo-Colonialism: The Last Stage of Imperialism*.

Since the main thesis of this book has to do with the economic underdevelopment of Africa, our concern here is primarily with economic imperialism. From our discussion so far, we can define economic imperialism as the economic subordination or domination of one country or a group of countries by another for the main purpose of formal or informal control of domestic economic resources for the benefit of the subordinating or dominating power, and at the expense of the local people and their economy. The imperialist powers control foreign exchange and public and private savings; and agricultural, mineral, transportation, communication, manufacturing, and commercial facilities and other assets. In other words, imperialist powers control both the liquid and real economic resources of the underdeveloped countries.[18]

In the final analysis, certain features of contemporary imperialism can be summarized thus:

> ... the further concentration and centralization of capital, and the integration of the world capitalist economy into the structures of the giant United States based multinational corporations, or integrated conglomerate monopolistic enterprises, and the acceleration of technological change under the auspices of these corporations.

... the abandonment of the "free" international market, and the substitution of administered prices in commodity trade and investment; and the determination of profit margins through adjustments in the internal accounting schemes of the multinational corporations.

... the active participation of state capital in international investment; subsidies and guarantees to private investment; and a global foreign policy which corresponds to the global interests and perspective of the multinational corporation.

... the consolidation of an international ruling class constituted on the basis of ownership and control of the multinational corporations, and the concomitant decline of national rivalries initiated by the national power elites in the advanced capitalist countries; and the internationalization of the world capital market by the World Bank and other agencies of the international ruling class.

... the intensification of all of these tendencies arising from the threat of world socialism to the world capitalist system.[19]

European Community — Third World Relationship

At this juncture, it is important to bring into this exposition John Galtung's European Community — Third World model of dominance or imperialism based on *exploitation* (that is, "vertical division of labour"), *fragmentation* and *penetration*.[20] As will become apparent shortly, the European Community by its action has added another dimension to contemporary imperialism.

Trade flows alone cannot be used as the criteria for exploitation. The better prices now received by the OPEC countries for their crude oil export to the rich countries is a bargain that takes place "within an old pattern, not a change of international structure." The price of the crude oil is still quite cheap for the rich countries. If the oil-exporting countries were to process their crude oil themselves and enjoy both the profits and the economic, research, educational, military, and psychological spin-off effects that accrue to the country where the processing is done, something very fundamental would happen which would have adverse effect on the rich nations. For example, research and education, among other things, would be affected.

The relationship between the Third World and European Community (the rich nations in general) "is *not* a relation aiming at even encouragement of a diversified spectrum of extraction and manufacturing leading to *horizontal* exchange between rich and poor countries, raw materials against semiprocessed and processed."[21] Should this have been the desired goal or if the parties to the association agreement were to treat one another as equals, there would necessarily be "a central authority, distributing important processing industries more evenly between member and associated countries, with special attention exactly to the spin off effects, to the amount of challenge and stimulus to the inspiration given to local research and education: in order to avoid having patterns developed in rich countries just slavishly copied or adapted by an expert team from the center."[22] This would then be the pattern found within any modern state, "encouraging its periphery through policies that are often *not* short-term economically rational."

Galtung has identified three factors which work against such a structure, based on "solidarity and equity." First, all the states that are now associated with the European Community in the Yaounde agreement are among "some of the poorest, least developed, least viable countries in the world."[23] Thus, it is easy for these countries to be made to play the role of suppliers of raw materials to the industrialized countries.

Second, the arrangement is made to protect European Community interests since the agreement they have made with the poor countries does not amount to "a real free trade area." The European Community institutes tariff and quota barriers for products that are "homologues et concurrentiels" or products likely to compete with products from European Community countries. This even affects foodstuffs. The agreement is such that enables members of the European Community to import just what they want and need from the poor associated states.

Finally, partly through the assistance of the European Development Fund and the European Investment Bank, the European Community is able to export more processed products to the associated countries. Through these two institutions West European countries are able to continue their subsidization of their own industry by paying for the infrastructure in the poor countries (roads, telecommunication, sewage, etc.), and "by giving grants tied to procurement of manufactured goods" from European Community countries.[24] As Galtung has demonstrated:

> During the first EDF (European Development Fund) only 0.7% of the funds disbursed were used by these states themselves to build local industry (for the local markets); during the second EDF it was 1.3%. The total amount of aid through the European Development Fund has increased from $581 million in the first period to $ 730 million in the second, but the level of tying is as high as 80% (82% of all French aid for instance) — i.e. capital goods are to be procured in EC (European Community). In this way, European governments subsidize not only their own industry but ultimately also themselves, because of what they get back in the form of taxes. This is also an old pattern, governments paying industry located in the center of the country so that they can build an infrastructure in the periphery, so that industry from the center can move into the periphery — all under the heading of "development." These grants that look highly attractive on a short-term basis will only be made available to countries willing to enter into an association agree-

ment. Of course such grants will be a major argument used by local elites arguing in favor of association.[25]

But in what Galtung calls the long run, there is going to be a surplus of semi-processed and processed goods for export to the rich countries. But it will take some time for the European Community countries to accept a situation in which such goods are brought into their countries in significant quantities. But eventually large-scale exports by the associated members to the European Community will take place under three very crucial assumptions. (1) The European Community would make sure that the processed goods do not compete with those from the European Community. Such goods will consist of such items customarily produced in the initial period of industrial development, e.g., "textiles and not-too-processed iron, and/or goods produced by highly polluting industries that EC (and other industrialized countries) would prefer to have outside its own borders."[26] (2) The European Community countries will insist that such processed goods be produced within global giants with headquarters within their borders. Thus, the ensuing economic cycles will tie "center to periphery in such a way that finance, administration and research will be located in the center."[27] Furthermore, "the extraction of raw materials, cheap labour and factories working according to old blueprints elaborated in the center will be located in the periphery."[28] Since all this will take place within the global giants, various financial manipulations will be possible. For example, "the corporation can fix internal prices such that the profit shows up where taxes are lowest." (3) Finally, the European Community countries will still find themselves at liberty to "export goods at a higher level of processing" than what they actually import from the underdeveloped countries. In fact, the European Community countries have succeeded in accomplishing exactly what they used to do by competition and by dividing the underdeveloped world into spheres of influence or empires. They now practice "collective colonialism." The EDF is an attempt to share the cost of infrastructure of the underdeveloped countries that enhance the profitability of the multinationals from the European Community countries.

The second component of dominance is "fragmentation" which is the same thing as what Kwame Nkrumah has referred to as "balkanization." Whereas the rich and exploiter countries are coordinated and unified, the poor, underdeveloped and exploited countries or what Galtung calls the "periphery" are disorganized and disunited. Little or no trade takes place among them, and added to this are indirect or very expensive communication and transportation. These problems are carried-overs from colonialism. The tendency is for the center to deal with the periphery nations individually, "particularistically" not in the presence of the others. Trade is also bilateral, between the dominant center and one of the periphery countries, without the benefit of institutions for "multilateral clearing."

Partly resulting from this situation, there is the absence of "a scarcity of multilateral organizations" to enable the periphery countries to deal with matters of common interest "in full view of each other." Fragmentation carries with it an element of monopoly. While the center establishes links in different directions, including other centre countries and groups of countries, the periphery or underdeveloped counries tend to concentrate their external activity in the direction of the center. This is seen as a natural event; anything different is a deviation against which the center countries could take an action the repercussions of which would be inimical to the interest of the periphery country concerned.

That the divisive effect on the Third World of the European Community was so intended cannot be debated. The basis of the European Community is "a system of selective preferences for the associated states, as opposed to other developing countries." The relationship between the periphery nations and the center must be viewed as a mere extention in time of the "particular relation" which existed between colonised countries and the metropoles; this relationship has refused to disappear after traditional colonialism. The very idea of "associated states" tells all of the story.

This particular label implies a "second-class membership" (a slap on the face of universalism) at a time when all nations are said to be first-class nations, much the same way as citizens of a country claim the right to the same first-class citizenship. It is important to emphasize that the European Community is exclusive in that membership with associate status is open only to "former dependencies." Although not explicitly stated, socialist countries that are former dependencies cannot join since "their entire theory and practice of economic relations are fundamentally opposed to capitalism" as practised by the European Community. Thus, Guinea and Algeria cannot be associate members, and those states that are members show little signs in the direction of nationalization, the exception here being Congo Brazzaville and Somalia. There is thus a wedge driven between underdeveloped countries that have selected different paths as their basic pattern of economic development.[29] As Galtung has noted:

> Less developed countries get their loyalties split because of the wedge driven between those that are former dependencies and those that are not, between socialist and those that are capitalist, and between continents. Most of the associated states will be African, making Africa to the EC what Latin America is to the U.S. So far the system has also had a fundamentally divisive impact *within* Africa, slowing down the move towards African unity, as well as the work of the UN Economic Commission for Africa. The same can be said for the Third World as a whole... the Yaounde agreement by and large tends to freeze the

status quo, it gives no impetus in the direction of solidarity. On the contrary, it plays up to the short-term interest of each developing nation, including the associated states, has in preserving its share of the export of raw materials, and in increasing it... for fear that any change will impair the present position. For that reason the associated states have tended to be the allies of the *regionalists* in the EC, the old "mother countries."[30]

The final aspect of the European Community dominance is "penetration." Penetration into the elites of former colonial territories is based on "ideological *identification* with the elites of the European Community and *dependency* on a continued relation with them."[31] The identification is achieved through education in institutions set up by the colonial powers. Dependency is accomplished in terms of "economic vested interest in a high... trade level between center and periphery countries."[32]

Taking together all the factors outlined above the inevitable conclusion one comes up with is that the European Community is pursuing the same old policies with new means. The old colonial policies had left the colonised societies exploited, penetrated, and fragmented. This, considering the fact that each of the countries of the European Community had their empire. But all of them have now combined their forces which are quite formidable. The individual former dependencies could not get equitable treatment from their former masters under colonialism and it would be folly on their part to expect it now. The association between the rich and powerful countries and the underdeveloped ones is necessary, perhaps essential. But the issue lies in the problem of equitable treatment. The European Community has added another dimension to contemporary imperialism.

The Dependency Model

Having outlined the main features of contemporary imperialism, how do we relate them to the economic underdevelopment of the poor countries? As suggested by Stratchey:

> The backward regions assumed a dependency status (the last step before outright control) in relation to the metropolitan powers chiefly because the former were in debt to the latter. What was significant about the shift from consumer goods to capital goods in world trade was that the colony-to-be needed long-term credits or loans to pay for the capital goods, and that finally, the relationship between the backward country and the metropolitan country one of debtor and creditor. And from this it was but a small step to dependence and domination.[33]

The question to be answered then is, what is dependency?

Dependency is the situation that the history of colonial imperialism has left and that modern imperialism creates in underdeveloped countries. As Dale Johnson puts it, "Dependency is imperialism seen from the perspective of underdevelopment."[34] Dependency is not an "external factor" as often erroneously believed. Dependency is a "conditioning situation" in which the specific histories of development and underdevelopment transpire in various societies. Specifically, as defined by Theotonio dos Santos, dependency is:

> a situation in which a certain group of countries have their economy conditioned by the development and expansion of another economy, to which the former is subject. The relation of interdependence between two or more economies, and between these and world trade, assumes the form of dependence when some countries (the dominant) can expand and give impulse to their own development, while other countries (the

dependent) can only develop as a reflection of this expansion. This can have positive and/or negative effects on their immediate development. In all cases the basic situation of dependence leads to a global situation in dependent countries that situates them in backwardness and under the exploitation of the dominant countries. The dominant countries have a technological, commercial, capital resource, and social-political predominance over the dependent countries (with predominance of some of these aspects in various historiical moments). This permits them to impose conditions of exploitation and extract part of the domestically produced surplus.[35]

Historical situations of dependency have conditioned contemporary underdevelopment in Africa and other underdeveloped societies. Thus underdevelopment is not an original state as modernization theorists want us to believe. The beginnings of African underdevelopment can be traced to the trans-Atlantic slave trade, the abandoning of that trade in favour of "legitimate trade" and the eventual partition of Africa. In other words, the basis of African underdevelopment can be found in slave trade and colonial imperialism. In the first the African supplied the white man with human cargo (often, at least at the initial stage, Europeans raided African coasts for captives whom they enslaved) who were taken to the American plantations to toil the lands stolen from the owners, the Indians. In return the African received guns, gunpowder and silky items that began his process of dependency.

In the second stage, the colonial imperialism stage, the African became oriented to the export of primary products (principally agricultural), under the control of metropolitan capital, and constituted as markets for imported manufactures from the same metropolitan countries. As already mentioned in the previous section, foreign capital came in to construct social overheads — transportation facilities and utilities that would enhance the exploitation of the people and their natural resources, and for the maintenance of law and order. With their economic and military power they successfully kept African countries as *de facto* colonies. Governments of the underdeveloped societies and their businessmen have no control over international markets for primary products, the prices of which fluctuate and quite often are manipulated by the rich and powerful nations. Such fluctuations almost always result in unfavourable terms of trade in relation to imports.

Dependency relations have also shaped the social structure of underdevelopment. In our discussion of imperialism it was stated that when the imperialist powers could not continue their occupation of their former dependencies, they decided to quit but made sure that they left the reins of power in good hands. They made sure that they handed power over to their internal collaborators. They did not hesitate to create and finance political parties in opposition to real nationalist ones; and they also rigged elections and used various other means to make sure that they handed over to those who would continue with the colonial policies. Thus a crucial problem of underdevelopment is the fact that in this process of dependency there has arisen a coincidence of interest between the local or internal bourgeois and the external capitalist oligarchies. The internal compradors greatly benefit from this dependency situation, and it would be tantamount to demanding too much of them to sever such a lucrative relationship. So after independence these national bourgeois have strengthened their relationship with their international allies. Their investments are geared towards exports and activities complementary to foreign industrial capital. They have connived with foreign interests to rob their countries of their much needed foreign exchange and have been involved in all sorts of unpatriotic activities that fail to aid economic development.

The implications of this sketch of the dependency model

are clear. Africa has played a definite role in the international economy, but the internal development of Africa has been severely curtailed or "conditioned" by the needs of the dominant economies within the world or international economy or market. No nation has ever developed completely outside of the world market nor has any nation operated without constraints upon policy choices. But the difference between dependent and interdependent development is that growth in the dependent nations occurs as a reflex of the expansion of the dominant nations, and is geared toward the needs of the dominant economies, i.e., foreign rather than national needs."[36]

In the dependent societies, foreign factors of production such as capital and technology have become the main determinants of economic progress and socio-political life. And while this same world market promoted the expansion of development in Europe and America, it has a tendency to limit development in the dependent societies.[37] This historical dependency has been the root problem of African underdevelopment.

> Dependency means, then, that the development alternatives open to the dependent nation are defined and limited by its integration into and functions within the world market. This limitation of alternatives differs from limitations in the dominant nations in so far as the functioning of the basic decisions in the world market... are determined by the dominant nations. Thus the dependent nations must make choices in a situation in which they do not set the terms or parameters of choice.[38]

The international system or world market upon which Africa depends implies a "structure," that is, a structure of institutions, classes, and power arrangements. The dynamic process that takes place within that structure is called "imperialism." "Imperialism," then, "is an institutionalized system of control which systematically shapes the institutions and structures of dependent, dominated countries and limits their freedom of action, if they are to avoid the system's sanctions, to system-defined alternatives."[39] The international system is not merely economic; it is a stratified system of power relations, as Irving Louis Horowitz has emphasized by the title of his book *Three Worlds of Development: The Theory and Practice of International Stratification.*[40]

At the core of this power relations within the international system are the multinational corporations. There are four main features of these global giants: (1) horizontal integration, the tendency to take advantage of a profitable opportunity to buy out their opponents who produce similar commodities, and vertical integration, the tendency to own the plant, produce their own raw materials, and also become their own wholesaler, thus monopolizing the three stages rather than one "stage of production"; (2) the tendency toward conglomeration or diversification; (3) mounting "internationalization" or "multinationalization" of the operation of capital; and (4) the growing cooperation among the capitalist world as opposed to the rivalry of about from 1870 to 1914, and the growing disunity of "the secondary capitalist powers thus far to offer a serious challenge to American hegemony."[41]

These characteristics of modern capitalism have prompted a need for cooperation among the multinational corporations with respect to their overseas operations. There has arisen a need to control the production process, from the sources of supply and processing of raw materials to markets or outlets for commodities. Their emphasis has turned to "long-range planning, maximum security and avoidance of risk, and preservation of a favourable climate (ideological, and social, as well as economic) for the *perpetuation* of corporate operations and for long-range profits."[42] Furthermore, increase in the scale, monopolistic concentration, conglomeration and internationalization of private capital leads to the reduced dependence upon immediate profit returns from overseas investments.[43]

Third, a limited measure of "development" takes place and the resulting moderate redistribution of income provides a wider market for metropolitan exports, and may even lead to relative stability. A relatively "developed" African economy is quite healthy for foreign investment and trade. In this respect contemporary capitalism has an ingredient of "welfare imperialism." The problem is that under these conditions African development is controlled fundamentally by the needs of foreign corporation, rather than response to African needs.

Fourth, there are efforts at regional integration of markets, such as the French Economic Community, the Commonwealth of Nations which tie African countries to their former colonial masters, the European Economic Market which former colonies can join only as associate members, and finally, the Organization of American States in which the United States dominates.

Since the nature of private corporate operations abroad is such that they need protection by the imperialist state, the multinational corporations have employed their power and influence to shape the foreign policies of their governments. In no other country is this more evident than in the U.S. Here the U.S. interests quite often are synonymous with the corporate interests of its firms abroad. This is demonstrated by this quotation:

> During the 25 years in which the United States was the most powerful nation on earth, the tighter and more notorious were the links between Washington, Wall Street, and Detroit, the better it was for the U.S. Companies. When the CIA removed Mohammed Mossadeq, an obstreperous Iranian premier who "irrationally" tried to interfere with Gulf's and Standard Oil's prospects for taking over his country's oil, or when the same agency rescued Guatemalan banana

land for United Fruit from a popularly elected "subversive" nationalist, these were U.S. patriotic initiatives applauded by businessmen. Capital and ideological purity were preserved together. The readier the Pentagon and CIA were to bring down or raise up governments in underdeveloped countries, the better the investment climate for U.S. corporations. U.S. military power was used to establish the ground rules within which American business could operate. The U.S. Government acted as consultant for rightist coups in Bolivia, Brazil, Chile, Greece, and Indonesia, and their generals opened their countries to U.S. investment on the most favourable terms. Wherever the flag has been planted around the world, in some 500 major military interventions, U.S. corporations have moved in. The construction of a world wide military empire has been good business.[44]

The names that are conspicuously absent from the above list are Congo (Zaire) and Lumumba and Mobutu, the latter being the "most successful" U.S. client in Black Africa. The same Pentagon and CIA brought down Lumumba and raised up Tshombe, later Mobutu, who has kept his commitment of allowing U.S. corporations to operate in Zaire uninterruptedly. We shall have an occasion to return to this point.

The relationship between the U.S. government and its multinationals became even stronger during the Nixon Administration. Nixon was a candidate put forward and also supported by the American conglomerates. Having been put in office by the business giants, Nixon had every reason to reward his backers. Thus, he went out of his way to demonstrate that his was a "Business Administration" and that he was all out to "protect American business."[45] Of course, Nixon could not have the courage to tell the American people that he was using the resources of the greatest power on earth to promote the interests of a few economic elites. The CIA was the instrument for implementing Nixon's economic policies. National interests became synonymous with the economic interests of the global giants. Of vital importance is the fact that the presence of U.S. business in a dependent country "entitles" it (U.S.) to become very actively involved in the domestic politics of the people, buying and selling local politicians.

Finally, before ending this review of imperialism and dependency, it is important to recognize a very important recent work in this area. Walter Rodney in his famous book, *How Europe Underdeveloped Africa*,[46] has given in great detail the information about how Western European Administrations and trading companies deliberately and systematically worked hard to bring about the underdevelopment of this continent. Rodney emphasizes that bringing Africa into the world economy may have had a few advantages but it did create the conditions for the present economic problems encountered by Africa. Integrating Africa into the international economic system at the time was premature and it was the beginning of the increasing disequilibrium between the poor and the rich economies. This was so because Africa was forced into the international market system at a competitive disadvantage. Since Africa did not, nor does it now, possess the kind of advanced technology known in the West and North America, it was virtually impossible for Africans to compete with the Europeans and the result was a one-way trade. Not only was the trade a one-way affair but the Europeans had made African societies their *de facto* colonies.

In their vantage position as the conqueror, the dominant powers—militarily, economically and politically—were able to exploit Africa's natural resources which they sent home without paying just prices; in addition Africa served as a dumping ground for their cheap and surplus products. The end product of all these events was that Africa became a dependent economy, serving European interests and thus externally controlled and regulated by the metropolitan countries.

The false decolonization which has resulted is the phenomenon of neocolonialism never solving these problems of underdevelopment. This, of course, is not to say that Europeans would have them if they had not been forced to leave, because solving these problems would not have served their imperialistic interests. My emphasis throughout this work, in the words of Joseph Wayas is:

> that the problem was not and has not been that Africa was brought into the world market system but rather, the manner it was introduced into it; having an economic relationship with Europe was not in itself a bad idea; what was bad was the nature of the relationship. The fight which African countries are waging today is therefore a fight not to eliminate the relationship but to change it so that Africa can move away from her present situation of economic dependence and subordination.[47]

What we have said is that development and underdevelopment are both comparable terms as well as having a dialectical relationship. By this is meant that the interaction of both produces each other. In the interaction between Europe and Africa the former was the master while the latter was the slave and the result was the transfer of wealth from Africa to Europe. This relationship has resulted in a great imbalance or disequilibrium which has remained the fundamental problem in African underdevelopment. It goes without saying that Africa must find a way to liberate herself from economic dependence. And this is what the struggle is all about.

REFERENCES

[1] Gus Hall, *Imperialism Today* (New York: International Publishers, 1972), p.13.

[2] Henry Patcher, "The Problem of Imperialism," *Dissent* (September-October, 1970), p. 463.

[3] George Lichteim, "Imperialism," *Commentary* XLIX/4 (April, 1970), p. 134.

[4] George Lichteim, "Imperialism in this Century, " *Commentary* XLIX/5 (May, 1970), p. 144.

[5] Ronald Stelle, *Pan Americana* (New York: The Viking Press, 1971), p. 19.

[6] James O'Connor, "The Meaning of Economic Imperialism," in K.T. Fann and Donald C. Hodges, eds., *Readings in U.S. Imperialism* (Boston: F. Porter Sargent, 1971), pp. 23-68.

[7] *Ibid.*, p. 74.

[8] *Ibid.*

[9] *Ibid.*, p. 25.

[10] *Ibid.*, pp. 25-26.

[11] *Ibid.*, pp. 30-31.

[12] V. I. Lenin, "Imperialism: The Highest Stage of Capitalism," in *Lenin: Selected Works* (New York: International Publishers, 1971), pp. 169-263.

[13] O'Connor, "The Meaning of Economic Imperialism," p. 32.

[14] "Neo-Colonialism," *Voice of Africa*, I/4 (April, 1961), p. 4; also cited by O'Connor, "The Meaning of Economic Imperialism."

[15] John Gallagher and Ronald Robinson, "The Imperialism of Free Trade," *Economic History Review*, Second Series, (August, 1953), pp. 5-6.

[16] O'Connor, "The Meaning of Economic Imperialism," p. 40.

[17] Reginald H. Green and Ann Seidman, *Unity or Poverty* (Baltimore: Books, 1968).

[18] For the discussion of the imperialistic control over money, see O'Connor, "The Meaning of Economic Imperialism."

[19] *Ibid.*, pp. 43-44.

[20] John Galtung, *The European Community: A Superpower in the Making* (London: George Allen & Unwin, 1973), Ch. 6.

[21] *Ibid.*, p. 69.

[22] *Ibid.*

[23] *Ibid.*, p. 70.

[24] *Ibid.*

[25] *Ibid.*, pp. 70-71.

[26] *Ibid.*, p. 71.

[27] *Ibid.*, pp. 71-72.

[28] *Ibid.*, p. 72.

[29] *Ibid.*, p. 78.

[30] *Ibid.*, pp.78, 79.

[31] *Ibid.*, p. 80.

[32] *Ibid.*

[33] O'Conner, "The Meaning of Imperialism," p. 33.

[34] Dale L. Johnson, "Dependence and the International System," in Cockcroft et al., *Dependence and Underdevelopment*, p. 71.

[35] *Ibid.*, pp. 71-77.

[36] Ira Katznelson et al, eds., *The Politics and Society Reader* (New York: David Mckay Co., 1974), pp. 175-76.

[38] *Ibid.*

[39] Cockcroft et al, *Dependence and Underdevelopment*, p. 9.

[40] (New York: Oxford University Press, 1972).

[41] Katznelson et al, *The Politics and Society Reader*, pp. 192-3.

[42] *Ibid.*, p. 194.

[43] *Ibid.*

[44] Richard Barnet and Ronald Muller, *Global Reach* (New York: Simon and Schuster, 1974), pp. 78-79.

[45] *Ibid.*, p. 83.

[46] Walter Rodney, *How Europe Underdeveloped Africa* (Washington D.C.: Howard University Press, 1974).

[47] Joseph Wayas, "How Independent are Sovereign African States? *Daily Times* (October 17, 1977).

4

DEVELOPMENT OF UNDERDEVELOPMENT: SLAVERY

Trading in African human cargo may be dated to ancient Egyptian and Roman days. During the period of Moslem ascendency it was practised also among Moslems in Arabia, Turkey, Persia, and India. But the military subjugation of the continent of Africa in modern times, and the enslavement of sections of its population, was begun by Portugal in about the middle of the 15th century. It was the Portuguese who introduced the Atlantic slave trade in the early 16th century when the discovery of the New World created a demand for more workers. Not long after this, the Spanish, French, Genoese, Dutch, and, after 1560, the English also joined the trade, and merchants from Liverpool were greatly involved as will become evident shortly. But the Portuguese were mainly responsible for setting up a string of fortified trading factories along the west coast from Cape Verde to the Congo by the time the famous Vasco da Gama had sailed around the Cape in 1497. Sure enough, Europeans did not start the African slave trade but "the sheer volume of the slave traffic across the Atlantic and the brutality with which African slaves were treated renders the European slave trade fundamentally different from anything that took place within Africa itself."[1]

The result of this was a triangular trade whereby England — as well as France and Colonial America — supplied the exports and ships; Africa, the human merchandise; the colonial plantations, raw materials. The slave ships sailed from the home country with cargoes of manufactured goods. These were exchanged at a profit on the west coast of Africa for black slaves,

> who were traded on the plantations, at another profit, in exchange for a cargo of colonial produce to be taken back to the home country... The triangular trade thereby gave a triple stimulus to British industry. The Negroes were purchased with British manufactures; transported to the plantations, they produced sugar, cotton, indigo, molasses and other tropical products, the processing of which created new industries in England: while the maintenance of the Negroes and their owners on the plantations provided another market for British industry, New England agriculture and the Newfoundland fisheries. By 1750 there was hardly a trading or manufacturing town in England which was not in some way connected with the triangular trade. The profits obtained provided one of the main streams of that accumulation of capital in England which financed the Industrial Revolution.[2]

The Atlantic slave trade started some 50 years before Columbus' voyage to the Western world. The trade started with Europeans invading the coast of Africa and capturing its inhabitants for sale on European markets, especially, at the initial stage, in Portugal and Spain. According to the earliest record of slave-catching kept by Azurara, leader of a Portuguese venture in 1446, after his ship had landed on the West-Central coast of Africa, soldiers swarmed ashore, seized a few curious and unsuspecting natives, and proceeded inland seeking more victims. They came to a settlement, and for the rest of the story, we turn to the diary:

> They looked towards the settlement and saw that the Negroes, with their women and children, were already coming as quickly as they could out of their dwellings, because they had caught sight of their enemies. But

they the Portuguese shouting out "St. James," "St. George," and "Portugal," at once attacked them, killing and taking all they could. Then might you see mothers foresaking their children and husbands their wives, each striving to escape as best he could.

Some drowned themselves in the water; others thought to escape by hiding under their huts; other stowed their children among the sea-weed, where our men found them afterwards, hoping they would escape notice. And at last our Lord God who giveth a reward for every good deed, willed that for the toil they had undergone in his service, they should that day obtain victory over their enemies, as well as payment for all their labour and expense; for they took captive of those Negroes what with men, women, and children, 165, besides those that perished and were killed.[3]

It is clear from this quotation that this business was very brutal and those who directed it very sanctimonious. It is not therefore surprising that two of the ships used by Good Queen Bets' favourite hero, Sir John Hawkins, in his slave trading enterprise were named *John the Baptist* and *Jesus*.[4]

This process of rapine and carnage went on for over four hundred years; for ferocity it has no parallel in the diabolical annals of human oppression. It constitutes a central feature of the process of the primitive accumulation of capital and a basic component of the history of capitalism, especially American capitalism.

For about the first fifty years, this cruel business supplied labour for plantations in southern Portugal, for Spanish mines, and for domestic service in those countries and in France and England. But with the discovery of the Americas whose greatest need was for strong labour familiar to the ways of mining and agriculture, the special function of Africa as a supplier of such labour was established.

Whites had no doubt that this was the predetermined

role that Africa had to play.[5] This role that Africa was forced to play was of particular importance to North America, especially the area that became the United States of America, because when the White Anglo-Saxons arrived there were about one million inhabitants known as Indians. This lack of an indigenous and exploitable population gave rise to the necessity for the mass importation of African slaves, direly needed in huge numbers in a plantation economy such as were to be established in the favourable climate and terrain found in what are today Florida and Maryland.

It was not possible to import slaves for labour in English America from the areas of Central and South America because these places were already dominated and exploited by Spain and Portugal. Africa was near enough to Europe and to America. Africa was at this point in an agricultural stage of civilization, had for centuries domesticated cattle, smelted iron (probably first in the world), woven cotton, and made soap, glass, pottery and blankets. The enslaved African was quite unlike the native Indian in that the African was taken away from his ancestral home to a strange land, where he was completely deprived of the opportunity to interact with his people as well as the ability of his social organization to act succor for him in flight or in resistance.

In the abominable trade fabulous profits, sometimes doubling and quintupling original investments in one or two voyages, were made by the slave dealers in Europe and, eventually, by the merchants of the New World, especially those of New England.

The triangular trade greatly stimulated shipbuilding in England. Special ships were constructed for the slave trade, "combining capacity with speed in an effort to reduce mortality. Many shipwrights in Liverpool were themselves slave traders. The outstanding firm was Baker and Dawson, one of the largest exporters of slaves to the West Indies, and engaged, after 1783, "in supplying of slaves to the Spanish colonies."[6] The slave trade also stimulated the export of woolen manufactures to the colonies. The woolen trade was so important that the British parliament in the 17th century used it as an important consideration in defense of the slave trade. The woolen trade was so lucrative that British companies fought among themselves for its control.

Slave trade promoted the production of rum, an essential component of the cargo of the slave ships, particularly the colonial American slave ships. Slave traders could not afford "to dispense with a cargo of rum. It was profitable to spread a taste for liquor on the coast. The Negro dealers were plied with it, were induced to drink till they lost their reason, and then the bargain was struck."[7] One African slave dealer is reported to have been invited to dinner by a slave ship captain just after the captain had paid the African for his slaves. In the ship the captain seized his bag of gold and consummated the process by enslaving his guest. In 1765 there were two distilleries at Liverpool, the express purpose of which was to supply ships bound for Africa.[8]

Another great item of every African cargo was guns and Birmingham was the center for the gun trade just as Manchester was of the cotton trade. The Birmingham guns "were exchanged for men, and it was a common saying that the price of a Negro was one Birmingham gun. The African musket was an important export, reaching a total of 100,000 to 150,000 annually. With the British government and the East India Company, Africa ranked as the most important customer of the Birmingham gun makers."[9]

Thus on the basis of this odious business, ports like Bristol and Liverpool, Perth Amboy and Newport flourished, to a considerable degree. On the whole,

> the enslavement of the African continent was of basic importance in the development of world capitalism, as Africa's intensified exploitation, beginning with the late 19th century, has been of consequence in the strength

of world imperialism. Indicative of the meaning of this business in money terms is the fact that the value of the over 300,000 slaves hauled in 878 Liverpool ships from 1783 to 1973 was more than 15 million pounds — and that is but one port, for one decade.[10]

Despite the lucrativeness of the slave trade, Africa's most important contribution to the development of European capitalism and of the American colonies — and of American capitalism does not lie on the trade itself. Africa's most important contribution lies "in slavery, in the unpaid and forced labour of million of Negroes for over two centuries."[11]

In explaining the speed and magnitude of the growth of the American capitalism, economic historians have enumerated several contributing factors. Among them are the stupendous size and great resources; its being separated from the perpetual and devastating wars of Europe, which set back its competitors and from which American bourgeoisie derived much profit; the immigration, for many years, of million of Europeans, Asians, and Latin Americans with their skills and strength (and their differences, making it easy for them to be dominated and exploited); the prolonged existence of a bourgeois-democratic republic, an ideal state form for the early development and ripening of capitalism. All these explanations are correct.

But of equal importance is the fact that within what has come to be known as the United States of America there lived Africans who were forcefully enslaved and who constituted between 10 to 20 percent of the American population. These mercilessly exploited and maltreated slaves "produced profits running into the multi-billions from the cotton, sugar, rice, tobacco, hemp, gold, coal, and lumber their labour created."[12] In terms of the economic conquest of America, and of the early accumulation of capital, the enslavement of the African was organic appearance and rise of American capitalism.

90

Now what did Africa get out of all this? It is quite difficult to convey the meaning of the slave trade in human terms. In the 400 years of the African slave trade not less than 15 million Africans were enslaved in the New World. For every one slave who arrived there alive, about five or six had died — in the wars in this continent, during the trek to the coast, while in the barracoons, waiting to be transported to the New World, in the frequent insurrections aboard ships, and in the course of the horrors of the six to ten weeks in the Middle Passage. Dr. DuBois, in his work *The Suppression of the African Slave Trade,* noted that the Royal African shipped about 60,000 slaves from 1680 to 1688, of whom over 14,000 died at sea.[13]

The implication here is that between the 15th and the 19th century, the African continent lost, in enslaved and killed, between 65 and 75 million people, and these were the most vital part of the population, since the aged, the lame, the sickly were not among those affected.

European and American writers have written that the slave trade was mutually beneficial; that it helped in the development of Africa. They have said that Africa acquired some food crops which became staples in the continent. They have also said that the abominable trade "enhanced the development of those states that benefitted from it largely by increasing the wealth available to the king of the state.[14]

We are told that slaves:

> constituted an increasingly major addition to the available exports — gold, silver, ivory, spices, skins, guns, grains, wax and other goods. In return for these goods, the rulers and their peoples received a large enough variety of European goods to support an economic base of great importance. The more goods, including slaves, that were produced in or channeled through his kingdom, the more imported goods a king and his people were able to acquire. With these imported

91

goods a ruler could equip at least some of his soldiers with European weaponry. This gave him an enormous advantage over neighboring peoples who fought with traditional African weapons. And the spread of attractive foreign goods served as a powerful inducement to the ruler's followers and vassals to support him in wars of conquest, which usually increased the supply of African goods, including slaves.[15]

That Africa had to be depopulated in order for her to acquire a few food crops does not stand to reason. There are various cases of diffusion the world over and the beneficiaries never had to become involved in slave trade in order to benefit from them. So it is nonsensical that acquiring a few food crops which have become African staples should be given as a justification for the odious trade.

It is very clear that in the trade Africans were in an inferior position; all that they could export were slaves and a few extractive materials while in return they bought manufactured European goods which included beads, trinkets, rum, guns and gunpowder, among other things. It is difficult to see how this trade aided the development of Africa as the apologists for slave trade have argued.

In 1976 I watched on the television screen David Brinkley and his colleague, John Chancellor, discuss the slave trade as part of the American bicentennial celebration. In their typical racist commentary, Mr. Brinkley and Mr. Chancellor commented that, despite shouts and screams to the contrary, that trade was mutually beneficial — European and American slave traders paid for their slaves and whatever the medium of exchange and whatever Africans did with it was not the business of the white man.

But my contention here is that the economic impact of the slave trade on Africa was negative. European traders in Africa made use of African and Asian consumer goods, indicating that their system of production was not very much superior. It is important to note that at the initial stage

Europeans used to buy cloths for resale in Africa and vice versa. Using Europeans as their middlemen, Morocco, Mauritania, Senegambia, Ivory Coast, exported cloths and other items to other parts of Africa. In fact, Professor John Flint in a lecture to the Interdisciplinary Seminar on Modernization, Purdue University, 1971, said that the quality of Yoruba cloths was far superior to that of the European invaders. Professor Flint stated that the Yoruba people refused to buy European cloths. As it was always the practice in the relationship between the two unequal partners, Europeans had to seek a way to destroy indigenous enterprise that stood in their way. The result was that while African trade with Europe contributed immensely to the development of the latter, the former became a victim of underdevelopment.

Thus, while African demand of cloths and other goods increased in the 15th and 16th centuries, Europeans were in control of the trade and could flood the African market with their own cloths. They learned the technique from Indians and perhaps Africans and in the process surpassed them. Certainly many varied social factors coming together determine very much when a society makes a breakthrough from small-scale craft technology to equipment designed to harness nature so that labour becomes more effective. Rodney tells us that one of such factors is the presence of "a demand for more products than can be made by hand, so that technology is asked to respond to a definite social need — such as that for clothes." But when the demand for clothes was increased Europeans seized the advantage and flooded the market with their own clothes and the African had no incentive to seek alternative means of production. The result was what Rodney calls "technology arrest" or stagnation, and in some instances real regression, since people even abandoned the simple technique of their forefathers.[16] An example is the abandonment of traditional iron smelting in most parts of Africa.

All the theories of modernization that we discussed earlier emphasize technology associated with scientific inquiry and the process of production. There is no doubt that this was the case during the capitalist development of Europe. But the slave trade had a disastrous effect on Africa by forcefully taking away Africans to till the lands stolen from Indians; such young adults and youths constitute the nucleus of any development. These are the young men who would probably have become leaders of invention. Africans were basically concerned with how to protect themselves and families from being enslaved abroad. Wars for slaves were daily exercise. Most of Africa was afire, everybody planning for an attack that could erupt anytime. Europeans were fond of backing various groups simultaneously. They would give this group guns and ammunition and warn them against an impending attack by the other group and vice versa. This was to make sure that one of the groups would strike first to prevent the other from attacking; this would ensure slaves for the European traders. This situation in which people lived in fear and speculation left no room for inventiveness. And the African was more concerned with trade than with production, and this situation was not propitious for the introduction of technological advance.

One might wonder why European technology was not eventually borrowed by Africa. The nature of the relationship between the two partners even in the post slavery period never permitted any transfer of technology. In fact, Europe was not willing to transfer technology to Africa. There are cases in which Africans appealed to Europeans to stop the slave trade and to introduce technical knowledge to the continent. Rodney has even cited certain correspondences to this effect.[17] The circumstances of African trade with Europe were quite unfavourable to creating a consistent African demand for technology relevant to our development; even when demands were made they fell on deaf ears as this would defeat the purpose of imperialism. Even today, the transfer of technology from the poor to the rich nations is not progressing smoothly.

Let me insert parenthetically that the only non-European country that has benefited from technological borrowing to become capitalist is Japan. We should note that Japan was a highly developed feudal society; it was never enslaved nor colonized by Europeans. It did not enter the international market with similar conditions as Africa. But now Europeans have forgotten how they have underdeveloped Africa. They have even forgotten that despite the civilising influences of Rome, they "progressed" with snail-like slowness for almost a thousand years after the fall of Roman civilisation.

We cannot end this discussion without stating rather emphatically that perhaps the most annoying, enduring, and the most pernicious effect of the slave trade

> lay in the attitudes that Europeans developed about Africa and Africans, and the sense of deep historic injury that modern Africans and "Africans of the diaspora" (as many Black Americans regard themselves) feel when they view the centuries of the trade and its aftermath.
>
> European attitudes about Africa developed into a complex set of derogatory myths. Africa was depicted as a Dark Continent of jungles and dark, mysterious swamps, and Africans were thought of as savages with no history and no "culture." European ignorance of the African interior contributed to the myth of African inferiority, but the slave trade played the more active role in creating myths. Most Europeans were exposed to African slaves (when they had contact with Africans at all) rather than to Africans who were free men. And the whole situation of the uprooted, enslaved African made him appear in an unfavourable light.[18]

Even today, this racist attitude continues and without this racism, I hesitate to find the reason behind their theorising that Africa lacks entrepreneurs who could spark off

95

economic development. This racist attitude has conditioned much of the contemporary white attitudes towards Africa and Africans. Such have been the prices Africans have paid as the result of the slave trade.

By way of summation, African dependency was consumated some five centuries ago. With the help of their naval fleet Europeans were able to travel to Africa and with the help of their superior weapons they were able to subjugate Africans. Of course, this was not the only method. Sure enough, ethnic rivalry and distrust existed among the different African groups. The clever Europeans exploited this unfortunate situation to their advantage. By setting up one group against another the slave traders were sure they would successfully keep the war going and this in turn would bring them the needed human cargo. Through this trade, Europeans and Americans made huge profits, produced the direly needed raw materials, stimulated their various industries and created the needed capital and all these contributed to their subsequent industrialization. America in particular benefited by keeping Africans as slaves for at least two centuries during which period they laboured to create the capital which eventually catapulted America into a capitalist state par excellence.

In return for all this Africa received trinkets, guns and powder and hot drinks which enabled them to constantly engage themselves in wars that provided the Europeans with slaves. Enterprising young men and women were stolen away into slavery to labour on lands stolen away from the Indians. Millions more young Africans were murderously slaughtered while others perished in various other ways. The European policy of setting one group or leader against another continued during colonial imperialism and it continues to be their foreign policy instrument in post independence Africa.

REFERENCES

[1] E. Jefferson Murphy, *History of African Civilization* (New York: Delta, 1974), p. 270.

[2] Eric Williams, *Capitalism and Slavery* (New York: Capricorn Books, 1966), p. 52.

[3] Quoted by Herbert Aptheker, *The Colonial Era* (New York: International Publishers, 1966), p. 14.

[4] *Ibid.*

[5] On this topic read Winthrop Jordan, *White Over Black* (Chapel Hill: University of North Carolina Press, 1968); and George M. Fredrickson, *The Black Image in the White Mind* (New York: Harper & Row, 1971).

[6] Williams, *Capitalism and Slavery*, p. 58.

[7] *Ibid.*, p. 78.

[8] *Ibid.*, pp. 78-79.

[9] *Ibid.*, p. 82.

[10] Aptheker, *The Colonial Era*, p. 17.

[11] *Ibid.*

[12] *Ibid.*, p. 18.

[13] Ph. D. dissertation, Harvard University, published as Vol. I of Harvard University Historical Series, 1896.

[14] Murphy, *History of African Civilization*, p. 292.

[15] *Ibid.*

[16] Walter Rodney, *How Europe Underdeveloped Africa* (Washington D. C.: Howard University Press, 1974), p. 104.

[17] *Ibid.*

[18] Murphy, *History of African Civilization*, p. 293.

5

DEVELOPMENT OF UNDERDEVELOPMENT: COLONIAL IMPERIALISM

It is difficult to say where slave trade ended and where *colonial imperialism* began because before slavery was extirpated in Africa, colonial imperialism had established roots in the continent. I refer to this latter phenomenon as colonial imperialism because our colonizers (exploiters or robbers to be specific) complimented themselves and rationalized away the inhuman treatment they meted out to God's sacred instruments by saying that we were racially, culturally, and/or religiously inferior to them. Thus they fashioned a relationship of unequals — rulers and ruled, superior and inferior — and also went ahead to establish political and legal systems meant to maintain and perpetuate this supremacy and domination. The purpose of this chapter is to chart a few of the events which took place under the era of colonial imperialism. We have singled out economic and educational underdevelopment for discussion.

Colonial Development (Underdevelopment)

Toynbee had predicted that future historians would say that "the great event of the twentieth century was the impact of the Western Civilization upon all other living societies of the world of that day. They will say of this impact that it was so powerful and so pervasive that it turned the lives of all victims upside down and inside out —

affecting the behaviour, outlook, feelings, and beliefs of individual men, women, and children in an intimate way, touching chords in human souls that are not touched by external material forces — however ponderous and terrifying."[1] Despite the exaggeration, there is some truth in this statement. The impact of western civilization is found everywhere in Africa and will be felt by generations yet unborn. In contrast to the argument of the cheerful school this section will try to demonstrate that colonial imperialism was not a civilizing mission. Although there may have been individuals and institutions that worked hard and sincerely for the good of Africans, their saving labours were palliative and peripheral. Let us take a look at how this European incursion affected Africans in the areas of economics and education.

Economic Development (Underdevelopment)

In precolonial Africa the most senior elder in the extended family made sure that everybody in the family had a piece of land to farm so that nobody would go hungry. The traditional African subsistence economies were able to provide sufficient diet for the African communities. And to the best of my knowledge, there is no historical evidence that any part of Africa ever suffered a chronic famine in the past.

But under colonialism the situation changed rather dramatically. Both the British and the French used what was essentially an *indirect* method of getting Africans to work for Europeans. The means by which they did this was the imposition of a money tax on peasants and the tax had to be paid in European monies. What this meant was to force the peasants to leave their homes, sometimes hundreds of miles away to work for Europeans since they alone had the money acceptable for tax purposes. Of course, if they did not pay

100

the tax they would be arrested and sent to work for the Europeans anyway.

Africans were not used to this situation and traditionally, it was not customary for people to work for others except for one's master (in the case of "slaves"), parents-in-law, one's parents and elders. Africans resisted this forced labour and this led to the Europeans fabricating various stereotypes about Africans — Africans were feckless, idle, lazy, irresponsible, brutish, ignorant, crafty, treacherous, bloody, thievish, mistrustful, and superstitious.

The result of this forced labour was that young and able bodied men were driven out of their homes to work for Europeans hundreds of miles away. Villages were denuded of their "fit adult males" for more than six months a year. The whole fabric of the traditional order was disrupted and many lives ruined. "The gross effect" of all this "was serious and continuous dismantlement of the pattern and structure of social life.... And this was compensated by no corresponding gain in understanding advancement by the men who went away to industrial work. For they went to the mines of the Rand or the Rhodesian Copperbelt, and there they worked as unskilled labourers beneath a colour bar of white enforcement. And this bar for long denied them access to any real participation in the new world of industry they were supposed to have entered."[2]

Africans were treated like beasts of burden. They were flogged constantly; they had no human rights, at least while in European factories, mines or plantations. In 1947 a senior Portuguese Inspector of Colonies said the situation in Angola "is in some ways worse than simple slavery. Under slavery, after all, the native is bought as an animal: his owner prefers him to remain as fit as a horse or an ox. Yet in Angola the native is not bought — he is hired from the state, although he is called a free man. And his employer cares little if he sickens or dies, once he is working, because when he sickens or dies his employer will simply ask for another."[3]

101

Apart from working in the mines Africans also worked in European plantations. Lands were alienated from Africans and given to Europeans to establish plantations; segregated quarters and churches were built. Africans were forced to plant export crops instead of their food crops. Describing the situation in Mozambique, Gabriel Mauticio Nantombo said:

> When the company came to exploit our region, everyone was forced to cultivate one field of cotton.... The time of cotton growing was a time of great poverty, because we could only produce cotton; we got a poor price for it, and we did not have time to grow other crops. We were forced to produce cotton. The people didn't want to; they knew cotton is the mother of poverty, but the company was protected by the government. We knew that anyone who refused to grow it would be sent to the plantations on São Tomé where he would work without any pay at all. So as not to leave the family and leave the children to suffer alone, we had to grow cotton. The company and government work together closely to enforce the system.[4]

The Mozambicans, Angolans and Guineans were largely bound to sell what they cultivated to concessionary companies. On the other hand, Europeans could sell theirs on the open world market at much higher prices. The companies that bought the cotton produced by Africans could set prices as low as they wished.[5]

Not only did the Europeans conspire to pay Africans the lowest possible prices for their products, they also paid them starvation wages. Uprooted from his village and thus denied the blessing of his subsistence economy, the African was bound to starve. John Maquival of Mozambique, describing his experience with colonial imperialism, said:

> the company paid money to the... government, and then the government arrested us and gave us to the

company. I began working for the company when I
was twelve... The whole family worked for the company; my brothers, my father... my father earned 150
escudos a month ($5.30). He had to pay 195 escudos
tax yearly. We didn't want to work for the company
but if we refused the government circulated photo-
graphs and a hunt was started. When they caught them
they beat them and put them into prison, and when
they came out of prison they had to go and work but
without pay... Thus in our own fields only our mothers
were left... All we had to eat was the little our
mothers were able to grow. We had to work on the
tea plantations but we didn't know what it tasted like.
Tea never came to our homes.[6]

As Blauner has correctly noted, "in a racial order a
dominant group, which thinks of itself as distinct and
superior, raises its social position by exploiting, controlling
and keeping others who are categorized in racial and ethnic
terms."[7] Accordingly, Africans under colonial tutelage fit
Marx's concept of an industrial reserve army, which meets
the system's need for an elastic labour pool.

The Portuguese were undoubtedly more brutal than the
British and the French. But even in Nigeria where subsistence economy as a means of livelihood still exists, the effects of the British occupation of the country was widely and
acutely felt. As late as 1951 an official report showed that
51 per cent of children in the Northern Region "died before
they were six, while 70 per cent of all children admitted to
the hospital in the Eastern Region were found to be suffer-
ing from malnutrition. For the country as a whole more than
20 million people (perhaps half the population) were thought
to be living on an everyday level of a very low order, with
widespread hunger and disease."[8] This story is the same all
over Africa except that it is worse in Rhodesia, South Africa
and Southwest Africa.

In fairness to the colonial powers it must be said that

103

they built roads, railroads and communication systems. However, the roads and railroads were designed primarily to serve the export-import trade and not to encourage internal trade and communication. In the case of Nigeria, the major lines ran from North to South, to and from the ocean, while east-west lines were few. There was no railway running between Eastern and Western Nigeria and the only decent road was built after Nigerians came to power. "As for communication with Nigeria's neighbors — the ex-French territories to the east, west, and north — both the British and the French were jealous of their preserves so that there were no railway lines and very few roads."[9] This situation is only now beginning to change under African leadership.

As part of the strategy of keeping Africans perpetually underdeveloped, the colonial imperialists also monopolized economic activities, thus preventing the rise of an indigenous entrepreneural class. Sir Taubman Goldie successfully eliminated Africans from the lucrative Niger trade by imposing taxes that Africans could not afford. In the export trade, Africans were very strongly discouraged. They were charged more export fees than Europeans.[10] In the late 1930's UAC (United Africa Company) alone controlled well over 40% of Nigeria's export-import trade, and in 1949 it controlled 34% of commercial merchandise imports in the country, and bought, on behalf of the Nigerian marketing boards, 43% of all Nigerian non-mineral exports. Furthermore, the UAC, John Holt, PZ (Paterson Zochnis) SCOA (the Sociate Commerciale del'Ouest Africa), CFAO (Compagnie Francaise de l'Afrique Occidentale), and UTC (The Union Trading Company), formed the Association of West African Merchants (AWAM) and through it made agreements and allocated export quotas. And this made it impossible for Africans to have a chance in the trading competition. The result was that in 1949 the AWAM controlled some 66% of all imports and almost 70% of the exports in Nigeria. They also controlled most retail and semi-wholesale trade all over the country. In the banking and shipping business, Europeans also pre-empted.[11]

In 1939 the British colonial government established a monopoly over the purchase, export and marketing of all West African agricultural products. It turned out that the large expatriate firms were the beneficiaries of that official monopoly, which lasted throughout the war. The banks which were exclusively in white hands, denied credits and loans to Africans. Let me elaborate on this a little further.

In British East Africa, credit to Africans was greatly discouraged by the Credit to Natives (Restriction) Ordinance of 1931. Insurance companies catered almost exclusively to the interest of white settlers and capitalist firms. The currency boards and central banks which performed such services denied Africans access to its own funds created by her exports. The various currency boards established in Africa were meant to issue and redeem the local circulating medium against sterling and other metropolitan currencies. Ideally, the currency board system required 100% backing of sterling for local currency. The East African Currency Board, for example, was established in 1919. Not surprisingly, it was staffed by British civil servants appointed by the Colonial Office, and apart from exercising financial control over British East Africa, it also financially controlled Ethiopia, British and Italian Somaliland, and Aden. The East Africa Currency Board was not given the authority to expand or contract local credit, and the result was that expenditures on local projects which required imported materials or machinary were limited to current export earnings, less outlays for crucial consumer goods, debt service and other fixed expenses. Thus, measures to increase exports were basic pre-conditions of local initiatives toward economic progress. What this means is that imperialism indirectly controlled the allocation of real resources.

In the early days of colonialism, the banks of Africa were small, but they were powerful and independent. The

Bank of British West Africa (later the Bank of West Africa in 1957, and subsequently renamed Standard Bank) and Barclays shared between them the largest share of the banking business of British West Africa. In the French West and Equatorial Africa the *Banque de l'Afrique Occidentale* (BAO) and *Banque Commerciale de l'Afrique* (BCA) emerged as the two most dominant. In 1949 the British and French West Africa Bank formed a union. The less dominant colonial powers were served by banks such as Barclays. In Southern Africa the most dominant bank appears to have been the Standard Bank. It made fantastic profits. For example, in 1960 it had a net profit of ₤ 1,181,000 and paid a 14% dividend to its shareholders. Most of the shareholders were in Europe or whites in South Africa. The reserves of these banks in Africa were exported to their metropolitan capitals where they were invested, for example, in the London money market.

In the particular case of Nigeria, it was the deliberate refusal by European banks to give loans to Nigerians, as the Foster-Sutton Commission of Inquiry had acknowledged in 1957, that prompted Dr. Nnamdi Azikiwe, then Premier of Eastern Nigeria, to divert some money from the public treasury into the African Continental Bank, in order to make funds available to African entrepreneurs. In the final analysis, the African, in the words of Professor Crowder:

> found himself the simple producer of raw materials for which Lebanese were the agents of sale and European companies the exporters. Conversely, these same companies imported the goods which Africans bought, mainly at the shops through the agencies of Lebanese traders, with money he earned from the sale of his crop. Only in rare cases did the African survive as an importer, almost never as an exporter, and in neither role was he significant after 1920. Except in the cocoa-producing areas of the Gold Coast (now Ghana) and Nigeria the African was squeezed out of his pre-col-

onial role of middleman between peasant producer and expatriate exporter by the Lebanese.[12]

The imperialists invested their money in plantations and mines and because of cheap labour, were able to make windfall profits. They bought raw materials and minerals which were shipped back to the metropolitan countries. They sold their manufactured products to their subjects at exorbitant prices; such products were often specially designed to last for a few days. A French writer, Dumont, recounted his experience thus: "In December 1949, in the northern Cœan (then Belgian), I picked up an alarm clock I wanted to buy in a little Greek shop. The proprietor quickly grabbed it out of my hands, saying 'That's a treaty article, it only works for a few days.' But it was sold to the Congolese at the same price as good European clocks."[13]

It is true that some form of "development" occurred under colonial rule, but this

> took place in sectors limited almost exclusively to production for export, the import trade, and related collection and distribution services. These sectors did not directly affect the bulk of the population, who continued to engage in low-productivity food and handicraft production predominantly for their own use or sale in local markets... What modern economic growth did occur... was directed to filling overseas market needs and providing markets for European manufactured goods. It took place within a framework which viewed metropolitan, not colonial interests as dominant. Indeed, the colonial economic structure tended primarily to serve the interests of a limited number of settler officials and the private foreign-owned exporting firms — not even necessarily, the overall economic interest of the colonial power.[14]

African colonies exported bauxite and imported

aluminium pots and pans; exported palm oil and imported soap, margarine and other related products; exported hides and imported boots and shoes; exported cocoa and imported chocolate and processed cocoa; exported rubber and imported tires; exported timber and imported processed timber and paper. In all cases, the price Africans paid for the finished products was many times the price for which they sold their raw materials because of the value added to the original raw material. Lamenting over this exploitative mercantilism, Kwame Nkrumah wrote that foreign monopoly interest had the entire African "economy completely tied up to suit themselves." In Ghana "whose output of cocoa is the largest in the world, there was not a single chocolate factory." While Ghana and other African countries "produce the raw materials for the manufacture of soap and edible fats, palm products, the manufacture of these items was discouraged." A British firm that owned lime factories in Ghana as well as in the West Indies, actually pressed "the juice from the fruit before shipping it in bulk to the United Kingdom and exporting it back" to the Ghanaians, "bottled, to retail in stores at a high price." Though Ghanaians "had the raw material needed for their manufacture, every bottle used in this country was imported. These facts have a kind of Alice in Wonderland craziness about them which many will find hard to accept. But they are implicit in the whole concept and policy of colonialism. Native initiative, where it was likely to endanger the interests of colonial power, was quickly stifled."[15] In this respect also, Gusfield has argued that "the decline of native Indian industries in the late eighteenth and nineteenth centuries was a consequence of the production of British textile manufacturers, then spearheading the Industrial Revolution in England."[16]

It had been maintained by the British that the Gold Coast climate was not suitable for growing potatoes. And they were not grown. But during the war, British troops were stationed in the Gold Coast. At the time shipping was quite severely restricted and potatoes, so valued by the British, were becoming scarce and the soldiers were becoming unhappy. The colonial administration quickly embarked on a "grow potatoes" campaign. Quite surprisingly, the Gold Coast climate which was said to be unsuitable for the growing of potatoes soon produced "magnificent crops." "Once the war was over, however, and normal shipping facilities were resumed, the Department of Agriculture changed its tune. Gold Coast potatoes... were unfit for human consumption. The result was that potatoes disappeared" from the Gold Coast fields and once more figured among European importers.[17] It may be of interest to know that Ghanaians have been growing and eating potatoes since that country became independent in 1957 and so far there has been no epidemic resulting from eating the potatoes.

It is important at this juncture to mention something about "ultra-colonial" territories for which Portugal qualifies outright. By ultra-colonial territories is meant those colonies owned by backwards European countries, which, because of their own metropolitan backwardness, did not "develop" their colonial territories. As Worsley states:

> Their history is a story of primitive and sterile robbery, through successive modes of exploitation. These range from brutal 'booty' capitalism through to latter-day authoritarian colonial systems in which the colonial territory is used as a 'solution' to misery at home via the export of unskilled and illiterate white peasants as primitive settlers, and by auctioning the resources of the colonial territory to international corporate capitalist enterprise (which then develops an interest in the regime's continuance and 'stability'). Underdevelopment, and the denial of democracy in Portugal, notably, reproduces themselves in chronic viciousness and backwardness in Angola and Mozambique.
>
>   Such 'ultra' colonialism have for long periods commonly allowed their nominal colonial 'possessions'

to vegetate (for example throughout most of the nineteenth century). During this phase, at least, economic exploitation has hardly occurred; indeed, nothing occurred. But without a *raison d'etre* of exploitation colonialisms of this kind would have eroded away. They revived and became virulent once more because other expanding colonial powers threatened to seize these areas. Then, their retention became a sacred national cause: prestige was threatened.[18]

It is sad to note that after 500 years of their occupation of Africa, the Portuguese never trained a single African doctor in Mozambique, and the life expectancy in Eastern Angola was less than thirty years. Having said this about the Portuguese, it is necessary to add that things in other colonies were not much better. For example, in Ibadan, Nigeria, there were about 50 Europeans before World War II. And yet there was a segregated hospital service of 11 beds, whereas there were 34 beds for about one-half-million blacks. The case of Ibadan was not an isolated one because in the 1930's 4,000 Europeans in the country had twelve modern hospitals while the African population of about 40 million had 52 hospitals.[19]

In the final analysis, colonialism was not merely a system of exploitation, but one whose main purpose was to repatriate the profits to the metropoles. By exporting the profits created by African labour to Europe, the development of Europe was assured while dialectically this meant the underdevelopment of Africa. It should be clear to the apologists for colonial imperialism that it is no ideological assertion, but a generalization supported by empirical observation, that the prime content of colonial political domination was economic exploitation.

Education

Just as the Europeans controlled African participation in the new economic order, they also carefully structured African education so as to perpetuate their underdevelopment and dependency. The colonial powers, mainly Britain and France, knew that the introduction of western education was the *sine qua non* for the exploitation of Africa and Africans. Without this education there certainly would not have been clerks and technicians to execute those essential tasks in the government and commerce, particularly those the white people could not carry out themselves. "Literate Africans were useful in many ways, although too much literacy was considered dangerous and undesirable. A certain amount of technical training was essential to provide cheap semiskilled labour, but it could not be allowed to continue beyond a given standard or the African would soon be competing with whites."[20]

It was the missionaries who introduced western education to the colonies but they did this because without it they would not have had the local preachers, interpreters and, later, clerks so crucial for keeping records and for other activities. "To all intents and purposes" the school was "the church"; the two were one and the same thing. "An appreciation of this fact is essential in all considerations of African education." Accordingly, in view of the fact that the school is an evangelistic agency, and that it is for the Christianity of the people that the missionaries are there at all, the moral life and character of the Europeans are of first importance in the work of running a school."[21]

African education consisted of learning the Bible, and how to read, write and calculate in English. In addition, health science, British Empire history, European geography, Shakespearean and Chaucerian works were taught. Empire Day, the day Africans' slavery was consummated, was always meticulously observed. All this was designed to impose upon

Africans the white man's mythical racial superiority and the African inferiority. Whatever Africans were taught about themselves was designed to enable them to internaliize their inferiority and to recognize the white man as their saviour. "As content, the schools equipped the African with little more than an elementary knowledge of the English language for an economic future in which a senior clerkship was the upper limit of his permissible advancement. In terms of need and desire, there were hundreds of candidates for every school vacancy."[22]

Tanganyika (now Tanzania) became a British trust territory in 1919. In 1959 its population had risen to almost 10 million. In the same year "the total number of secondary school enrollments for standard 12 the last in the four-year secondary course was 318, while the total number of School Certificates gained was 245."

Kenya was luckier than Tanganyika. Out of a population of eight million, 799 African boys and girls took School Certificate, and 654 achieved it. In Uganda with a population of about six million, 860 African pupils won School Certificates in 1960.[23] What this reveals is that in a population of 24 million in British East Africa, after many years of colonial rule, there was an annual total of less than 2,000 School Certificates, that is, less than one for every 12,000 of the population.

Was this due to lack of funds? This writer says no. Northern Rhodesia, with all its enormous copper earnings annually and with a population of more than two million, had only one secondary school offering a complete course to Senior Cambridge level. In Southern Rhodesia, another rich territory, "12,148 African boys and girls entered school at the very bottom of the scale, in substandard A, but those who reached the top of the scale, standard 12, *numbered only thirteen*."[24] "Higher education in the Belgian Congo had produced fewer than a score of African graduates by the year [1960] in which the Belgian retired; in this vast country of peasant-farmer, there was only one Congolese graduate in agriculture."[25]

In the case of Nigeria Table 5.1 tells the story. The expenditure for education during the pre-World War II

TABLE 5.1

Expenditure for Education in Nigeria 1877-1952

Year	Expenditure for Education £ stg.	Total Expenditure £ stg.	Percent of Total Expenditure
1877-1882	200	*	*
1883-1895	*	*	*
1896	2,000	3,459,774	1.0
1897-1913	*	*	*
1914	47,900	3,684,615	1.3
1915	46,303	3,561,769	1.3
1916	46,312	3,562,462	1.3
1917	46,298	3,307,000	1.4
1918	45,744	3,519,000	1.3
1919	49,216	4,474,419	1.1
1920	69,444	*	*
1921-1922	87,494	*	*
1922-1923	100,063	*	*
1923-1924	109,203	*	*
1924-1925	116,301	*	*
1925-1926	125,251	*	*
1926-1927	158,454	*	*
1927-1928	198,838	*	*
1928-1929	232,396	*	*
1929-1930	263,456	*	*
1930-1931	286,521	*	*
1931-1932	271,712	8,063,142	3.4
1932-1933	252,984	*	*
1933-1934	237,732	*	*

113

1934-1935	225,038	*	*
1935-1936	229,058	*	*
1936-1937	247,795	*	*
1937-1938	289,284	*	*
1938-1939	269,152	*	*
1939-1940	264,461	*	*
1940-1941	259,546	7,254,325	3.6
1941-1942	282,882	7,026,894	4.0
1942-1943	352,896	8,998,795	3.9
1943-1944	481,226	9,998,795	4.8
1944-1945	481,226	9,998,795	4.8
1945-1946	615,663	10,132,599	6.1
1946-1947	861,135	14,051,688	8.1
1947-1948	1,390,700	17,185,941	6.1
1948-1949	1,467,744	23,898,427	8.1
1949-1950	2,308,530	28,253,090	6.1
1950-1951	*	*	*
1951-1952	8,324,000	49,131,000	16.9

* Data not available

Sources: James Coleman, *Background to Nationalism* (Berkeley and Los Angeles: University of California Press, 1958); Otonti Nduka, *Western Education and the Nigierian Cultural Background* (Ibadan, Nigeria: Oxford University Press, 1964). George Padmore, *Pan-African or Communism?* (London: Dennis Dobson, 1936).

period was rather meagre. In the 1931-32 budget while the colonial government spent only £ 271,712 on education and £ 441,589 on medical and public health service, it spent £ 694,904 on police, military and prisons out of a total expenditure of £ 8,063,142. It is no surprise that the government expenditure on education and on medical and public health services should be less than that for the police, the military and prisons because colonialism was very strongly resented by the people, and in order to continue to exist the military and police had to be strong.

114

Although expenditure for education began to increase somewhat in 1943, it was not until during the 1951-52 fiscal year that this increase became significant. It is of paramount importance to note that it was in that year that a new constitution gave Nigerians a larger say and share in the running of their government. Concerned about the inadequacies of the colonial education, it was no surprise then that universal primary education was introduced in the West and East by the mid-1950's. The importance they attached to education can be demonstrated in the 1952-53 education expenditure for the federation — Table 5.2.

TABLE 5.2

Expenditure for Education in Nigeria, 1952-53

Government	Total Expenditure £ stg.	Expenditure for Education £ stg.	% of the Expenditure
Federal	52,447,250	3,240,175	6.1
Northern Region	14,949,000	1,805,992	12.0
Eastern Region	6,653,000	2,118,414	31.8
Western Region	12,807,000	4,052,221	31.6
Total	86,854,250	11,216,802	

Source: Otonti Nduka, *Western Education and the Nigerian Cultural Background* (Ibadan: Oxford University Press, 1964), p. 116.

Colonial education was not designed to benefit Africans and to help prepare them to participate meaningfully in the economic exploitation of their country. They did not encourage Africans to have advanced education. The few they encouraged or sent to study in Europe were those they were sure would return to be their stooges and act as their protégés. As Nkrumah has noted in his *Consciencism*, such compradors were not exposed to the kind of education that would liberate them mentally and otherwise.

Finally, apologists for colonial imperialism have argued that the money for education and hospitals were paid by the metropoles taxpayers. This is a rather nonsensical argument when one notes the fact that colonial imperialism exported millions of pounds from the continent every year. Even the hospital facilities were given almost exclusively to those the imperialists exploited directly. The purpose of educating Africans, as already pointed out, was not to get the African educated in order for him to benefit in the colonial exploitation of his country; the basic reason for educating the African was to facilitate his exploitation and that of his motherland. Thus, everything done in the colonies were designed for the benefit of the imperialists and merely allowed crumbs to the exploited as incidental by-products of exploitation.

The people were aware of the fact that they were being exploited and that they did not benefit from the exploitation of their natural resources and the surpluses they created. They embarked on all forms of radical action to compel their exploiters to return whence they came. But before they fled, the colonial powers imposed upon the people constitutions that would ensure conflicts among the different groups, as in Nigeria. They worked hard to place in power those who would continue to promote their interests after they had gone. The formal ending of colonial imperialism has ushered in neocolonialism. This results from "false decolonization," the preservation of colonial relationship of western dominance and African dependence by means other than direct political control, after granting them pseudo political independence.[26]

REFERENCES

[1] Arnold Joseph Toynbee, *Civilization on Trial* (New York, 1948), p. 214.

[2] Basil Davidson, *Which Way Africa?* (Baltimore: Penguin Books, 1971), p. 42.

[3] Cited in *ibid.*

[4] Quoted in Elsa Roberts and Nancy Barnes, *Race to Power* (New York: Anchor Books, 1974), p. 44.

[5] For similar treatment of Nigerians and Ghanaians, see Daniel A. Offiong, "The Cheerful School and the Myth of the Civilizing Mission of Colonial Imperialism," *Pan African Journal* IX/1 (Spring, 1976), pp. 35-54.; Michael Crowder, *West Africa Under Colonial Rule* (Evanston, Ill.: Northwestern University Press, 1968); James Coleman, *Nigeria: Background to Nationalism* (Berkeley: UCLA Press, 1958).

[6] Quoted in Roberts and Barnes, *Race to Power*, pp. 47-8.

[7] Robert Blauner, *Racial Oppression in America* (New York: Harper and Row, 1972), p. 22.

[8] Davidson, *Which Way Africa?*, p. 84.

[9] Frederick A. O. Schwartz, *Nigeria: The Tribe, the Nation, or the Race* (Mass.: M.I.T. Press, 1965).

[10] Crowder, *West Africa Under Colonial Rule.*

[11] P. T. Bauer, *West African Trade* (New York: Augustus M. Kelley, 1963).

[12] Crowder, *West Africa Under Colonial Rule*, p. 345.

[13] Rene Dumont, *False Start in Africa* (London: Deutsch, 1966), p. 40.

[14] Reginald Green and Ann Seidman, *Unity or Poverty? The Economics of Pan Africanism* (Baltimore: Penguin Books, 1968), pp. 31-32.

[15] Kwame Nkrumah, *Africa Must Unite* (New York: International Publishers, 1970), pp. 26, 27, 30.

[16] Joseph Gusfield, "Tradition and Modernity: Misplaced Polarities in the Study of Social Change," *American Journal of Sociology*, 72 (January, 1967), p. 353.

[17] Nkrunah, *Africa Must Unite.*

[18] Peter Worsley, *The Third World* (Chicago: The University of Chicago Press, 1967), pp. 45-46.

[19] Rodney, *How Europe Underdeveloped Africa.*

[20] Colin Turnbull, *The Lonely African* (New York: Claredon, 1968), pp. 96-97.

[21] Victor A. Murray, *The School in the Bush* (New York: Barnes and Noble, 1967), p. 65.

[22] Coleman, *Nigeria*, p. 116.

[23] Davidson, *Which Way Africa?*, pp. 45-46.

[24] *Ibid.*, p. 46.

[25] *Ibid.*, p. 44.

[26] Green and Seidman, *Unity of Poverty.*

6

DEVELOPMENT OF UNDERDEVELOPMENT: NEOCOLONIALISM

European powers did not establish colonial states to carry out a programme of political development or change, but to erect efficient and effective administrative states for purposes of economic exploitation and this largely explains many of the problems faced by African nations after independence. "Withdrawing in deep water, colonial powers left behind them far greater problems than any they had ever proposed to solve. This is not to suggest, of course, that they would have done better to withdraw later, since there was never any sign that they would allow the real problems to be tackled on a realistic basis."[1] This conclusion is borne out by the fact that the main solutions they "proposed" and also "promoted" are in themselves a large part of the troubles, difficulties and problems faced by Africans today.

> For what the colonial powers thought wise and necessary was the formation and promotion to power of 'leading elites' or 'middle classes' (those whom the French have so revealingly called *interlocuteurs valables* — 'negotiators worth talking to'): groups of men who would ensure that post-colonial government should be 'moderate and responsible' — should be, that is, a reflection of colonial government. And it is here in no small part, that the seat of the trouble has lain.[2]

Although generalization is always unfair, such "leading

elites" and "middle classes" have largely crumbled under the strain of political independence.

> Some have retired into profitable corruption, others into a more or less sterile defense of the *status quo*. For others, again, traditionalist separatism (we may call it, with reservations, tribalism) has become a major outlet for their energy. And given their often great authority among ordinary people, the example of these educated 'elites' and 'middle classes' has echoed down the ranks of African society with curious results.[3]

Apart from their corruption, their alliance with the international exploiters in the industrialised societies is a great factor in African underdevelopment. It is a fact that corruption exists in both the industrialised and nonindustrialised societies; and as the Watergate revelations made it abundantly clear, a society like the U.S. is rife with corruption. However, the marked difference is that while the monies stolen from the American people are reinvested in America, those of Africa are reinvested abroad and vast amounts find their way into Swiss banks. This alliance between domestic and international exploiters is a serious problem in African underdevelopment, a fact known to Latin Americans a long time ago.

The policy by which the colonial powers proposed and promoted solutions favouring their long-term interests was quite in keeping with their policy of balkanization. By this is meant the colonial policy of fostering regional and ethnic particularism (e.g., Nigeria and the Sudan); their tendency (particularly France and Belgium), during the phase of transfer of formal political power to allow the break-up of large political systems (e.g., the French West African Federation), or to support separatist movements (e.g., the Congo); and finally, "the fact that the present political configuration of Africa, as a mosaic of petty states extremely vulnerable to external pressures, clearly accords with the general interest of the Western Powers."[4] All these are some of the aspects of neocolonialism that are discussed in an earlier chapter.

NeoColonialism and Nkrumah

It is not possible to discuss neocolonialism in the African context without coming face to face with Kwame Nkrumah. Lenin has greatly influenced Nkrumah's conception of imperialism. In Lenist context the paramount motivation behind colonial imperialism was the economic exploitation of the countries which were annexed. All arguments about the "civilizing mission" were a mere camouflage of the imperial profit motive. This Lenist thesis appears in Nkrumah's *Towards Colonial Freedom.*[5] Nkrumah writes:

> The imperialist powers need the raw materials and cheap native labour of the colonies for their own capitalist industries... The problem of land ownership in the colonies has risen because the colonial powers have legally or illegally seized valuable mining and plantation rights. The British are more careful than other imperialists to legitimize their seizure, but even their semi-legal methods do not disguise the fact that they have no right to rob the native of his birthright.[6]

But Nkrumah subsequently retreated from this Marxist doctrine of economic determinism. He then urged all Ghanaians to "Seek ye first the political kingdom and all things will be added to it." He once noted that "political power is the inescapable prerequisite to economic and social power."[7] Thus, it was no longer economic power that determined political relationships.

But it was not long before Nkrumah was reconverted to economic determinism, because according to him, "political independence is but a facade if economic freedom is not possible also?"[8] Nkrumah's *Neo-Colonialism: The Last Stage of Imperialism*[9] is to show that African attainment of independence, when not followed by a change in economic relationships, gave rise to *client states*. Nkrumah states that his reason for writing the book was "to expose the workings of international monopoly Capitalism in Africa in order to show the meaninglessness of political freedom without economic independence."[10]

Nkrumah has defined neocolonialism in several ways. For example, he has referred to it as "the process of handing independence over to the African people with one hand, only to take it away with the other hand"; he has defined it as "clientele sovereignty, or fake independence: namely, the practice of granting a sort of independence by the metropolitan power, with the concealed intention of making the liberated country a client-state and controlling it effectively by means other than political ones." In his *Africa Must Unite*, Nkrumah writes that "the greatest danger at present facing Africa is neocolonialism and its major instrument, balkanization."[11] Nkrumah argues that under colonial imperialism there was something like public accountability. But neocolonial imperialism was the most irresponsible form of imperialism because of the lack of inner constraint of accountability. According to Nkrumah:

> Where neocolonialism exists the power exercising control is often the State which formerly ruled the territory in question, but this is not necessarily so... A state in the grip of neocolonialism is not master of its own destiny... Neo-colonialism is the worst form of imperialism. For those who practice it, it means power without responsibility and for those who suffer from it, it means exploitation without redress. In the days of old-fashioned colonialism, the imperial power had at least to explain and justify at home the actions it was taking abroad. In the colony those who served the

ruling imperial power could at least look to its protection against any violent move by their opponents. With neocolonialism neither is the case.[12]

Thus, if Lenin has used his *Imperialism: The Highest Stage of Capitalism* to explain why the proletarian revolution predicted by Marx never came, Nkrumah used his *Neo-Colonialism: The Last Stage of Imperialism* to explain why the revolution predicted by Marx and Lenin will not occur. The reason lies in neocolonialism. In the *Revolutionary Path* in which Nkrumah summarizes his writing, he has these words about neocolonialism: It "is a stage in the development of imperialism;" it

> is more insidious, complex and dangerous than the old colonialism. It not only prevents its victims from developing their economic potential for their own use, but it controls the political life of the country, and supports the indigenous bourgeoisie in perpetuating the oppression and exploitation of the masses. Under neocolonialism, the economic systems and political policies of independent territories are managed and manipulated from outside, by international monopoly finance capital in league with the indigenous bourgeoisie... a single productive process is divided between states. Communications, banking, insurance, and other key services are controlled by neo-colonialists. The regional economic groupings in Africa have been encouraged, controlled by neo-colonialists, which therefore further strengthen international finance capital. Backing up these processes, the power of international monopoly finance is used to force down the price of raw materials, and to keep up the price of foreign manufactured goods.[13]

Multinationals: Engines of Growth?

What Nkrumah seems to be saying is that at the centre of neocolonialism lies the multinational corporations. He appears to disagree with the Euro-American notion that the multinationals are the engines of growth in the underdeveloped societies. Could Nkrumah be right? It is necessary to examine this proposition rather carefully. What are these multinationals?

> Though globe-girdling business concerns are at least as old as the British Empire's East India Company, the multinational corporation is largely a phenomenon of the post-World War II era, and its emergence has become spectacular in the past decade. There is no universally accepted definition, but the multinationals generally are agreed to be those companies having production facilities in many lands, having access to capital world-wide and having a "global-outlook" among their managements. That encompasses some 200 U.S. based multinationals including General Motors, RCA, IBM, Dow Chemical and other blue chips.[14]

In the early part of this decade the U.S. Library of Congress ranked tables for a Senate Committee investigating the role of giant corporations in the world economy. The Library ranked 100 largest entities in the world — countries and companies — for the years 1960, 1965 and 1970. The companies were interspersed with the countries to show their "huge clout." Each country was ranked by its gross national product, and each company was ranked by its annual sales volume.

This exercise revealed that the business corporations were gaining on the countries. In 1960, the top-100 list consisted of 59 countries and 41 companies; in 1965, there was a change in the compositions as there were 57 countries and 43 companies; by 1970, there were 49 countries on the list and 51 companies.

The U.S. and the Soviet Union topped the roster for all three periods. The significant changes in the top level ranking were the rise of Japan and the decline of Britain. In 1960, Japan ranked seventh and Britain fourth, but in 1970 Japan ranked third while Britain ranked seventh.

General Motors had sales of $18.8 billion in 1970 and ranked 24th, just behind Switzerland which had a GNP of $20.6 billion. Other standings in 1970 were: 25 — Yugoslavia, 26 — Pakistan, 27 — South Africa, 28 — AT and T, 29 — Standard Oil of New Jersey (now Exxon), 30 — Denmark, 31 — Ford. The first non U.S. company to appear on the list was Royal Dutch Shell which ranked 36th with sales of $10.8 billion. Sears, Roebuck ranked 41st ahead of Turkey, Chile, and Colombia. IBM ranked 47th, just behind Chile but ahead of Mobil and Colombia.

In previous ranking no Japanese companies appeared on the list but in 1970 there were two — Nippon Steel (70th) and Hitachi (83rd). Previously (1960), there were no German companies on the list but in 1970 there were six — Volkswagon (64th), Siemens (86th), Farbwerke Hoechst (86th), Daimler-Benz (91st), August Thyssen-Hutte (93rd) and BASF (95th). Sadly enough, Nigeria, Algeria, Ghana, and Iraq, among others, were displaced from the list during the decade.[15]

The role of the global giants in world economy has been so alarming that even the arch-priest of the free enterprise ideology, the U.S., has itself become worried. In 1974 it held hearings to try to determine "the future shape of the international oil industry."[16]

In 1975 there were various hearings still trying to determine the direction of the multinationals in world economics. It was found that: (1) U.S. direct investment abroad in 1973 amounted to well over $ 100 billion; (2) these direct investments involving U.S. ownership and control had accounted for nearly 80 percent of the U.S. long-term capital outflow; (3) two-thirds of the direct investment

125

abroad went to the technically-advanced countries and for the remainder, almost one-half went into petroleum, that investment in the underdeveloped countries accounted for less than 20 percent of the total; (4) a great number of the investments are in the form of wholly or largely owned foreign affiliates of U.S. global giants; (5) foreign investment is dominated by a few global giants; (6) in 1973, the return flow of capital income from direct investment abroad amounted to $12.3 billion as against an outflow of new investment of $4.9 billion, reinvested earnings of $8.1 billion not included in both cases; (7) profits of foreign affiliates of U.S. companies in 1972 were about 22 percent of domestic profits of all U.S. corporations; (8) U.S. investment abroad, by increasing foreign income also raises foreign demand for U.S. products and thus strengthens the U.S. terms of trade.[17] There were many other findings but the above suffice for our purposes here.

In the same year, 1975, there was yet another inquiry to determine, if any, the role the U.S. global giants played in the devaluations of the dollar. The basis of the hearings was because for seventeen days in March of 1973, the international money markets of the so-called free world were almost shut.

> It was the first peace time suspension of virtually all foreign exchange markets. When the markets were reopened the currency alignment which had been agreed on a month earlier on February 12, was abandoned, and the currencies of the Western world were allowed to float, that is, to change parity. Fixed exchange rates were abandoned for the moment, although some European countries attempted to keep their currencies in step with each other.[18]

The suspicion of the U.S. Senate was that the theory of coverage of exchange risks by multinational corporations was in operation. According to this theory, multinationals do operate across national boundaries and exchange controls in order to maximize their profits from a currency devaluation or revaluation, or to protect themselves from its consequences. Thus the enormous volumes of exchange that global giants generate through inter-company payments, either trade-related or financial, are maneuverable. "The object of money management is to place cash in lands whose currency is appreciating and place debts in those where they can be repaid with depreciated currency."[19] The study concluded:

> It seems unlikely that the anticipation of a devaluation of the dollar did not play a part in these transfers of funds. Which in turn intensified the growing currency crisis. Liquid assets denominated in strong currencies of the sample... rose by 73 percent in the January 31, 1973 report from the year earlier; at the same time, their Eurodollar U.S. deposited in banks outside the U.S. holdings fell by 16.5 percent.[20]

I have provided the above information because of my belief that the U.S. herself is afraid of the monster that she relies upon for the exploitation and domination of the world. If the U.S., the richest and most powerful country in the world, is afraid of her own corporations, how much more the poor, underdeveloped countries? The impression derived from the various hearings of the U.S. Senate on the global giants seems to be that the multinationals are out to exploit and to even create situations that would enhance their exploitation. Or can they be engines of growth under these circumstance?

On the basis of the available evidence, the claim that global corporations are the major sources of foreign capital to the underdeveloped nations is more "metaphor than reality." The global corporations largely "use scarce local capital of their local operations rather than to bring capital from either the United States or Europe."[21] In the particular case of Latin America where data are available, between

1957-65, "U.S. based global corporations financed 83 percent of their Latin American investment locally, either from reinvested earnings or from local Latin American savings."[22]

Thus, only about 17 percent of U.S. investment during the period 1957-1965 represented a transfer of capital from rich countries to poor. Barnet and Muller have presented massive data to demonstrate that as much as 52 percent of all profits of subsidiaries operating in foreign countries are repatriated to the metropolitan countries; that the profitable practices of these foreign corporations rather than representing an import of capital, actually decrease the availability of local capital for local industry; that the argument for foreign investment as a supplier of new capital through which the superior management skills of global corporations can be channeled into productive facilities is contradicted by data; and that it is not true that the global corporations make greater contributions to development than local entrepreneurs.[23]

The impression one gathers from the much talked about investment in the underdeveloped countries is that the balance of payment situation in these countries are improved. This is obviously not the case.

In the 1978-79 Budget Speech on March 31, 1978, His Excellency, Lt. General Olusegun Obasanjo, then Head of State of the Federal Military Government and Commander-in-Chief of the Armed Forces of Nigeria, said:

> During the year 1977, Nigeria's exports increased to around ₦8 billion. During the same period, by comparison, the total value of merchandise imports into Nigeria has been put at about ₦6.7 billion. Taken together, these figures suggest a surplus of some ₦1.3 billion in merchandise trade. However, when payments for personal home remittances, dividend repatriation and services such as shipping and insurance are taken into account an over-all balance of payments deficit of about ₦600 million is indicated. As a result of these

unfavourable developments in our over-all balance of payments position, our foreign reserves which had stood at about ₦3.7 billion at the end of 1975 declined to about ₦3 billion at the end of December 1977.[24]

It is not known to this writer what the balance-of-payment situation was at March 30th, the end of the 1977-78 financial year. But in September, 1978, Chief S. B. Falegan, Director of Research, Central Bank of Nigeria said that at that time the total foreign exchange of the country was just ₦ 1.0 billion and that on the basis of the rate of importation and the rate of capital outflow, the end of the year's financial operations might end up in a balance of payments deficit of about ₦ 2.0 billion. A great part of the deficit is attributed to the export of profits, gains from loans and monopoly prices, and all forms of unethical methods designed to evade taxes.

.

To make sure that their profits are as high as possible, the global giants in collusion with their domestic compradors and frontmen, become involved in anti-government activities like falsely declaring profits in order to evade taxes and for short-landing of imported goods and services for which pre-payments before delivery have been effected. Through such practices the host government loses heavily through local revenue and foreign exchange leakages.

In Nigeria, for example the *Daily Times* investigative report stated that one global giant engages in the practice of importing and selling tires operating "under a system whereby it apparently pays for its goods before they arrive and before the shipping documents have been fully submitted." It was further stated that on quite a few instances, this company "had received only half the goods it had already paid for in foreign exchange, thus exporting more than it should."[26]

In Egypt, a multinational was reported to have exported to the U.S. a net profit that was calculated as four times the GNP of Egypt for the year 1974. The figures for the British-Royal Dutch Shell and the U.S. Ford Motors were stated as three times Egypt's GNP respectively for the same year. The same source, basing its calculations on the U.S. official statistics for the years 1974 and 1975, concluded that $ 23,300 million was the amount which "the branch offices of various U.S. companies shipped out of the developing countries."[27] Another report has it that in the past three decades De Beers has exported from Tanzania 30 times more capital that it had originally invested there.[28]

There are various other means by which foreign companies dupe us and thereby perpetuate our underdevelopment. The so-called experts from parent companies abroad are made to visit the subsidiary company at the expense of the domestic company. The entire cost, including the cost of the tickets, is footed by the local company. If the visitor is not made to stay indefinitely he is made to return home with briefcases stocked with the domestic currency.

There is a particular case reported about a Briton who visited Nigeria and within a short time stole ₦10,000 cash and tactfully passed it through Nigerian Customs check at the airport in a Kingsway Stores bags. Somewhere during his flight to Europe he showed the money to a Nigerian and told him that the naira would be quickly bought by British banks. And they would be quickly resold to Nigeria through link companies operating in Nigeria. The same money could be sold to Nigerian students in Britain who in turn bring back the money into Nigeria by sending it to their relatives or by bringing it home when coming on vacations. "All link companies operating in Nigeria generate their funds here through trade of the banks and devise ways of repatriating the money home. When a link company says it is bringing capital from abroad, it is usually in the form of machinery or materials the costs of which are inflated sufficiently to enable the company repatriate large repayments home."[29]

When global giants purchase from and sell to their own subsidiaries, they set prices that often have little or no relationship to the market price — "transfer prices," as they call it. For example, if a refrigerator manufacturer with operations in other countries wishes to export from a manufacturing subsidiary it owns in one country to a distributing company it owns in another country, it is advantageous for tax purposes to the exporting subsidiary to undervalue its exports. A common reason for this action is that taxes in the manufacturing country may be higher than taxes in the importing country. The result is that the "artificial price" charged on the export reduces total taxes for the global giant and increases its global profits, while this, to the manufacturing country, means a loss of foreign exchange (not to mention tax revenues) it would have collected had this type of transaction taken place between independent buyers and sellers.

Multinationals get their subsidiaries in the underdeveloped countries to pay for services given by the parent body abroad; but the parent body does not reciprocate by paying for the services rendered it by its subsidiaries.

> The most glaring example of this practice is to be found in the advertising industry where services such as colour separation, filming, dubbing, writing tune to words, consultancy are rendered by some third parties in London to whom the Nigerian Companies owe their loyalties as illegal subsidiaries. Of course, the front in Nigeria is clearly Nigerianised; clauses in the transfer of ownership agreement or by gentlemen's agreement still tie the Nigerian company financially through payment for services to the parent company.[30]

To still enable them to export more money from the

underdeveloped world, they inflate the cost of raw materials and machinery by at least 200 per cent. The argument given by the multinationals is that they need to do this because of "inflation in Europe" and the uncertain position of clearing facilities at wharf.

Foreign companies, as a rule try to import everything that they need even those things that are present locally. Even where the host government restricts such practice there is always a way. The locally-based foreign-owned company will arrange and write the other company a letter informing them that they will be unable to supply what they need. On the basis of such a letter the other company can then acquire license to import what it wants, of course, after receiving permission from the government concerned.

Link companies get their allies abroad to prepare for them fake invoices for non-existent services which they present to the government concerned for permission to export their money. Bulk purchases abroad earn some commission but this is never shown on invoices presented to the government. Such commission is paid into a foreign bank (usually Swiss) and this encourages the drain on foreign exchange.

In Nigeria there is a decree banning the hiring of buying agents abroad, but link companies continue this practice either by making provisions in financial estimates or by simply employing such agents. Such agents are generally retired officials of the company and are located in the head office of the parent companies to prevent suspicion. These are the men who supervise all purchases from the buying of raw materials to machinery on commission basis used to inflate invoices.

Using expatriate salaries repatriation, the multinationals ravage the foreign exchange of the host country. The Nigerian government allows expatriates to repatriate 50 percent of their salaries. But what their employers, the multinationals, do is to inflate the salaries of their expatriate employees by as much as five times the actual salary. The salaries paid to expatriates in this country have no relevance to the nature of the work they do. When one compares the salaries they earn here to those of their counterparts in their home countries, one finds it difficult to believe what he sees. The purpose of all these dirty tricks is to enable the companies to steal away as much money as possible, thus draining the foreign exchange of the countries concerned.

For reasons well known to the rulers of Nigeria, foreigners are allowed to repatriate their pension contributions. This practice is not allowed in Britain. In the U.S. one is not allowed to take away a penny, in fact, you cannot even apply until you are 65 or so. By allowing the repatriation of pension contributions, Nigeria adds further problems to her exchange problems.

There may be other means whereby the multinationals repatriate money from the underdeveloped countries. But even on the basis of the few methods of repatriation and avoidance of taxes well known, it is difficult to say that multinationals are engines of growth in the underdeveloped countries. Because of the various dubious methods they employ to steal money from the host countries, it is in fact impossible to know exactly how much money they take away every year.

Closely related to their myth of being the engines of growth is their claims of transferring technology to the underdeveloped societies. In one of the 1975 Senate hearings on the role of American multinationals in the world economy and what should be U.S. foreign policy, Jacobs Clayman had this to say:

> The propensity of American multinationals to export America's comparative advantage in high-technology manufacturing production ought to be subject in its own right to rational control in the national interest. The pell-mell rush to take unique American know-how

overseas for production at higher rates of private profit causes too much social damages to be left uncontrolled. If technology exports are not rationalized with a view to the comprehensive national interest, American productivity, economic growth, employment and foreign trade will continue to suffer from the wholesale loss of technological leadership.[31]

On the basis of what we now know Clayman has nothing to fear as far as the underdeveloped countries are concerned. The multinationals do not make any meaningful transfer of technology to those societies.

Technological dependence is a great obstacle to development. An inevitable factor in the process of development is for a society involved to be able to develop the right kind of technology for its local needs; the very purpose of a pattern system is to promote the inventiveness of one's citizens. But when technology is controlled from abroad, the funds needed for research and development go to the metropolitan firm to develop its technology still further and this is technology designed for global profit maximization, not the development of the underdeveloped countries.[31]

The conditions under which global corporations transfer technology to underdeveloped countries are not conducive to development. A study of some 409 "transfer of technology" contracts between the global corporations and their subsidiaries in various countries reveals that almost 80 percent of them completely prohibited the use of the transferred technology for producing exports. United Nations studies in India, Pakistan, the Phillippines, Mexico, and Iran show a pattern of what the U.N. calls "restrictive business practices." Only in a few cases do the global giants permit local firms to export to neighboring markets considered too small to interest them, or to far away markets far beyond their reach.[32]

The control of technology in the developing countries gives the global giants immense power (in the poor countries) and such power can be abused, and it often is. The type of technology transferred to the poor countries is the type being abandoned or on the verge of being abandoned by the metropolitan countries. Quite often the technology transferred to the underdeveloped countries is the type least needed by them. What poor countries need may not be expensive Euro-American four-wheel tractors which very few can buy, operate and repair, but better hoes and ox plows.

The transferred technology is not of much assistance to the recipients because the executives of the global giants define these needs in terms of Euro-American criteria. There is great emphasis on individual refrigerators, washing machines, cars, expensive medical technology, etc. Most of their technology is designed for private consumption and not for solving social problems — e.g., a better source of water and sewage system which would drastically reduce illness, and public transportation. Rather than develop labour-intensive technology for poor countries, the global giants export capital-intensive and labour-saving technology. The result is the worsening of the already very high unemployment situation.

The problem does not end there. If the technology they bring to the host country is advanced, they will not allow the indigenes any meaningful· participation so as not to master the job. The essence of encouraging foreign companies to come in is with the expressed hope that the foreigners will train the indigenes to man the machinery and other techniques with a view to eventually taking over completely, or at least taking over a commanding share of the enterprise. But without this training not much is transferred by the multinationals.

Finally, despite much talk in the U.S. and other Western quarters about the export of advanced technology to the underdeveloped countries, much of the technology is what is obsolete in the metropoles. The result is that when the machine goes bad there are no spare parts. There is no underdeveloped country that has not had this experience. This is not helpful to economies that are struggling to get out of underdevelopment and it is difficult to see, with all the exposes above, why the multinationals should be regarded as engines of growth in the underdeveloped societies of the Third World.

Monks without Hoods

To all of the above practices by the multinationals must be added that of maintaining discriminatory personnel policies towards indigenes. They refuse to confer effective managerial positions and power at the senior management level to the indigenous executives. In the words of Sani, "the indigenous executives of multinationals are little more than glorified clerks who, like monks without hoods, are generally dressed in borrowed robes while occupying the token executive chairs assigned to them."[34]

During the colonial era, Africans, no matter how qualified, were not allowed to advance beyond chief clerkship. Africans better qualified than Europeans were made to serve under the latter; and even when Africans had Europeans under them — and these were very rare cases — the Europeans' salaries would be much higher than those of the former. But under contemporary imperialism, neocolonialism, the practice is to theoretically allow Africans to advance to a managerial level but without any responsibility. The multinationals will provide the indigenous "mock executives" with cosy offices and expensive desks and chairs. But power, which is all that matters, is not conferred on the Africans. They are, in fact, glorified clerks.

It is sad that a recent investigative report in Nigeria concluded that no Nigerian employee of a multinational was classified among senior management. The report, befittingly entitled "Mischief at Michelin,"[35] touches a chord of the problem of the underdeveloped countries.

It was stated that the Director of Michelin makes Nigerians work under the most primitive conditions. The Director and his European colleagues live comfortably in Ikoyi and there is a bus provided to take their children to and from school. When confronted with a question as to why such a privilege could not be extended to children of Nigerian employees, he replied that they were scattered all over Lagos and it was impossible to give them the same service. When asked why his senior Nigerian employees did not live in Ikoyi, he pretended not to know the answer. The Director's house costs Michelin ₦28,000 a year while the highest paid Nigerian employee gets only ₦780 a year housing allowance. This is less than 3 per cent of what his expatriate director receives.

On December 30, 1977, he sent out memos to his Nigerian colleagues to the effect that none of them belongs in the coveted senior management category; included among these is a Nigerian who earns the equivalence of a deputy secretary's salary. By denying them the senior executive status, the Director keeps them away from the workings of the company. This, of course, does not mean that he would have allowed Nigerians any meaningful participation had they been categorized as senior executives. There is no handbook outlining the conditions of services for employees and the implication of this is the application of arbitrary rules here and there. Recently two of his most senior Nigerians resigned out of frustration with the company.

Finally, the report complains about the business practice of Michelin. This company imports most of its tires from France. The usual practice is for import costs to be paid after all the relevant documents have been tendered. But Michelin chooses to pay for its goods before they arrive and before the shipping papers have been completely submitted. The practice is for this company to receive about half the goods it has paid for in foreign exchange, thus exporting more money out of the country than it should. When the

137

investigators confronted the Director with this ostensible anomoly, his response was that his company's goods were stolen somewhere before they reached Lagos. It is ridiculous to believe that about half of his company's goods should get lost each time they are shipped to Lagos.

Michelin began operations in this country in 1962 in prefabricated and temporary buildings. Sixteen years later this company does not have a permanent site, a clear indication that it does not feel it has a permanent stake in this country. It may be added that in 1977 this company sold tires for more than ₦40 million.

Another story of exploitation and mismanagement has to do with Calcemco of Calabar and its former director, Dr. A. P. C. Cumming, an expatriate.[36] He was fired for allegedly engaging in activities inimical to the interest of the company. Among the allegations against this expatriate were:

> (1) That he went to Europe in January, 1978 and renegotiated for clinker at $ 47.25 per ton, without any authority from the Board; and this was done after the Board itself had negotiated and agreed to a price of $41.00 per ton with the suppliers. The result of this transaction was that the company lost ₦149,840. Who received this difference is not known.
>
> (2) The director "tried to bull-doze the Board into ordering a second-hand (scrap) cement mill at ₦1,200,000... when two existing cement mills at the company's plant had never been utilised to full capacity."
>
> (3) The director bought a new Mercedes Benz car immediately upon arrival in Calabar when in fact there was already another Mercedes Benz car in good condition and a new Peugeot 504 available for his own use. He subsequently bought a third car, all for his own use.

(4) The director was given free house, cars, over-generous allowances and salary and yet he still "coerced" the accountant to give him ₦100 a week for food, something not provided for in the contract. (5) The company previously leased a house for a senior staff at ₦170 per month. Eventually, the director used ₦9,300 to refurnish and renovate the same house and then leased it to his girlfriend at ₦ 40.00 per months.

(6) The director's "vindictive, inhuman and authoritarian management" forced more than 69 "highly-trained Nigerian technicians and professionals" to resign within nine months after the director took over.

(7) He asked the Accounts Department of the company to open a bank account in Lagos, "to which he should be the sole signatory, and to transfer funds to it, so that he could draw out money at will whenever he visited Lagos." But this idea was quickly dropped when the Accounts Department asked him to seek the approval of the Board.

(8) The director "was more enthusiastic to order materials from overseas, than to use local materials to produce cement..."

Michelin and Calcemco are only cited as examples; there are literally many Michelins and Calcemcos. And needless to say, these situations are not confined to Nigeria; they exist in all underdeveloped countries. The success of the economic and financial manipulations by these companies are aided by their internal compradors. In relation to this, Olowoporoku and Sonaike have noted that one of the general disadvantages of reliance on external economic contacts is:

The creation and propagation of official corruption and corruptive practices. This arises partly from the inducement by foreigners who believe the African can sell his father for money. Many foreign business men have been the source of embarrassment to many African leaders, as attested to by recent events. For example, in Nigeria several foreign businessmen have been deported for wielding corrupting influence on policy makers in Nigeria and boasting about it. The massive importation of cement which nearly destroyed the Nigerian economy is an aspect of this influence which encourages Nigerians to want to get rich at all costs. The global reverberations of the Lockheed scandal is another example.[37]

The Nigerian cement importation scandal of 1975-76 needs a little elaboration. During this period Nigeria was receiving 1.6 million tons of cement a month; the shipments were more than twice the unloading capacity of all Nigeria's ports combined. The massive orders resulted in an armada of ships anchored off the Lagos coastline. In September, 1975 there were more than 420 freighters, many of which were decrepit bulks manned by very small crews sent by shipowners to collect demurrage costs of $4,100 a day per ship. Some of these ships had to wait for seven months, and even for a year. The result of this was that in the moisture-ridden hulls, the cement lost its binding quality after six months, thus becoming completely useless for construction. Although the intention of the government was to destroy the worthless cement, it still found its way into the hands of contractors who made use of them. It is difficult not to believe, at least suspect, that the collapsing of a two-story building nearing completion at the University of Ife in 1976, killing one workman and injuring 18 others, was not connected with the use of the ruined cement.

The Government appointed a tribunal to inquire into the scandal. "But it seems to have made little progress in untangling a web of kick-backs and bribes involving Government officials, foreign ship owners, corrupt purchasing agents, unscrupulous middlemen, phony corporations, dubious letters of credit and Swiss bank accounts."[38]

In its report the tribunal complained of lack of cooperation from the public; people who had information refused to come forward to give it to the tribunal. The tribunal however accused nine public officials. One of the accused was a secretary in the Ministry of Defense who said he merely carried out orders from General Gowon. Others included a former ambassador to the Netherlands. The names of prominent Nigerian businessmen that figured in the rumours about who were involved were not mentioned in the report.

The tribunal reported that the proper price of cement per ton at the time was $53 per ton instead of $60 that was paid. The result was that the Government lost $57 million, excluding the demurrage costs which were estimated at $240 million. This still does not include the cost of hiring an American company under a $45-million contract to use barges for floating the ships.

Sure enough, the exploitation of Nigeria and Nigerians has been aided and in some cases spearheaded by the so-called elites, the compradors. As Dr. Ronald Walters, Director of Social Science Research, Howard University has observed:

> it is the function of these elites... to preserve outposts of Western culture and civilization in Africa as a cluster of superior values and behaviour patterns; to serve as the social transmission belt for contact between the West and the masses of Africa; to function as figureheads and midlevel technicians in a system of economic exploitation, and to develop an indigenous and a wealthy black elite class amidst the vast poverty of the masses... This is not the whole picture, but the model, as it functions in one sector, works practically the same way in other sectors of society except where in recent years some countries have succeeded in

141

nationalizing talents of the elite by nationalizing the institutions which they traditionally serve.

In his broadcast on September 21, 1978, Lt. General Obasanjo said that some political aspirants to the offices to be vacated by the military in 1979 were parading foreign lands in search of support. He said further that this is unpatriotic and that their activities were closely monitored. He warned that future leaders should not sell the country to foreign powers in order to gain political power.

This particular behaviour of our political aspirants clearly points to the crux of the matter, the extent of our dependency upon neocolonialist powers. This further confirms our thesis that much of the exploitation of Africans is engendered by Africans, the internal allies of the neocolonial imperialists. The contemporary history of Africa is replete with cases of Africans gaining political power through the assistance of their external allies. Tshombe and Mobutu quickly come to mind. Idi Amin took the reigns of power from Milton Obote through the assistance of Israel that masterminded the whole military coup. Although this had been rumoured at the time Idi Amin staged his successful coup, the confirmation came from Col. Baruch Bar-Lev, an Israeli who headed a military mission in Kampala. In an interview with the *New York Times* on July 17, 1979, the Colonel said that he helped Idi Amin plan and execute that coup. The Colonel could not have been involved without the approval of Israel.

Two more cases of how our elites collaborate with international capitalists to exploit us. As of now there is an agreement between Peugeot of Nigeria Ltd. (a Nigerian-owned company), and UTA (a French airline), to airfreight completely knocked down (CKD) parts of the Peugeot cars from France to Nigeria. The Peugeot company is projected to produce between 32,000 cars and 50,000 cars a year between 1978 and 1981. If all the CKD parts are to be airfreighted then the cost is going to be astronomical, in the neighbourhood of ₦70-80 million a year. This is bound to be a drain on foreign exchange reserves of our country. But could not Nigeria Airways perform this function? One cannot but suspect some kickback scheme being involved in the deal.

The final case concerns a recent advertisement asking tender for the supply of furniture for army barracks and the new international airports. There are certainly enough domestic furniture manufactures whose services can be fully utilised and thus save depleting our tiny foreign exchange reserve still further. It is absurd that NECCO (a Federal Government-owned company) should ask tenders for airport furniture from importers and not from domestic manufacturers. The fantastic costs of such imported manufactures and the commission payable to the parent company will mean unnecessary drain on foreign exhange reserves. But whether or not those who draw up such agreements benefit financially from them, the very absurdity of the nature of the agreement is bound to raise questions about their propriety.

Aid and Third World Indebtedness

We now turn our attention to the issue of foreign aid and indebtedness of the underdeveloped world. U.S. interests and those of its multinational giants are synonymous. And as can be expected, there is a great "partnership" between the state and the global giants. By singling out the U.S. Agency for International Development (AID) and U.S. dominated international agencies such as World Bank and International Monetary Fund, we can see some of the functions the U.S. performs for its corporations.

Take foreign aid for example. As defined by President John Kennedy, foreign aid is "a method by which the United States maintains a position of influence and control around the world, and sustains a good many countries which would definitely collapse, or pass into the Communist Bloc,"[40] Foreign aid consists of loans and gifts, and in the words of a Presidential Commission, "gifts to prove our esteem for foreign heads of state, hastily devised projects to prevent Soviet aid, gambles to maintain existing governments in power."[41]

But the ramifications of this *aid* are great. Foreign aid goes far beyond a mere transfer of capital; loan monies are generally stipulated for specific uses such as education, labour unions, transport and communication facilities, and are often accompanied by a large number of American "experts." What is apparent here is that apart from the foreign debt and balance of payment problems, among others, "aid programmes affect political decisions about development, the socialization and training of certain sectors of the population, and so on."[42] Contemporary imperialism or neocolonialism seeks to avoid direct political control or military intervention, especially after Southeast Asia where they suffered their first major defeat. Western interests are then preserved through "the reinforcement of the infrastructure of dependence" — African institutions and social classes which are geared toward foreign interests. This is accomplished in large measure through aid agencies.

Foreign aid agencies provide an "opening wedge" or "point of entry" for private capital. They do this in several ways: (1) they make loans directly to the global giants, both for feasibility studies and for actual implementations; (2) they actually conduct these studies for the corporations; (3) they sponsor aid programs such as Food for Peace (under which the U.S. government makes loans to its corporations in American currencies, acquired from the sale of surplus agricultural commodities, in order to provide funds for local costs of investment. Foreign aid helps to "socialize the indirect costs of private investors" such as setting up programs in African or American universities, technical institutes, "productivity centers," to train managers and skilled labour for the local subsidiaries of the global giants; subsidizing university research projects in the poor countries and in the U.S. — mostly involving technological and scientific problems of the global giants, and promoting and making funds (loans) available for infrastructure such as roads, communications facilities, and so on, all of which would benefit the foreign corporations more than the local population.[43]

Foreign aid places the metropolitan firms in an advantageous position over local ones in several ways: by refusing loans to indigenous firms which might compete with foreign firms; by feeding U.S. firms with vital information denied to local firms; by lobbying and sometimes pressurizing the host government to pursue policies and take positions favourable to the U.S. or the Western world in general; by specifying that loan contracts for various construction projects be given to a U.S. firm or a local one but simultaneously adding such conditions which virtually eliminate local firms from competition.

Foreign aid makes it easy for the global giants to settle down and make long-range corporate planning and it also lessens the risks to the corporations of long-range overseas investment. This is accomplished through various ways. There are many investment guarantee programs designed to insure U.S. corporations against losses from war, insurrection, expropriation, incontrovertibility, and revolution. Thus, any dispute arising between any African state and American corporations certainly involves the U.S. government.

Foreign aid promotes the local investment climate through various programmes which include training local labour leaders to become ardent anticommunists: the U.S. trade unions with the assistance of the U.S. government have built pseudo labour institutes in several African countries, including Nigeria and Zaire, where local labour leaders are indoctrinated in the art of labour depoliticization;[44] by infiltrating local organizations such as trade unions, peasant, and community organizations; by using the mass media and educational institutions to promote the ideology of capitalism — their task is facilitated because many of the teachers, bureaucrats and others have been educated either in America or Europe where they had already been bombarded with capitalist advertisements; by sending experts to African governments to supervise the implementation of the aid programs; as a corollary, the U.S. government and its corporations acquire enormous control over policy formulation and development strategies. Furthermore, they persuade and pressurize host government planners to gear their development policies to the long-range needs of U.S. corporations.[45]

Outright bribes, as have been revealed in various countries, are often employed to get local policy makers to take U.S. positions. Foreign aid itself is a form of bribe, because if a country does not take positions at the U.N. and its agencies and O. A. U. favourable to the U.S. it is not likely to be favoured with foreign aid. Daniel P. Moynihan, the obstreperous, boisterous, and flamboyant former U.S. Ambassador to the U.N. successfully created a special department within the State Department to track down those countries which were voting against "U.S. interests," which meant that not only would such countries not be able to get "aids" from the U.S. but would also find it extremely difficult, if not virtually impossible, to get loans from the World Bank and could even be subjected to "destabilization" programmes.

Because of its firm control over the World Bank and I.M.F., the U.S. can centralize and rationalize the world capital market. But above all, foreign aid accomplishes the function of preserving American capitalism beyond the specific interest of any single U.S. corporation. In other words, it ensures that any kind of economic development in the recipients' country "is firmly rooted in capitalist ways and practice."[46]

The question that a curious reader may raise is why the

U.S. makes great use of the international financial institutions, mainly the World Bank, for its aid purposes much less
than through bilateral programmes? For example, between
1960 and 1964-65 loans of the World Bank to African
countries increased from $40 million to $213 million. It
again rose to $345 million in 1969. Thus, from about one-
seventh of the total amount expended by the U.S. on bilateral aids in 1960, the World Bank's loans and credits rose
to one-half in 1965, and surpassed it by the end of the
decade.[47] While the intention of the U.S. has been to decrease its bilateral aid in this decade, the Bank promised to
treble its lending to African countries. The answer to the
question posed above is provided by Smith:

> Decreasing U.S. bilateral aid and increasing ac-
> tivity of the international institutions are not spontane-
> ous unrelated tendencies, but reflect Washington's
> policies and ability to implement them. In the World
> Bank, which was organized and financed initially by
> the subscriptions of the capital-exporting countries, the
> United States, with some 28% of the Bank's govern-
> ment subscriptions and 25% of the vote in 1967, is by
> far the dominant power. Britain is second with 11% of
> the subscribed capital and 10% of the vote, followed
> by the FRG and France, each with about-half of the
> latter. Only some 10% of subscriptions are actually
> paid in, e.g., the United States had paid in $635 mill-
> ion in 1967.
> Presiding successively over the Bank since its for-
> mation have been representatives of the amalgam of
> U.S. big business, finance and government: John J.
> McCloy — from Assistant Secretary of War to IBRD,
> then to U.S. High Commissioner for Germany, to
> chairman of Chase National Bank and director of big
> corporations; Eugene R. Black — from vice president
> of Chase National Bank to IBRD, then to director of
> big corporations and foundations; George D. Woods
> Chairman of First Boston Corporation to IBRD, then

to corporations; Robert McNamara — Ford Corporation to secretary of defense, then to IBRD. U.S. and British nationals make up 50% of the Bank's regular professional staff. It would be difficult to find a body which more typifies the U.S. oligarchy and its world finance relationships.[48]

The political and economic interests of the international finance and the monopolies, especially the U.S. as the major capital exporter, are well protected by the World Bank. For example, the Bank itself has stated that its function is that of acting "as a safe bridge for the movement of private capital into international investment.[49] The Bank promotes this by advising governments to change "inequitable and restrictive legislation" to attract private capital and service hard loans; and it hates to see any government ownership on the pretext of "management considerations;" and it does not lend even at conventional terms for purposes, which in its own judgment could be so financed by private capital. The U.S. asks the World Bank "to establish basic policy criteria for a country's tax structure, the allocating of budgetary resources and pricing policies."[50] For example, the President of the Bank, Mr. McNamara, advises African countries to undertake "tax measures" and "choice of projects that might be politically unpopular," and to show a "willingness to accept and implement advice from outside experts."[51]

What this advice seeks to accomplish is to promote and underpin profitable foreign investment, notably that of U.S. and Britain, as can be established in the structure of, and decisions concerning the granting of bank loans. There is a great emphasis on transport. By the early 1960's loans worth $860 million had been made to Africa and of this, 55% was allocated to transport. By 1967 this had declined to 43% but still the highest, while electric power consumed 28% and the rest went for industry, agriculture and education.[52]

African countries have complained about a number of things associated with aid. They include: (1) that unlike the massive aid given to West Germany after World War II under the Marshall Plan, the aid given to the underdeveloped countries has been a drop in the ocean; (2) that negotiations for the tiny aid are always protracted and frustrating; (3) that they resent the tying of aid to the procurement of goods and services from the donor countries regardless of cost and quality; (4) there is invariably an incongruency between their perception of development priorities and that of the donor countries who rather than support their development plans and programmes tended to pick out and support low priority and politically attractive projects which have the effect of distorting their development objective and priorities; and (5) that this aid has forced them into more debts.

In connection with this last complaint, Dr. Adebayo Adedeji, former Economic Commissioner of Nigeria said in September 1978, that African countries owe about ₦25,641,000,000; this does not include the recent $1 billion loan Nigeria is currently collecting from the NATO countries. Dr. Adedeji went further to say that African States still depend on foreign ships to import and export about 90 percent of their cargoes.

In 1967 the World Bank gave out about $870 million to underdeveloped countries. At the same time disbursements net of amortization, subscriptions, and contributions, and of changes in holding of the funded debt of the IBRD amounted to $545 million. Interests exacted by the World Bank amounted to more than $200 million — that is 23% of gross disbursements. What we see here is that the real net transfer of resources amounted only to $345 million, or about 40% of gross disbursements.[53]

Between 1956 and 1965 the outstanding external public debt of some 97 underdeveloped countries jumped from $10 million to over $39 billion. Their estimated service payments on external public debt also rose from under $1 billion to $3.5 billion, nearly all of which had to do with export credits. For 81 underdeveloped countries their external public debt outstanding rose by 38% over the period 1965-68, from $37.78 billion to $53.36 billion. Within the same period estimated payments of interest and amortization also jumped by about 38%, to $4.67 billion in 1968.

Figures for unguaranteed export credits, debt repayable at the option of the borrower in local currencies, or commercial areas are not included in the World Bank data. "If we further take into account the possibility that even the data on public and publicly guaranteed debt may be understated to some extent, the total outstanding debt of the developing countries could well have exceeded $45 billion at the end of the year 1966 and debt service could have amounted to more than $5 billion."[54] Outstanding public debt of underdeveloped countries for 1966 as estimated by the World Bank was $4 billion. The inevitable conclusion that one comes to, on the basis of our analysis, is that investment by the global conglomerates, foreign aid by the so-called friendly nations, and loans (which I have simply included among aid) tend to perpetuate underdevelopment. In fact, their positive impact on African economic development is at best minimal. In particular, foreign investments have created in the underdeveloped societies a phenomenon which has been called "growth without development."

Growth Without Development

We find "marginals" in every underdeveloped country. Marginals refers to those people who live on "the edges of the new zones of prosperity." The marginals are in majority in every African society. In other words, we have a very few people who have benefitted from the exploitation of the multinationals and all forms of aid while the majority languish under abject penury. There is no sign of the "trickle-down-effect" or the "spread effect" manifesting itself. This situation is characterized by "growth without development" — that is, "growth engendered and kept up from the outside, without the construction of socioeconomic structures that would enable automatic passage to a still further stage, that of a self-centered and self-maintained new dynamism."[55] There is real growth in terms of conventional economic indicators, but its concomitant problem is the coexistence of a relatively well-off and dynamic sector and a sector of stagnant and even growing misery. The observable economic change is not complemented by structural changes in lines of production, by employing more efficient techniques in government or economy, by meaningful involvement of indigenous personnel in the economy other than the unskilled labour category, or by "new social achievements and new levels of economic aspiration."[56] The examples that readily come to mind are those of Liberia and Ivory Coast. We begin with Liberia.

Following Tubman's Open Door Policy — the policy of allowing unrestricted foreign investments in Liberia and of allowing the indigenes of Liberia formerly excluded from the mainstream of Liberian life by the Americo-Liberians to participate — foreign capitals began to flow into Liberia. In the 1960's foreign capital flow into that country was $75 million per year. In 1943 the government budget was $750,000, but in 1963 it was $50 million. The ruling oligarchies — Americo-Liberians — are politically probic. The capital and the high level skill needed to exploit the resources of Liberia come from outside. Firestone plantations, various mining and a host of other concessions, are owned and run by Americans, Germans, Scandinavians, Swiss and other non-Liberians. Lebanese and Syrians monopolize merchandising of commodities. Large rubber and fruit plantations owned by the Americo-Liberians are run by Indians, Sierra Leonians, and other non-Liberians.[57] In the words of Clower et al:

> It is only a slight exaggeration to say that the professional, managerial, and entrepreneural labour force in Liberia is divided neatly into two groups: Liberians work for government, are owners of rubber farms, transport facilities, and building, provide legal services, and to a small extent medical and commercial services. Foreigners are overwhelmingly predominant in staff positions in iron ore, rubber, and timber. Where Liberians are employed by concessions, they most frequently act as non resident advisers in law, public relations and advertising.[58]

This was the pronouncement of a group of American experts after studying economic development in Liberia for about a year. It was their belief that "the lives of all Liberians could be markedly improved within a generation," provided that the government changed and decided to operate "an intelligent and honest development policy." The economic experts further discovered that "the relinquished developmental opportunities because of prestige outlays are very great. Government expenditures on diplomacy amounted to 8 per cent of the 1960 budget, while those on education amounted to only 10 per cent. Some $50 million have been spent during the past five years on expensive public buildings... The primary obstacles to economic progress in Liberia are not technical but social-political and institutional residues of an earlier era."[59] In spelling out the real nature of the trouble, these experts, sent to Liberia by the U.S. Agency for International Development (AID), asserted that "Liberia is being run and run inefficiently, in terms of development — by a handful of people. Close family ties developed in response to earlier pioneer conditions inhibit efficient conduct of government by encouraging nepotism and large-scale outlays for unproductive purposes."[60]

Although this assessment was made in the 1960 s and

while Tubman was President, nothing changed in the era of President Tolbert. A few gluttonous elites intractably aligned themselves with the international capitalists to exploit the masses of Liberia. There were certainly some observable signs of growth in Liberia prior to the coup that toppled the Tolbert government but the masses are yet to benefit from it.

The situation in the Ivory Coast offers an infernal parallel to that of Liberia. According to U.N. data, the Ivory Coast of President Felix Houphouet-Boigny has recorded an economic growth rate well above 6%, and an annual national income much higher than the African average. There has been a steady increase in investment; recurrent budget surpluses have enabled the government to spend on development; expenditures for administration have been lower than in many other countries. But all these developments are very deceiving because they are not a result of any basic structural change from colonial times, nor on subsequent closing or reducing of the gap between the elite and the poverty-striken majority, nor on definite advance to self-determination.

Sure enough, there has been a significant rise in agricultural production, as Samir Amin has noted, but this is very much according to the colonial pattern. The only difference being that the earlier pattern was "elaborated" over a longer period of time.[61] Amin has stated that "it will probably be impossible to continue to advance in the area of agricultural development without radical changes in policy. The fundamental reason for this is that an expensive plantation economy (whose results have been too easily obtained without direct transportation infrastructure), thanks to the introduction of a foreign-salaried work force, has fashioned a regressive social structure."[62]

Economic financing in Ivory Coast has taken the form of partnership with French and other European Common Market investors; this partnership has exacted its price both in direction of development and in sovereignty. "The domination of foreign capital is exercised in an absolute manner over the entire economy of the country. Its remuneration at very high rates indicates the external dependence of this growth."[63] There are many more capitalists in the Ivory Coast than before, but few of them are indigenes, even Africans. Here, as in Liberia, the economy is in the hands of foreigners. "If one can speak, therefore, of the development of capitalism in the Ivory Coast, one cannot likewise speak of the development of an Ivory Coast capitalism. Ivory Coast society does not have its own autonomy: it is not included in the European society that dominates it; if the proletariat is African, the true bourgeoisie is absent, domiciled in the Europe that furnishes capital and cadres."[64]

These words were written in 1967 but nothing of significance has changed in Ivory Coast since then. What has been said about Liberia and the Ivory Coast can be said about almost every African country. Political independence has not ended economic exploitation and domination, only the methods have changed somewhat plus the fact that the U.S. which never had any outright colony in Africa has emerged as the greatest economic neoimperialist power.

Before ending this chapter, I consider it important to briefly look at what Frantz Fanon sees as the role of the African intelligentsia and bourgeoisie in post colonial exploitation of the continent. It provides a sort of explanation for the role of the bourgeoisie that we have discussed above.

Fanon on the Intelligentsia and Bourgeoisie

In those colonial countries where nationalist struggle has occurred, "where the blood of the people has flowed and where the length of the period of armed warfare has favoured the backward surge of intellectuals towards bases grounded in the people" there has taken place "a genuine

154

eradiction of the superstructure built by these intellectuals from the bourgeois colonialist environment."[65] But it is the national bourgeoisie that takes over from the imperialist power. This class of people runs the country very much in the same way that their previous masters had run it. The country is rife with internal contradictions. And since there is no homogeneity of caste, many intellectuals condemn the regime which is based on domination of the few — Michels Iron law of Oligarchy. In the same society are some intellectuals and civil servants, who sincerely "feel the necessity for a planned economy, the out-lawing of profiteers and the strict prohibition of attempts at mystification. In addition, such men fight in a certain measure for the mass participation of the people in the ordering of public affairs."[66]

These are the "honest intellectuals" with "no precise ideas about politics." Their timidity and indecisiveness are partly due to "the apparent strength of the bourgeoisie."[67] Consequently, after independence, in order to avoid the installation of corruption within the country, economic regression and the introduction of a tyrannical regime, "the road to the national bourgeoisie" must be closed. This is "the only means towards /progress."[68] Fanon is very contemptible and hostile towards the bourgeoisie because as far as the struggle for national independence is concerned, their force is completely negative. Fanon sees the bourgeoisie resorting to reforms thus preventing the attainment of genuine national liberation.

As Fanon sees him, "the national middle-class which takes over power at the end of the colonial regime is an under-developed middle-class."[69] It has "no economic power, and in any case it is in no way commensurate with the bourgeoisie of the mother country which it hopes to replace."[70]

The most enlightened section of the new state, which consists of the university and merchant classes is small and concentrated in the capital; this section is also concentrated

155

in the type of activities in which it is engaged — business, agriculture, and the liberal professions. It lacks financiers and industrial managers.

> The national bourgeoisie of under-developed countries is not engaged in production, nor in invention, nor building nor labour; it is completely canalized into activities of the intermediary type. Its innermost vocation seems to be to keep in the running and to be part of the racket. The psychology of the national bourgeoisie is that of the businessman, not that of captain of industry; and it is only too true that the greed of the settlers and the system of embargoes set up by colonialism has hardly left them any other choice.[71]

Thus, Fanon tells us that the African bourgeoisie is a sort of phantom bourgeoisie, merely clinging on to capitalism that the masters introduced to the colony; it is not financially strong, nor does it possess the capability to build its own capitalist economy. The fact of the matter is that colonialism does not allow the indigenes to have meaningful participation in the domestic economy and thus it is not possible for the new bourgeoisie to accumulate enough capital to be able to embark on economic adventures. The bourgeoisie class continues with the production of raw materials for export to the metropolitan countries. Thus, it perpetuates its economic dependence. Often, the financing of the production of raw materials is done abroad and the tendency is to encourage development of underdevelopment and the exportation of scarce reserves.

Lacking in both sufficient material and intellectual resources, the national bourgeoisie

> limits its claims to the taking over of business offices and commercial houses formerly occupied by the settlers. The national bourgeoisie steps into the shoes of the former European settlement: doctors, barristers,

traders, commercial travellers, general agents and transport agents. It considers that the dignity of the country and its own welfare require it should occupy all these posts. From now on it will insist that all the big foreign companies should pass through its hands, whether these companies wish to keep on their connections with the country, or to open it up. The national middle-class discovers its historic mission: that of intermediary.[72]

As perceived by the national bourgeoisie, its mission does not include the transformation of the nation; its only mission is becoming "the transmission line between the nation and a capitalism, rampant though camouflaged, which today puts on the masque of neocolonialism." It is quite happy in its role as the "Western bourgeoisie's business agent." By accepting this cheap-jack's function that it carries out without any complexes in a most dignified manner, the middle-class absconds from its historic role.

Unlike its Western counterpart, the African bourgeoisie is not an inventor and the discoverer of new worlds. The African bourgeoisie is dominated by the spirit of indulgence, and this occurs because it "identifies itself with the Western bourgeoisie, from whom it has learnt its lessons. It follows the Western bourgeoisie along its path of negation and decadence without ever having emulated it in its first stages of exploration and invention, stages which are an acquisition of that Western bourgeoisie whatever the circumstances."[73] Thus the African bourgeoisie is eminently qualified for its role as colonial imperialism's internal collaborator, comprador, in the post-independence game of neocolonialism.

In order to be able to fulfill its role, the African bourgeoisie creates the single national party. Fanon writes:

> Powerless economically, unable to bring about the existence of coherent social relations, and standing on the principle of its domination as a class, the

157

bourgeoise chooses the solution that seems to it the easiest, that of the single party. It does not yet have the quiet conscience and the calm that economic power and the control of the state machine alone can give.[74]

With the establishment of the single party system comes "the modern form of the dictatorship of the bourgeoisie, unmasked, unpainted, unscrupulous, and cynical."[75] At the head of this party is the man who had earlier enjoyed the affection of the masses as one genuinely interested in their welfare. But now this man is interested in becoming "the general president of that company of profiteers impatient for their returns which constitutes the national bourgeoisie."[76] The party is used as a means of private advancement, and it is both objectively and subjectively made "the accompliance of the merchant bourgeoisie." But Fanon makes no mistake in revealing what the African middle-class really is: "only a sort of little greedy caste, avid and voracious, with the timid mind of a huckster, only too glad to accept the dividends that the former colonial power hands out to it."[77]

The African bourgeoisie fails to possess something crucial to a bourgeoisie, and that is "money." So he bècomes for quite a long time "a bourgeoisie of the civil service." If he is given enough time and opportunity, this bourgeoisie will embezzle enough money to stiffen its domination. But this sort of bourgeoisie is "incapable of giving birth to an authentic bourgeois society with all the economic and industrial consequences which this entails." He therefore turns his attention to "trade and small business enterprises, and securing commissions. It is not its money that works, but its business acumen. It does not go in for investments and it cannot achieve that accumulation of capital necessary to the birth and blossoming of an authentic bourgeoisie."[78]

The political leader increasingly becomes alienated from the masses who fret and fume because independence has brought them no tangible gains. Because he feels the resentment and hostility of the people, he tends to bend towards the national bourgeoisie. He eventually "knowingly becomes the aider and abettor of the young bourgeoisie which is plunging into the mire of corruption and pleasure."[79]

> The economic channels of the young State sink back inevitably into neo-colonialist lines. The national economy, formerly protected, is today literally controlled. The budget is balanced through loans and gifts, while every three or four months the chief ministers themselves or else their governmental delegations come to the erstwhile mother countries or elsewhere, fishing for capitals.
> The former colonial power increases its demands, accumulates concessions and guarantees and takes fewer and fewer pains to mask the hold it has over the national government. The people stagnate deplorably in unbearable poverty; slowly they awaken to the unutterable treason of their leaders. This awakening is all the more acute in that the bourgeoisie is incapable of learning its lesson. The distribution of wealth that it effects is not spread out between a great many sectors; it is not ranged among different levels, nor does it set up an hierarchy of half-tones. The new caste is an affront all the more disgusting in that the immense majority, nine-tenths of the population, continue to die of starvation. The scandalous enrichment, speedy and pitiless, of this caste is accompanied by a decisive awakening on the part of the people, and a growing awareness that promises stormy days to come.[80]

Frantz Fanon wrote his *The Wretched of the Earth* more than a decade ago. Events in Africa and the Third World as a whole have vindicated his predictions. His writing is a great indictment against African leaders who took over from their colonial overlords only to perpetuate the master-servant relationship.

The next chapter examines how the U.S. State Department, through the instrumentality of the Central Intelligence Agency (CIA), has promoted and continues to promote and protect U.S. multinationals' interests in the underdeveloped world. In fact it will be clear that without the CIA it would be difficult for the U.S. to implement its foreign policies and it would be extremely difficult for the multinationals to penetrate, dominate and exploit the Third World the way they have done and continue to do.

REFERENCES

[1] Basil Davidson, *Which Way Africa?* (Baltimore: Penguin Books, 1971).

[2] *Ibid.*, p. 131.

[3] *Ibid.*

[4] Reginald H. Green and Ann Seidman, *Unity or Poverty?* (Baltimore: Penguin Books, 1968), p. 14.

[5] Kwame Nkrumah, *Towards Colonial Freedom* (London: William Heinemann, 1946, 1960).

[6] *Ibid.*

[7] Kwame Nkrumah, *I Speak of Freedom* (New York: Frederick A. Praeger, Inc., 1961), p. 162.

[8] *Ibid.*, p. 44.

[9] Kwame Nkrumah, *Neo-Colonialism: The Last Stage of Imperialism* (New York: International Publishers, 1966).

[10] Kwame Nkrumah, *Revolutionary Path* (New York: International Publishers, 1973), p. 310.

[11] Kwame Nkrumah, *Africa Must Unite* (New York: International Publishers, 1970), p. 173. This book was published posthumously.

[12] Nkrumah, *Neo-Colonialism*, p. 1.

[13] Nkrumah, *Revolutionary Path*, p. 313.

[14] *The Wall Street Journal* (January 13, 1972).

[15] *San Francisco Chronicle* (1972).

[16] U.S. Senate *Hearing Before the Subcommittee on Multinational Corporations*, 1974.

[17] Peggy B. Musgrave, *Direct Investment Abroad and the Multinationals: Effects on the United States Economy* (Washington, D.C.: U.S. Government Printing Office, 1975). This monograph was prepared for the Subcommittee on Multinational Corporations, U.S. Senate.

[18] *Multinational Corporations in the Dollar Devaluation Crisis: Report on Questionaire* for use of the U.S. Subcommittee on Multinational Corporations, June 1975, p. 6.

19 *Ibid.*

20 *Ibid.*, p. 1.

21 Richard J. Barnet and Ronald E. Miller, *Global Reach* (New York: Simon and Schuster, 1974), p. 152.

22 *Ibid.*, p. 153.

23 *Ibid.*, p. 160.

24 *Sunday Times* (April 2, 1978).

25 *Daily Times* (September 21, 1978).

26 Habibu Sani, "The Invisible Governments: Multinationals in the Third World, " *Daily Times* (April 16, 1978).

27 Eugene Onwumere, "Africa and Multinational Corporations," *Daily Times* (August 2, 1978).

28 Naiwu Osahon, "How Foreign Companies Cheat Us" *Daily Times* (September 18, 1977), 18.

29 *Ibid.*

30 *Ibid.*

31 Hearings before the Subcommittee on Multinational Corporations of the Committee of Foreign Relations, United States Senate, 94th Congress, July 21 and December 9-10, 1975.

32 Barnet and Muller, *Global Reach*, p. 1.

33 *Ibid.*

34 Sani, "The Invisible Governments."

35 *Daily Times* (March 27, 1978).

36 *The Nigerian Chronicle* (July 21, 1978).

37 Bode Olowoporoku and Olayinka, "A Critique of African Development Strategy with Reference to External Economic Relationships," *African Development Studies* (March, 1977), p. 92.

38 *New York Times* (June 28, 1976).

39 *The Nigerian Chronicle* (August 24, 1977).

40 Harry Magdoff, *The Age of Imperialism* (New York: Modern Reader, 1968), p. 117.

41 *Ibid.*

42 Ina Katz Nelson et al., *The Politics and Society Reader* (New York: David Mckay Company, Inc; 1974), p. 195.

43 *Ibid.*, p. 197; See also Green and Seidman, *Unity or Poverty?*.

44 Daniel A. Offiong, "The AFL-CIO Foreign Policy in Latin America and Africa," *The Third World Review* II/1 (Spring, 1976), pp. 36-48.

45 *Ibid.*

46 Magdoff, *The Age of Imperialism*, p. 117.

47 Stewart Smith, *U.S. Neocolonialism in Africa* (New York: International Publishers, 1974), p. 86.

48 *Ibid.*, pp. 86-87.

49 Quoted by *Ibid.*, p. 87.

50 *Ibid.*, p. 88.

51 *Ibid.*

52 *Ibid.*

53 Paul Streeten, *Aid to Africa* (New York: Praeger Publishers, 1972), pp. 69-70.

[54] *Ibid.*, p. 70.

[55] Samir Amin, "Capitalism and Development in the Ivory Coast," in Irving Leonard Markovitz, ed., *African Politics and Society* (New York; The Free Press, 1970), p. 288.

[56] J. Gus Liebenow, *Liberia: The Evolution of Privilege* (Ithaca: Cornell University Press, 1969), pp. 174-175.

[57] Daniel A. Offiong, "Controlled Social Change: The Case of Liberia," an unpublished paper, p. 28.

[58] R.W. Clower et al, *Growth Without Development: An Economic Survey of Liberia* (Evanston, Ill.: Northwestern University Press, 1966).

[59] *Ibid.*

[60] *Ibid.*

[61] Amin, *"Capitalism,"* p. 279.

[62] *Ibid.*

[63] *Ibid.*, p. 280.

[64] *Ibid.*, p. 287.

[65] Frantz Fanon, *The Wretched of the Earth*, translated by Constance Farrington (New York: Grove Press, Inc; 1966), p. 37.

[66] *Ibid.*, p. 42.

[67] *Ibid.*, p. 142.

[68] *Ibid.*

[69] *Ibid.*, p. 122.

[70] *Ibid.*

[71] *Ibid.*

[72] *Ibid.*, p. 124.

[73] *Ibid.*, pp. 124-25.

[74] *Ibid.*, p. 133.

[75] *Ibid.*

[76] *Ibid.*

[77] *Ibid.*, p. 141.

[78] *Ibid.*, p. 144.

[79] *Ibid.*, p. 135.

[80] *Ibid.*

7

THE CIA AND U.S. CAPITALISM

Connor Cruise O'Brien believes that the Hobsonian and Leninian version of imperialism no longer applies, if it did apply, and that there is no adequate economic motive for imperialist activities. For O'Brien, imperialism is a mere desire on the part of powerful nations to dominate the poor, powerless and underdeveloped nations.[1] Thus, if France, for example, dominates the political scene of Upper Volta, it is not because the former needs resources or the market both of which are not there — of the latter, "but on the contrary, because France annually makes up the deficit in the Upper Volta budget."[2] This is what O' Brien refers to as "Uneconomic imperialism."

O'Brien states further that "it is a declared goal of the United States, not merely to prevent Soviet and Chinese territorial expansion, but to check the spread of a political doctrine: Communism."[3] Doing this requires close surveillance of the domestic politics of the poor and weak countries which the U.S. feels are susceptible to communism; discreet guidance of these politics when considered necessary; employing economic pressure and in the penultimate recourse to intervention by resort to methods such as bribery, blackmail and political assassination. In the words of O'Brien:

> The Congo [Zaire] is an obvious case in point. I have myself heard a senior and responsible American official state that it was not America's responsibility to prevent

163

the Congolese from massacring each other, but it *was* America's responsibility to keep Communism out of the Congo. In practice, American officials, some employed by the C.I.A. and at least one by the United Nations, actively intervened in Congolese politics in order to bring about the downfall of Lumumba and the triumph of his enemies; his subsequent murder and the murder of his principal associates at the hands of these enemies were then regarded as an internal Congolese affair...

The Congo in some ways is an extreme case, *a cas limite*, and the limit it stands for, in the eyes of many Africans and Asians, is the limit to their own freedom. From this example they see that if their government shows what are, in the eyes of U.S. officials, Communist tendencies, the diplomatic, political, secret service, and financial resources of the greatest of world powers may be turned against them and that a political receiver nominated by Western interests — a Tshombe — may be put in charge of their affairs. They know further that if they withstand the political shock — which few of them indeed feel strong enough to do — they may have to face actual military intervention, as those other *cas limites*, Santo Domingo and Vietnam, have demonstrated. If there are sizeable Western business interests in their territory they will know that their position in relation to these interests will be among the criteria of their non-Communism, that is to say of their continued existence. But even if they have little or nothing, like many of the so-called French-speaking African territories, this does not exempt them from Western surveillance, for even these wastelands form part of that "reservoir of strategic space" which is Africa.[4]

What O'Brien describes is what has come to be known as the policy of "containing Communism." But this writer does not believe that the U.S. and its Western allies want to dominate the Third World simply for the sake of domination. Does O'Brien really believe that France has no economic justification for dominating the Upper Volta? It can equally be said that the U.S. had no economic justification for underwriting one-quarter to one-third of the Bolivian budget for many years. Or did the U.S. economic interests in the Dominican Republic justify the military expenditure in U.S. invasion and occupation of the island? The fact is that it is in the economic interests of the Western world to control the underdeveloped societies; these are their plantations. Much of the money involved in the intervention in Bolivia was spent in the U.S. — a lot of aid to U.S. business. As has become clear in this work, most of the foreign aid money is spent in the donor's country. In the U.S., for example, contracts for the materials to be supplied to the recipient country are awarded to friendly companies. So it is a way by which American Presidents say "Thank you" to those companies that supported their election. On the other hand, "the U.S. search for power, prestige and security is inseparable from the U.S. interest in free trade throughout the world. As the most powerful and advanced capitalist nation, the United States stands to benefit from free trade, just as Britain did when it was the leading world capitalist power."[5] In this great international enterprise, the CIA, agent of the U.S. State Department, is crucially important. This chapter reviews the role of this agent in making the world safe for capitalism.[6] And since the relationship between the CIA and the multinationals is symbiotic, we shall also discuss how the latter serve as cover for the CIA and also justify U.S. involvement in internal politics of the underdeveloped world.

The CIA and the Global Giants

As discussed earlier, the interests of the U.S.-based multinationals and those of the U.S. government are substantially identical. For the Marxists, the government is the instrument of the dominant economic power in the society. After all, beneath the sonorous speeches of the politicians, the paramount business of politics has to do with mundane economic issues, such as tariffs, taxes, monopolies, franchises, licenses, over which people struggle and bargain for the opportunity for economic gain. According to Marx, the state is nothing more than the "executive committee of the ruling class" and this implies that the interest of the multinationals and those of the state could not clash. Furthermore, for the U.S. and other Western societies, "What is good for General Motors [a multinational] is good for the country" and vice versa. The riches and power of the global giants redound to the benefit of their government. And, as already pointed out, wherever the U.S. government has successfully intervened militarily, the multinationals have freely moved in to plunder the conquered territory, the pillage by way of profits and raw materials are taken back to the U.S.

But it is also important to mention that the U.S. multinationals are not just extensions or instruments of the U.S. government; nor is the U.S. State Department a mere follower of the multinationals. The reason for this is that neither the nation-state nor the corporation is a monolithic entity. Having said this, however, it must be pointed out that it would be no exaggeration to say that when it comes to the exploitation and domination of the non-white societies, there is a near unanimity among the ruling elite. In other words, racism encourages the worst form of exploitation of people of colour. Thus, despite the fact that the U.S. claims to be the bastion of world democracy, it has gone out of its way to support white supremacist regimes in Southern Africa, vetoing U.N. resolutions aimed at liberating the oppressed masses of that area.

Wherever the U.S. national flag has been planted around the world, in some 500 major military and naval bases and in the command posts of over a dozen military interventions, America multinationals have moved in. The construction of an international military empire has meant good business. Thus it is not correct, as O'Brien has done, to say that economic consideration is not an overriding factor in U.S. foreign policy. Through public subsidies, U.S. multinationals have constructed roads, harbours, airports, hotels, and banks around the globe. The military budget provides the best illustration of the "compatibility of patriotism and profits." During the Cold War era the Department of Defense distributed about $50 billion a year to U.S. corporations through procurement contracts.[7] The Pentagon had $6 billion a year to spend on research.[8] Much of this money went to finance development costs of civilian products like the Boeing 707. When electronics and aircraft companies bought full pages of newspapers and magazines to advertise and warn the U.S. of Soviet threat, they were, as they claimed, responding to a patriotic duty as well as business opportunity. In other words, the business enterprises exploited the obsessive fear of communism by Americans and the government then had a good excuse to pump in billions of dollars into the private sector. Exploiting the underdeveloped countries and bringing back the plunder to enrich their country is an excellent act of patriotism. Thus, the U.S. government is duty-bound to protect these multinationals in their plundering expeditions, and as will be demonstrated below, there is absolutely no doubt that the U.S. government has been doing exactly that.

The extent to which the U.S. government and its multinationals can go to exert and maintain their control over another country is illustrated by what happened in Chile after Salvador Allende had been elected President of that country. Even before his election, the CIA had in 1964 intervened against Allende, when he was a presidential candidate running against Eduardo Frei Montalva of the Christian Democratic Party, which had the support of the U.S.[9]

Allende campaigned in 1970 for the presidential office

as a Marxist-Socialist who opposed the domination of the Chilean economy by the U.S.-based multinationals, such as International Telephone and Telegraph, copper-mining operations, and oil companies. Not long after his election to the Presidency, Allende embarked on fulfilling his campaign promises by nationalizing many industries, including the copper mines on which the U.S. depended for large amounts of its copper resources.[10]

On the eve of the election in 1970, John McCone, the President of ITT and former head of the CIA offered a million dollars for clandestine operations to prevent the candidate from winning the election.[11] The offer was promptly and politely rejected. But on September 15, the U.S. State Department asked Ambassador Edward Korry "to do all possible short of a Dominican type action" to prevent Allende's inauguration.[12] This included a $350,000 bribe money to be distributed to members of the Chilean Congress in an endeavour to overturn the results of the election.[13]

The State Department also rejected ITT's timetable designed to topple the Allende govenment. The ITT's timetable concerned the spreading of "economic chaos." Jack D. Neal, an ITT staff member with 35 years' service in the State Department, had submitted an 18-point programme aimed at stimulating a *coup d'etat.* He suggested concerted economic pressure through the cut-off of credit and aid and the support of local opponents of the regime. In the final analysis all his methods were adopted, but not his schedule. Neal had wanted the destabilization and the consequent overthrow of the Allende regime to be completed in three weeks but the State Department took three years to accomplish it. When the feat appeared to take much longer time to accomplish than Neal had envisaged, he complained bitterly in a memo to his boss, Vice-President W.R. Merrian. "Why should the U.S. try to be so pious and sanctimonious in September and October of 1970, when over the past few years it has been pouring the taxpayer's money into Chile admittedly to defeat Marxism. (According to a former U.S. Ambassador to Chile, the CIA and other Agencies spent $20 million to defeat Allende in 1964). Why can't the fight be continued now that the battle is in the homestretch and the enemy is more clearly identifiable?"[14]

The reason was that both the U.S. government and the rest of the business community felt that the ITT plan for fighting Allende would not succeed! On October 9, 1970, Merrian reported to John McCone thus:

> Practically no progress has been made in trying to get American business to cooperate in some way so as to bring on economic inventory on hand in Chile to take any chances and that they keep hoping that everything will work out all right.... According to my source [CIA contact] we must continue to keep the pressure on business.[15]

In a year's time the Nixon Administration's "game plan" for economic warfare against Allende's regime began to shape up. John Connally, Secretary of the Treasury, was charged with the responsibility of formulating Chilean foreign policy. Chile now became a major U.S. concern because Allende had nationalized Anaconda's and Kennecott's copper mines.

In October, 1971, the Secretary of State, William Rogers, was sent to brief a closed meeting of executives from ITT, Ford, Anaconda, Purina, the First National City Bank, and Bank of America, among many others, that "the Nixon Administration is a business Administration. Its mission is to protect American business." The "new ball game with new rules," as Assistant Secretary of the Treasury, John Petty, had characterized it, included cutting off EX-IM Bank credits on which vital imports from the U.S. depended; pressurizing multilateral institutions such as the World Bank and the Inter-American Development Bank not to approve more loans to Chile; encouraging private banks to cut off credit (this was particularly effective because the line of short-term bank credit shrank from $220 million to $35 within the first year of Allende's regime); and ending the aid programme excepting military aid (which rose from $800,000 in the last pre-Allende regime to more than $12 million within two years of Allende's government).[16]

Thus, Allende was correct when in December, 1972, he complained to the U.N. about "large-scale external pressure to cut us off from the world, to strangle our economy and paralyze trade and deprive us of access to sources of international financing."

In addition to all this, Henry Kissinger, who was then a special adviser to President Richard Nixon, directed the CIA to spend $8 million in an effort to undermine and ultimately overthrow Allende's government. The $8 million was handled through the black market, and was used to pay off labour unions (with the help of the American Federation of Labour-Congress of Industrial Organizations) to strike and boycott the government, and to pay newspapers and politicians hostile to Allende's regime to keep the heat on. U.S. corporations eventually abandoned their initial reticence and joined the ITT to refuse to sell spare parts for trucks and machinery even for cash while Kennecott conducted a worldwide campaign to keep Chile's expropriated copper off the world market. I doubt if there are many, if any, developing (underdeveloped) countries that can survive such a situation for a long time.

The Chilean case illustrates the extent to which the U.S. is prepared to go whenever it feels the interest of its corporations are threatened. However, the U.S. is not willing to publicly acknowledge its responsibility for its role. According to former CIA director, William Colby, "the presumption under which we conduct this type of operation is that it is a covert operation and that the United States' hand is not to show."[17] Thus, Mr. Colby defines what is known within the

CIA circles as the "Doctrine of Plausible Deniability." The mundane activities of the CIA are conducted in such a way that the U.S., as in the case of the Congo (to be discussed) can deny responsibility for the reprehensible deeds of the CIA. Even within the U.S. government itself, orders are given in such a way that it is quite often impossible to trace the origin of the instruction to carry out a particular covert operation. All these come within the definition of the Doctrine of Plausible Deniability. But despite the State Department's denial that the U.S. was involved in the overthrow of the democratically elected government of Salvador Allende, a U.S. Senate Select Intelligence Committee in a 62-page report (written by its staff) released on December 4, 1975, stated quite categorically that the U.S. had ended a ten-year, $13.4 million effort to deny Allende power in Chile by "advocating and encouraging the overthrow of his democratically elected government."[18]

The report of the Committee released on November 20, 1975 (a 347-page document) stated that President Richard Nixon personally issued the order to the CIA to get rid of Allende. The CIA station in Santiago and U.S. military personnel helped to plan and provide weapons for the kidnapping of the Chilean armed forces Commander-in-Chief, Rene Schneider, who had refused to go along with CIA-supported plans for a coup to prevent Allende's election.[19] Schneider, for refusing to support the overthrow of the legitimate government of his fatherland, was murdered in a bungled kidnapping attempt in the early morning of October 22, 1970, by a group of military abductors. The abortive coup was ordered by President Nixon because "an Allende regime would not be acceptable to the United States."[20] The implication here is that for a government in any underdeveloped country not to be toppled by the CIA, whoever is in power must be a marionette amenable to the whims of the U.S. Testifying at the hearings of the Committee, a former CIA director, Richard Helms, said that at his meeting with President Nixon, it was his impression that "the President came down very hard that he wanted something done, and he didn't much care how and that he was prepared to make money available."[21] The report went on to quote Mr. Helms as saying "If I ever carried a marshal's baton in my knapsack out of the Oval Office [U.S. President's Office] it was that day."[22]

Helms handwritten notes at the meeting with President Nixon reflected these instructions and reactions from Nixon: "one in 10 chance perhaps, but save Chile... not concerned risks involved... no involvement of Embassy... make the economy scream... 48 hours for plan of action."[23] In the same report former Deputy Director of Plans, Thomas Karamessiness, testified that Kissinger, then serving as national security adviser, "left no doubt in my mind that he was under the heaviest of pressure to get this accomplished."[24] The pressure to block Allende's election was "as tough as I ever saw it in my time there, extreme," testified a CIA agent in Latin America.[25]

The report further revealed that Korry sent a message to former President Frei to join American efforts to deny the election to Allende. Korry wrote: "not a nut or bolt will be allowed to reach Chile under Allende. Once Allende comes to power we shall do all within our power. to condemn Chile and the Chileans to utmost deprivation and poverty, a policy designed for a long time to come to accelerate the hard features of a Communist society in Chile."[26]

The report also confirmed that the Nixon Administration had sought to goad the Chilean army into taking an independent course of action, to pre-empt the 1970 election. On October 7, 1970, Korry had received a cable from Washington authorizing him

> to inform discreetly the Chilean military through the channels available to you that if a successful effort is made to block Allende from taking Office, we would

reconsider the cuts we have thus far been forced to make in Chilean MAP (military assistance program) and otherwise increase our presently programmed MAP for the Chilean Armed Forces. If any steps the military should take should result in civil disorder, we would also be prepared to deliver support and material that might be immediately required.[27]

The report went on to say that the activity of the U.S. in Chile was representative of six major covert operations studied during the Committee's investigation. The six operations in turn, were quite representative of "thousands" by the CIA.[28] The Committee concluded that (1) the ITT put $ 350,000 of its own money into the Chilean presidential election of 1970, that it gave $ 250,000 to the campaign of former President Jorge Allende's Party, and that $ 350,000 had come from other U.S. businesses; (2) the CIA successfully effected the content of a *Time* magazine story in 1970 through "briefings requested by *Time* and provided by the CIA in Washington" and the briefings "resulted in a change in the basic thrust of the *Time* story on Allende's September 4 victory and in the timing of the story"; (3) after President Nixon had ordered a stepped-up effort to prevent Allende from being elected in September, 1970, the CIA covertly channeled $ 11.5 million to *El Mercurio*, the largest daily paper in Chile, to insure anti-Allende coverage and to keep the paper solvent, and it should be added that *El Mercurio* was published by Augustine Edwards, a close friend of Donald Kendall, president of Pepsi Cola, Inc.[29] In the final analysis, the Committee concluded that while it could not establish any direct operational involvement by the CIA or the U.S. Embassy in the 1973 coup, the members agreed that the U.S. policy towards Chile had "created the atmosphere" in that country for Allende's destruction in the coup.[30]

Kissinger's argument had been that the U.S. had wanted

to stop Chile from getting a repressive regime. But the military junta that murdered Allende and took over power have established one of the most repressive government's under the face of the sun. United States companies have returned to Chile and the economic warfare fought against Allende's regime was quickly ended immediately after the overthrow and murder of Allende.

Thus, Richard Falk is correct in his obervation that "the CIA's role has been to keep repressive governments in power and to overthrow or harass more progressive ones,"[31] the reason being that "the less totalitarian the society, the easier it is to influence what goes on there."[32] For example, Allende's "tolerance of forces opposing him made it easy for the CIA and other intelligence agencies to work with them to hasten his downfall."[33] "Perjury, subordination, torture, property destruction, assassination, fraud, impersonation and a variety of other acts for which ordinary citizens go to jail become the dictates of duty" and "National Security is the holy oil that converts felonious acts into patriotic exploits."[34]

In the case of Africa, Lemarchand has cited seven instances in which CIA played a "central, or at least significant" role.[35] (1) The CIA played a significant role in influencing the decision of Kasavubu to depose Patrice Lumumba as the "impartial arbiter" of the conflict between the President and Prime Minister. (2) CIA operations which included the hiring and training of mercenaries and the procurement and maintenance of Skyraider bomber fighters and B-265, were undoubtedly instrumental in defeating Soumialot's Popular Liberation Army during the 1964 Zairean rebellion. (3) CIA agents operating mostly from Rwanda, kept close contacts with opposition leaders in Burundi and also provided them with "technical advice as well as financial support'" in an attempt to turn back the tide during the "pro-Chinese" interlude of 1964-65. (4) CIA agents planned the hi-jacking in June, 1967 of Moise Tshombe's plane, and "therefore were indirectly responsible for the abortive anti-Mobutu mercenary-led coup that followed Tshombe's surrender to the Algerian Authorities." (5) CIA agents manipulated the outcome of the 1967 elections in Somalia. The "rise to power of Prime Minister Muhammed Egal was said to have been 'facilitated' by thousands of dollars in covert support to Egal and other pro-Western elements in the ruling Somalia Youth League Party prior to the 1967 presidential elections." (6) The CIA was greatly involved in catapulting Colonel Richard Ratsimandrava to power in Madagascar in February, 1975. This man was killed by members of the model police group which replaced him with Didier Ratsinaka. (7) The CIA was deeply immersed in the events in Angola by shipping massive quantities of arms and ammunition through Zaire, making cash payments to Holden Roberto and Jonas Savimbi, hiring of mercenaries in Europe and the U.S., and supervising of logistical operations on the ground, both in Zaire and Angola.

Since Mobutu is regarded as the CIA's most "successful" client in Africa, and since the case of Zaire is often cited by U.S. officials as a prime example of successful covert intervention, it is used as an example of the CIA's intervention in Africa.

The Congo, renamed Zaire, "was not only a wealthy nation strategically placed in the heart of Africa: it was also presumed to be a symbolic battleground between East and West, where the success or failure of one's clients would have repercussions throughout Africa and the developing world."[36] As Emerson, one of the defenders of the U.S. intervention in Zaire, has testified, perhaps unwittingly, "throughout Africa, and far more widely in the world at large, Lumumba, the Congolese first Prime Minister, was hailed as the outstanding champion of Congolese national unity and independence and as a martyr in the anticolonial struggle."[37] But because of his friendly relations with the Soviet Union, and his socialist ideas, the U.S. came "to take

175

an increasingly hostile attitude toward him."[38] The U.S. and its NATO allies quickly embarked on a programme designed to promote a pro-Western Zairean regime that would protect American and Western economic investments in the absence of the Belgians. Even before Zaire became independent in June, 1960, the CIA had been carrying out covert activities in the form of political manipulation and cash payments to particular politicians.[39] As Marchetti and Marks have written, the CIA "became deeply involved in the chaotic struggle which broke out in the Congo in the early 1960s. Clandestine service operators regularly bought and sold Congolese politicians, and the agency supplied money and arms to the supporters of Cyril Adoula and Joseph Mobutu."[40]

The CIA got one of the marionettes in the person of Moise Tshombe to declare the seccession of Katanga Province because Lumumba was going to establish a "ruinous and Communist state."[41] After the Belgian troops had invaded the country, Lumumba called upon the U.N. for assistance in order to keep down the rebellion and to get Belgian troops out of his country, supposedly a sovereign state. But assured of the firm backing of the U.S. and other NATO Allies, Belgium adamantly refused to remove its troops from Zaire.[42]

At a very crucial time the CIA "discovered" Mobutu and gave him every support that would ultimately lead to the death of Lumumba. The CIA had allegedly tried to poison Lumumba but failed and it then decided on another line of action.[43] On November 27, 1960, a CIA agent, Michael Mulroney, succeeded in inducing Lumumba to leave for Stanleyville without U.N. protection. On January 17, 1961, Lumumba's plane was diverted to Katanga where he was murdered by his fellow Congolese.[44]

Meanwhile, the U.S. used its influence to get money from the U.N. for Mobutu to pay his troops and the mercenaries recruited for him by the CIA. They also made sure that Mobutu's superior, General Lundula, suspected of being loyal to Lumumba, was barred, through U.N. control of the Zaire's airports, from returning to the capital at the critical time.[45] As Roger Morris noted:

> The fall of Patrice Lumumba in 1960 to the coup installing General Joseph Mobutu in 1965; CIA cash payments to politicians; manipulation of unions and youth or cultural groups; and a rising investment in planted propaganda all helped establish increasingly pro-Western regimes, ending in the military dictatorship that has governed the country for the last [twelve] years.
>
> Perhaps the most dramatic instance of CIA intervention came in the 1964 Stanleyville revolt when Cuban Bay of Pigs Veterans were contracted to fly vintage B-26 bombers and white mercenaries were recruited by the Agency in South Africa and Rhodesia. The revolt was crushed, though not before fifty-eight European hostages were killed by the rebels in the wake of the CIA bombing and the Belgian-United States airdrop on Stanleyville. [Ten thousand Blacks were killed by the Belgian-U.S. troops.]
>
> More often, the intervention continued quietly in the passage of money and advice. Mobutu succeeded in a blood-less coup in late 1965, and has reportedly kept up a close liaison with his former patrons.[46]

Sure enough, Mobutu has kept up a close liaison with his former patrons and this underscores his extreme dependence on the U.S. In 1967 President Johnson was quick to send in arms to help restore order during an anti-Mobutu mercenary-led coup. In 1977 and 1978, Mobutu had to depend on the U.S. and its Western allies to repell the invasion of exiled Zaireans in Angola.

At the end of the invasion of the exiled Zaireans in which Moroccans and French troops, and hundreds of mercenaries recruited by Western governments and multinationals became involved, Mobutu found his treasury empty. He quickly embarked on the usual trip to the metropoles, hat in hand, begging them to replenish his treasury for him. The U.S. and other Western countries were very quick to grant him loans. In fact, since this marionette came into power the U.S. Congress has had to vote special funds to keep the Zairean government functioning. Zaire is to the U.S. what Cuba is to the Soviet Union. As Table 7.1 shows, of all the 32 African countries listed, by 1968 Zaire received the highest amount of aid coming into Africa from the U.S.

This trend is bound to continue so long as Mobutu is in power.[47] The reason is that his unpopularity at home and poor management of the national economy will continue to force him to depend more and more on the U.S. and its NATO allies, since this is the only way he can continue to hold on to power. Of course, Mobutu must continue, like pre-revolution Cuba, to be a caretaker of Western capitalist interests. Despite the natural wealth of this Central African country, poor management and collaboration with neocolonial forces have kept the country underdeveloped and one of the poorest countries in Africa.

With the help of Mobutu, the U.S. was "heavily involved" in the Angolan civil war of 1976. That was the conclusion of a Congressional Report on the CIA activities in Angola; but President Ford censored the report to prevent it being made public.[48] The U.S. began its involvement in Angola as far back as 1962 when on the advice of the CIA and Mobutu, Mr. Roberto, the brother-in-law of Mobutu was selected as a future leader for Angola.[49] U.S. support was subsequently extended to Jonas Savimbi, the leader of the National Union for the Total Independence of Angola.[50]

But in 1975 the U.S. went out of its way to see that the course of nationalism in Angola was the same as in Zaire. In early June, 1975, the CIA asked the U.S. government for a $6-million aid for pro-U.S. groups in Angola.[51] The aid was revised upward — $14 million — and was

TABLE 7.1

Total U.S. Economic Aid to Sub-Saharan Africa
Through 1968
(in Millions of U.S. Dollars)

Country	Value
Zaire	405
Liberia	252
Ghana	240
Ethiopia	229
Nigeria	229
Sudan	107
Guinea	74
Somalia	73
Ivory Coast	67
Kenya	63
Tanzania	62
Zambia	41
Sierra Leone	39
Senegal	32
Uganda	30
Cameroon	27
Malawi	23
Mali	19
Botswana	16
Niger	15
Togo	14
Dahomey	11
Upper Volta	11
Chad	8
Gabon	8
Burundi	7
Rwanda	7
Central African Republic	5
Lesotho	4
Mauritania	3
Congo (Bra)	2
Gambia	1

*Includes grants, loans, Food for Peace, and all other forms of U.S. aid.
Source: *Black Africa* by Donald George Morrison, Robert Cameron Mitchell, John Naber Paden, Hugh Michael Stevenson. Copyright ©1972 by The Free Press, a Division of Macmillan Publishing Co., Inc., p. 134.

approved by both the Forty Committee and President Ford in July.[52] The aid was further increased to $25 million in August and to $32 million in November.[53] The CIA admittedly told the Committee that it had spent only $31 million in military hardware, transportation costs, and cash payments.[54] But the consensus of the Committee members was that U.S. expenditure on Angola far exceeded what the CIA was willing to tell them.[55] The beneficiaries of the U.S. aid were the FNLA and UNITA. The third movement, the MPLA, was supported by the Soviet Union, Cuba and Nigeria. The principal client of the U.S. was the National Front, headed by Holden Roberto. In fact, in 1975 Mobutu had contacted Kissinger and succeeded in getting the CIA to give Roberto $300,000 for bribes and other activities. The Committee believed that the "infusion of U.S. aid, unprecedented and massive in the underdeveloped colony" may have panicked the Soviet Union into arming their MPLA clients, and the joining of the war by Cuba.[56]

The U.S. did not stop at its own support for the National Front but went to the extent of persuading South Africa to intervene on behalf of the National Front.[57] On January 11, 1976, when African leaders met in Addis Ababa to consider the Angolan crisis, President Ford arrogantly wrote all African heads of state asking for Soviet and Cuban withdrawal from Angola as the *quid pro quo* for South African disengagement.[58] The U.S. thus allowed its policy to converge with that of white supremacist South Africa. Even at the meeting in Addis Ababa Mobutu did not disguise himself as the number one American client in Africa; he was the leader of the faction that supported the U.S. position. According to the *New York Times*, the U.S. State Department was so delighted with Mobutu's role in the Angola civil war that it asked the Congress to increase Zaire's aid from $20 million to $60 million. These additional funds consisted of $20 million in development aid, $20 million in Export-Import Bank loans, and $20 million in Food for Peace credit.[59]

Another reward for Mobutu's anti-Angola stance was the invasion of the Shaba Province of Zaire by Zairean exiles in Angola. This was a sort of counter-action by the MPLA after the civil war; needless to say, this invasion was very costly for Mobutu as he had to call in the French and Moroccans to send back the invaders and after that he had to rush to Europe and the U.S. begging for money. It was very interesting when about two years ago both Angola and Zaire signed an agreement not to allow dissident elements residing in their two territories to use their country as a staging ground against each other.

Why all this U.S. involvement in Africa? Is the sole purpose to contain communism, as Cruise O'Brien would want us to believe? In the *Kissinger Study of Southern Africa*, the famous *Memorandum 39*, economic factors were given great consideration in trying to determine U.S. policy in Africa. According to that document:

> U.S. direct investment in Southern Africa, mainly in South Africa, is about $1 billion and yields a highly profitable return. Trade, again mainly with South Africa, runs a favorable balance to the U.S. (our exports to South Africa were about $450 million in 1968 against imports $250 million.) In addition, the U.K. has indirect economic interest in the key role which South Africa plays in the U.K. balance of payments. U.K. investment in South Africa is currently estimated at $3 billion, and the British have made it clear that they will take no action which would jeopardize their economic interests. The U.S. has an important interest in the orderly marketing of South Africa's gold production which is important to the successful operation of the two-tier gold price system.[60]

Africa accounts for a significant proportion of U.S. imports — 100% of industrial diamonds; 58% of uranium; 48% of cocoa; 44% of manganese, used in producing steel;

40% of antimony to harden metals; 39% of platinum; 36% of cobald, for jet engines and high-strength alloys; 33% of petroleum; 30% of beryl, used in weapons and nuclear reactors; 23% of chromite, used in gun barrels; 21% of

TABLE 7.2

Production of Minerals in Southern Africa[1]
as a Percentage of World Production

	1967	1968	1969
Gold	68.3	68.8	68.8
Gem diamonds	62.2	64.0	63.6
Industrial diamonds	54.4	52.9	64.3
Cobalt (contained)	55.9	57.0	56.7
Chromite	32.1	31.7	31.5
Vanadium[2] (ore and concen.)	31.1	25.9	29.4
Platinum group metals	26.4	25.5	28.4
Vermiculite	30.2	29.0	30.7
Antimony	21.5	27.3	27.9
Copper (ore and concen.)	23.4	21.8	22.0
Uranium[3] (contained)	17.9	17.1	17.0
Manganese[4] (ore)	12.8	13.9	14.4
Beryllium[5] (Beryl)	7.0	8.7	10.4

1. Includes South Africa, Namibia, Botswana, Lesotho, Swaziland, Rhodesia, Angola, Mozambique, Zambia, Zaire and Malagasy Republic.
2. Namibia production is of lead vanadate concentrate. South African production is of vanadium pentoxide.
3. "Free world" production only.
4. Percentage of manganese concentrate differs according to country.
5. 1967 figures for Rhodesia taken from U.S. import data.
Source: *Minerals Yearbook,* 1968 and 1969, U.S. Department of U.S. Interior. Cited in Mohamed A. El-Khawas and Barry Cohen, eds., *The Kissinger Study of Southern Africa* (Westport, Conn.: Lawrence Hill and Co., 1976).

The CIA and U.S. Capitalism

TABLE 7.3

The Number and the Value of Aircraft
Sold to South Africa, 1965-1972

Year	Number	Value U.S. $
1965	235	34,548,530
1966	208	4,519,595
1967	333	23,438,380
1968	200	30,398,139
Total	1,076	92,904,644
1069	284	42,503,604
1970	180	25,627,562
1971	135	70,357,608
1972	144	80,485,712
Total	743	218,974,486

Source: *Implementation of the U.S. Arms Embargo* (Against Portugal and South Africa, and Related Issues) Hearings of the Subcommittee on Africa, House Committee on African Affairs, 93rd Congress, 1st Session, March 20, 22 and April 6, 1973 (Washington D.C.: U.S. Government Printing Office, 1973 p. 89. Cited in Mohamed A. El-Khawas and Barry Cohen, eds., *The Kissinger Study of Southern Africa* (Westport, Conn.: Lawrence Hill and Co., 1976).

columbium-tantalium, for heat-resisting alloys in missiles and rockets; and 21% of coffee.[61] Tables 7.2 through 7.8 show to what extent Africa is economically important to the U.S. and this is equally true of other Western countries of the NATO alliance.[62] Table 7.2 shows production of minerals in Southern Africa as a percentage of world production. Table 7.3 shows the number and the value of aircraft sold to South Africa between 1965 and 1972, in spite of the U.N.

183

arms embargo against South Africa and of which the U.S. was a signatory. Table 7.4 further shows the extent to which the Nixon Administration went out of its way to help South Africa militarily. We recall that this very Administration had informed American businessmen shortly after Nixon had been sworn in that it was going to give special attention to them. It declared itself a business administration. South Africa is the place in Africa where the U.S. investment is

TABLE 7.4

C-130 Aircraft/SAAF Support Program

I. Licensed export of spare parts, associated ground equipment and technical data - by Calendar Year

Year	Value U.S. $
1963	1,282,000
1964	2,070,646
1965	857,000
1966	1,346,000
1967	2,728,439
1968	3,880,091
1969	3,777,815
1970	2,752,175
1971	2,798,836
1972	1,677,185
1973 (through Apr. 4, 1973)	92,387

II. Center Wing Repair Program (April, 1970-June, 1971) Program Price, $3,472,000.

III. T-56 Engine Overhaul Program (engines to be imported into U.S. for overhaul and re-exported upon completion).

    (1) Total of engine repair Program:

        (a) 46T-56 engines to be imported-$552,000

        (b) Replacement parts during overhaul (estimated) - $1,066,602

    (2) Portion of total program in (1) achieved up to 4 April, 1973.

        (a) 10T-56 engines imported 1972-$720,000.

        (b) 12T-56 engines imported 1973-$144,000.

        (c) 10T-56 engines re-exported 1973-$351,870.

Source: Ibid. Cited in Mohamed A. El-Khawas and Barry Cohen, eds., *The Kissinger Study of Southern Africa* (Westport, Conn.: Lawrence Hill and Co., 1976).

concentrated. South Africa is the bastion of Western colonialism and racism in Africa and the substenance of apartheid means good business and profits for the U.S. conglomerates. Tables 7.5 through 7.7 show to what extent President Nixon went out of his way to Americanize the Portuguese colonial wars in Africa. In fact, after Portugal had decided to accept her defeat in Africa President Nixon, apparently because of pressure from the multinationals, urged the Portuguese leaders to continue with the war. Under the pretext that it was arming its ally against the Communist East, the

TABLE 7.5

*Exports of American Aircrafts and Helicopters to Angola,
Mozambique, and Portugal: 1965-1972*

Year	Angola		Mozambique		Portugal	
	No.	Value	No.	Value	No.	Value
		$		$		$
1965	5	209,940	1	23,177	5	7,021,428
1966	7	248,196	-	-	1	14,667
1967	16	360,647	-	-	7	14,132,912
1968	11	303,556	1	105,122	14	25,370,505
1969	5	211,056	2	7,576,956	9	7,753,035
1970	12	477,797	21	808,030	10	16,458,548
1971	23	513,908	1	5,143,175	9	10,487,256
1972	-	-	13	881,678	10	57,936,468
Subtotal 1965-68	39	1,122,339	2	128,299	27	46,539,512
Subtotal 1969-72	40	1,202,761	37	14,409,839	38	92,635,307

Source: Bureau of the Census, FT-410 Export Statistics. Cited in Mohamed A. El-Khawas and Barry Cohen, eds., *The Kissinger Study of Southern Africa* (Westport, Conn.: Lawrence Hill and Co., 1976).

TABLE 7.6

Number of Portuguese Military Personnel Trained by the U.S.
Fiscal Year 1968-1972 Inclusive

Year	Army		Air Force		Navy		Total
	U.S.	Overseas	U.S.	Overseas	U.S.	Overseas	
1968	6	4	1	-	63	-	74
1969	3	25	7	-	95	-	130
1970	8	29	2	-	49	-	88
1971	6	31	3	45	18	-	103
1972	6	30	10	17	16	-	79
1973	15	35	12	17	15	-	94
Total	44	154	35	79	256	-	568

Source: Implementation of the U.S. Arms Embargo (Against Portugal and South Africa, and Related Issues). Hearings before the Subcommittee on Africa of the Committee on Foreign Affairs, House of Representatives, 93rd Congress, 1st Session, March 20, 22; April 6, 1973 (Washington, DC: U.S. Government Printing Office, 1973), p. 89. Cited in Mohamed A. El-Khawas and Barry Cohen, eds., *The Kissinger Study of Southern Africa* (Westport, Conn.: Lawrence Hill and Co., 1976).

U.S. pumped into Portugal tons of military hardware which were transported to Portuguese colonies to continue with her genocidal wars. Table 7.8 shows the extent of U.S. trade in Africa. As already noted, this trade is concentrated in South Africa and the U.S. has a great advantage.

Economic considerations have been the vital force behind the foreign policy of the U.S. in Africa, despite the constant pronouncements that they are after communism. What this means is that the U.S. must prevent any attempt to jeopardize their sources of raw materials, and the CIA has been extremely important in making the world safe for capitalism. As Lemarchand has noted:

186

TABLE 7.7

U.S. Exports of Herbicides to Angola, Mozambique and Portugal, 1962-72
(in millions of dollars)

Year	Angola	Mozambique	Portugal
1969	2	-	57
1970	43	28	344
1971	-	88	115
1972	39	413	151
Total	84	529	667

Source: "Portugal Afrique: La Guerre de L'OTAN" *Jeune Afrique* No. 705 (July 13, 1974), p. 64. Cited in Mohamed A. El-Khawas and Barry Cohen, eds., *The Kissinger Study of Southern Africa* (Westport, Conn.: Lawrence Hill and Co., 1976).

Mobutu owes a very large personal and political debt to his C.I.A. mentors (particularly to Lawrence Devlin who has since emerged as one of the wealthiest men in Kinshasa, and whatever efforts and resources were "spent" on Mobutu turned out to be a highly productive investment from the standpoint of U.S. corporate interests. While the C.I.A. continues to play a critically important role in making Zaire "safe for U.S. capitalism," the very magnitude of U.S. corporate interests there ($800 million) constitutes an additional motive — as well as an excellent "cover" — for the maintenance of an extensive C.I.A. network on the scene. If the case of Zaire is any index, the relationship between Agency activities and U.S. corporate interests is a circular one: while the C.I.A. operations may play a decisive part in preparing the ground for the intrusion of U.S. corporate interests, these in turn provide further justification for C.I.A. involvement — as well as the alibis and technological facilities deemed necessary for the conduct of intelligence operations.[63]

TABLE 7.8
U.S. Trade with Africa and South Africa
(in millions of dollars)

	Exports						Imports					
	1960	1965	1970	1972	1973	1974	1960	1965	1970	1972	1973	1974
Total Exports and Imports	793	1,229	1,580	1,577	2,306	3,659	534	878	1,113	1,595	2,583	6,617
Algeria	28	21	62	98	161	315	1	8	10	104	215	1,091
Angola	11	13	38	26	38	62	26	48	68	90	167	378
Cameroon, Federal Rep. of	*	7	19	37	15	20	*	13	25	24	30	27
Central African Republic	*	1	1	1	3	1	*	10	6	7	8	7
Egypt	151	158	77	76	225	455	32	16	23	17	26	70
Ethiopia	12	22	26	24	25	33	27	64	67	58	79	64
Gabon	*	5	7	13	19	33	*	11	9	11	12	162
Ghana	17	36	59	44	63	77	52	59	91	80	90	126
Ivory Coast	*	11	36	22	69	49	*	46	92	92	108	95
Kenya	*	24	34	26	39	49	*	13	23	27	26	39
Liberia	36	39	46	41	46	70	39	51	51	52	72	96
Libya	43	65	108	85	104	139	**	30	39	116	216	1
Malagasy Republic	3	4	7	11	15	7	13	29	32	37	40	60
Mauritania	*	4	4	5	9	11	*	2	1	1	1	**
Morocco	36	56	89	58	113	184	10	6	10	11	14	20
Mozambique	10	9	22	16	23	32	5	7	18	26	34	45
Nigeria	26	74	129	114	161	286	40	60	71	271	652	3,286
South Africa, Republic of	288	438	563	602	746	1,160	108	226	290	325	377	609
Sudan	7	15	7	18	39	64	5	11	12	12	9	27
Tanzania	*	7	12	12	11	51	*	2	24	21	27	26
Tunisia	22	44	49	55	60	87	*	43	3	8	33	21
Uganda	*	2	4	3	2	8	*	38	48	49	57	67
Zaire	*	71	62	37	110	145	*	*	41	43	71	68
Zambia	*	*	31	34	39	68	*	*	2	3	6	6
Other	103	103	89	119	163	253	174	77	59	110	213	226

* Not applicable

** Less than $ 500,000

Source: U.S. Department of Commerce, Bureau of Census, Statistical Abstract of the United States, July, 1975. Cited in Mohamed A. El-Khawas and Barry Cohen, eds., *The Kissinger Study of Southern Africa* (Westport, Conn.: Lawrence Hill and Co., 1976).

Even in the case of Angola, the House Committee concluded that "control of resources" was crucial to U.S. involvement in that country's civil war. So O'Brien is wrong to believe that the kind of imperialism described by Hobson and Lenin no longer exists. We turn to the CIA's corporate shell game.

The CIA's Corporate Shell Game

Business corporations return favours to the CIA — corporations provide intelligence cover for the CIA. About 200 CIA agents abroad make use of such a cover. There is what is known in the U.S. as "Delaware corporations," or, simply, "proprietaries." These are private institutions and businesses financed and controlled by the CIA. Most of them are incorporated in Delaware because of lenient regulation of corporations in that state.[64]

The CIA has used its proprietaries to establish influence over many of the world's airlines, particularly in the underdeveloped societies. In Libya a proprietary, United Business Associates (UBA), had a deal to finance a national airline for Libya.[65] They lent money for the simple purpose of controlling the airline. The cost was several millions of dollars and the way this was done, according to a former CIA agent was: "We had to offer them control over 20 per cent of the stock of the corporation and we would lend them the money. Then we would have to put one of their natives alongside every American in a similar position. Talking about kickbacks, that's the name of the trade over there. That's how we covered the men of the cabinet... And if we ever called that note, they would have taken the franchise away."[66]

The CIA is the owner of one of the largest fleets of "commercial" airplanes in the world. Apart from those mentioned above, CIA-owned airlines include Air America, Air Asia, Iran Airline, Civil Air Transport, Intermountain Aviation, Southern Air Transport, and many others in the world. Why should the CIA own all these airlines and planes? The answer lies in the fact that its mercenaries and its foreign troops need air support to fight their undeclared and mundane wars. As Orvis Nelson, a former CIA agent, has put it:

> If I were sitting in a position where I was curious about what was going on in troubled areas, there are two things I would be damned well interested in. The first is information. The second is transportation to get in and out, to get any information and, perhaps, to do some other air activities. You have mobility. You know who and what are going in and out. You know who people's associates are. You are in a position to move your people about.[67]

There are many other proprietaries all over the underdeveloped world. The CIA hire and place a manager into a company and he will then report back to the CIA as far as financial records are concerned. According to Barnet and Muller, "the CIA has a special office that does nothing but maintain contact with corporations overseas... placing agents on corporation payrolls, frequently without the knowledge of top management.[68] Of interest also is the number of high ranking CIA officials recruited from the private corporate sector. An examination of recruitment patterns from 1944 to 1960 shows that out of a combined total of thirteen top CIA officials, five were recruited from key law firms, one from a banking and investment firm, one from an industrial corporation and seven from "miscellaneous business and commercial corporations."[69]

Finally, the CIA in recent years has set up consulting firms in the international energy field. The CIA-owned consultant firms have won "governmental and private contracts in the Middle East as management experts and use these positions to gather secret economic intelligence... These data are then passed on, at least in part, to American companies in position to profit from it."[70] The CIA proprietaries generate revenues of well over $30 million per year and this is never included in CIA's approved budget, which, of course, is a strict secret.

Impact on Third World Development

The impact of all this on the development of the underdeveloped societies is negative. Let us take the case of national integration in the African societies. When Africans become stooges of the CIA they raise their stock of resources and expectations and also feel confident with the help of their boss, to create new parties, instigate coups and do all sorts of things. They simply refuse to compromise where this would be the most meaningful and even only thing to do. This is what happened in Angola, Zaire, Burundi, Madagascar, and other places. As noted by Barnet:

> The deliberate disorientation of societies by means of bribery, assassination, black propaganda, subordination and other methods helps keep [underdeveloped societies] poor and dependent. When they are manipulated for United States foreign policy purposes rather than their own development purposes, their capacity even to begin to deal with the overwhelming problem of mass poverty is undermined. Unfortunately, United States foreign policy purposes in most areas of the Third World have been defined in such a way as to conflict directly with local development needs. The crushing problems of Asia, Africa and Latin America — mass poverty, unemployment and growing inequality — require structural changes in those societies, polite terminology for overthrowing local elites that run them as personal holding companies or throwing out foreign business interests that are often equally exploitative. Consequently, the CIA's continuing secret war has

191

been in support of foreign local interests threatened by structural change, the maintenance of a repressive "stability" that stifles hope for the majority of the population. The capability of the United States to support reactionary regimes, and its clear interest to do so wherever possible, has been a powerful political factor in preserving a highly inequitable and ultimately explosive status quo.

For the most part, CIA intervention has not been successful against countries with capacity to destroy the United States... But in the weak countries of the Third World, the CIA can make a crucial difference in setting political direction and it often has...[71]

By way of conclusion, the U.S. has supported murder, arson, larceny and deceit abroad; it has maintained a bureaucracy of hired hitmen (killers), thieves and con men for use against foreigners. The U.S. has even established a department of "dirty tricks" run by people who have been trained to have no respect for the law but the command of the superior. There is absolutely nothing wrong about a country having an intelligence agency but the CIA has operated as a criminal enterprise. Interestingly enough, the U.S. had felt that it could maintain a system of law and order within its borders in such a schizophrenic environment in which government subsidizes assassination and crop contamination abroad. But the revelations attending the Watergate political scandal have proved them wrong.

Every military and political act undertaken by the CIA and the multinationals — "the corporate state" — is not based on strict cost-accounting rules. These very costly acts are designed to enable them to control as much of the globe as possible for international expansion by finance capital. In fact, there is an economic reason in every ostensibly uneconomic act. They are an expression of what C.W. Mills calls "gambling."[72] The aim of the economic and political policies that constitute " imperialist gambling" is to expand the control, power, resources, and profits of the financial oligarchy; this concern permeates U.S. foreign policy. The U.S. seeks to control as much as possible of the known and potential sources of raw materials, to maintain open doors to safe and lucrative investments, to maintain decisive influence over "conquered" societies in the politico-economic arena in order to exercise a favourable investment and profit environment, to cream off local surpluses for investment and ease the problems of exporting home capital and balancing payments, to stifle state or national industrial development which would compete with neocolonial imperialism, to block national reform movements threatening to pass social legislations and organize labour, and to promote dependence on capitalist nations and development along capitalist lines.

The chief opponent of these aims is socialism, that is, the nationalization of the development process. Self-determination and independent development, whether socialist or not, is not tolerated by the neocolonial imperialists. All reform movements are viewed as communist, that is "evil" and must be nipped in the bud. According to David, "the corporate demand for government spending that avoids redistribution by servicing the external empire has been maintained, justified, and buttressed by the ideology of the anticommunist mission of the cold war."[73] The U.S. bourgeoisie that were once a great champion of democracy and self-determination in an era of its own push for autonomy against older colonial power "now stand exposed as the main opponents of their own articulated principles" and in the process the Americans "have ranged ourselves against nearly every movement that might have led men toward a better life, on the grounds of our opposition to communism."[74] Paul Baran and Paul Sweezy have noted that "all revolutionaries are automatically suspect; no regime is too reactionary to merit all-out United States backing."[75] Finally, as Senator Frank Church of Idaho stated to his colleagues in 1972, "a government may torture and terrorize its own population but — from the standpoint of U.S. foreign policy — as long as it remains anticommunist, provides 'stability,' generally supports American foreign policy and is hospitable to U.S. investment, it qualifies, for purposes of U.S. aid, as a 'Free country.'[76] Foreign aid, contends Church, is designed "to serve private business interests at the expense of the American people." And in voting against the foreign aid programme in 1971, Senator Church stated rather succinctly that "there is abundant evidence that our foreign aid program is much less philantropic than we have cared to portray... 93 percent of AID funds are spent in the United States for products supplied as part of foreign aid programs."[77]

There is no exaggeration in saying that economic considerations dominate U.S. foreign policy. And although the U.S. has been singled out for analysis here, there is no doubt that in most of the U.S. ventures in Africa, members of the European Community almost always join hands to work together. Examples are the Congo crisis and the Angola civil war. Like the U.S., economic considerations tend to pervade the foreign policy of the European Community.

REFERENCES

[1] Connor Cruise O'Brien, "Contemporary Forms of Imperialism," in K. T. Fann and Donald C. Hodges, eds., *Readings in U.S. Imperialism* (Boston: Porter Sargent Publisher, 1971), pp. 1-12.

[2] *Ibid.*, p. 7.

[3] *Ibid.*, p. 8.

[4] *Ibid.*, pp. 8-9.

[5] Timothy F. Harding, "The New Imperialism in Latin America," in Fann and Hodges, *Readings in U.S. Imperialism*, pp. 14-15.

[6] For other functions, see Jerome H. Skolnick and Elliott Currie, eds., *Crisis in American Institutions* (Boston: Little, Brown and Company, 1976), pp. 90-91.

[7] Barnet and Muller, *Global Reach*, p. 79.

[8] *Ibid.*

[9] *The New York Times*, (September 8, 1974).

[10] *Ibid.*

[11] Barnet and Muller, *Global Reach*, p. 81.

[12] *Ibid.*, p. 82.

[13] Excerpts from the report, "Covert Action in Chile, 1963-1973," prepared by the staff of the U.S. Senate Select Committee on Intelligence, as carried in the *New York Times*, (December 5, 1975).

[14] Quoted by Barnet and Muller, *Global Reach*, p. 82.

[15] Quoted by *Ibid.*

[16] *Ibid.*, p. 83.

[17] The *Washington Post* (October 11, 1973).

[18] Excerpts of "Covert Action in Chile," *New York Times* (December 5, 1975).

[19] U. S. Senate Select Committee on Intelligence Report, as excerpted by the *Washington Post* (November 21, 1975).

[20] *Ibid.*

[21] *Ibid.*

[22] *Ibid.*

[23] *Ibid.*

[24] *Ibid.*

[25] *Ibid.*

[26] Select Committee on Intelligence Report, as excerpted in the *New York Times* (November 21, 1975).

[27] *Ibid.*, as excerpted by the *Washington Post* (November 21, 1975).

[28] Select Committee on Intelligence Staff Report, as excerpted by the *New York Times* (December 5, 1975).

[29] *Ibid.*

[30] *Ibid.*

[31] Richard A. Falk, "CIA Covert Action and International Law," *Society*, Vol. 12, No. 3 (March/April, 1975), p. 41.

[32] *Ibid.*

[33] *Ibid.*, p. 54.

[34] *Ibid.*, p. 53.

[35] Rene Lemarchand, "The C.I.A. in Africa: How Central? How Intelligent?," *The Journal of Modern African Studies* Vol. 14, No. 3 (1976), pp. 413-414.

[36] Roger Morris, "The Aftermath of CIA Intervention," *Society*, Vol. 12, No. 3 (March/April, 1975), p. 78.

[37] Rupert Emerson, *Africa and United States Policy* (Englewood Cliffs, N. J.: Prentice-Hall, 1967), p. 65.

[38] *Ibid.*

[39] Victor Marchetti and John D. Marks, *The CIA and the Cult of Intelligence* (New York: Alfred A. Knopf, Inc., 1974), p. 31.

[40] *Ibid.*, see also Fann and Hodges, *Readings in Imperialism*, Ch. I.

[41] *Ibid.*

[42] *Ibid.*

[43] Select Committee on Intelligence Report, as excerpted in the *Washington Post* (December 21, 1975).

[44] *Ibid.*

[45] Fann and Hodges, *Readings in Imperialism*, Ch. I.

[46] Morris, "The Aftermath of CIA Intervention," p. 78.

[47] For example, in 1973 President Richard Nixon toasted President Mobutu Sese Seko, announcing "Zaire is a good investment," The *New York Times* (January 4, 1976).

[48] M. A. El-Khawas and Barry Cohen, eds., *National Security Study Memorandum 39: The Kissinger Study of Southern Africa* (Westport: Lawrence Hill and Company, 1976), p. 183.

[49] *Ibid.* In a CBS television interview in the U.S. on May 8, 1978, John Stockwell, the man who was in charge of CIA operations in Angola during the civil war, said that President Mobutu "pocketed the money" — about ₦1.4 million — entrusted to his care for the use of the pro-West factions in the Angolan conflict. About ₦400,000 of that money was for the use of President Mobutu. The *Daily Times* (Lagos) (May 10, 1978).

[50] El-Khawas and Cohen, *Memorandum 39*, p. 184.

[51] *Ibid.*

[52] *Ibid.*

[53] *Ibid.*

[54] *Ibid.*

[55] *Ibid.*

[56] *Ibid.*

[57] Two things suggest that the U.S. persuaded South Africa to intervene on the side of the pro-West faction. First, the then South African Foreign Minister, Mr. Pik Botha said in 1976 that the U.S. had betrayed them by leaving them to fight Cuba and Russia alone. Second, President Ford addressed a letter to all African heads of state giving conditions under which South Africa would withdraw her troops from Angola. That letter caused a great furor among the Black Congressional Caucus. For example, see the *Washington Post* (January 12, 1976).

[58] *Ibid.*

[59] The *New York Times* (September 25, 1975).

[60] El-Khawas and Cohen, *Memorandum 39*, p. 87.

[61] *U.S. and World News* (May 3, 1976), p. 29.

[62] Tables 7.2 through 7.7 have been taken from El-Khawas and Cohen, *Memorandum 39*. For a fuller picture of U.S. contribution to the oppression of blacks in Southern Africa, read: William Pomercy, *Apartheid Axis* (New York: International Publishers, 1971); Elsa Roberts and Nancy Barnes, *Race to Power* (New York: Anchor Press, 1974).

[63] Lemarchand, "The C.I.A. in Africa," p. 410.

[64] Marchetti and Marks, *The CIA and the Cult of Intelligence*, p. 134.

[65] John Marks, "The CIA's Corporate Shell Game," *The Washington Post* (July, 11, 1976). John Marks is the co-author of *The CIA and the Cult of Intelligence*, already cited in this work. The contents of his article were confirmed by the findings of the Select Committee on Intelligence, November, 1975.

[66] *Ibid.*

[67] *Ibid.*

[68] Barnet and Muller, *Global Reach*, p. 102.

⁶⁹ Gabriel Kolko, *The Roots of American Foreign Policy* (Boston: Beacon Press, 1969), p. 20.

⁷⁰ The *Washington Post* (July 11, 1976).

⁷¹ Richard J. Barner, "Dirty Tricks and the Intelligence Underworld," *Society*, Vol. 12, No. 3 (March/April, 1975), p. 54.

⁷² Charles H. Anderson, *The Political Economy of Social Class* (Englewood Cliffs: Prentice-Hall, 1974), p. 270.

⁷³ Quoted by *Ibid.*, p. 271.

⁷⁴ *Ibid.*

⁷⁵ *Ibid.*

⁷⁶ *Ibid.*

⁷⁷ Frank Church, "Why I Voted No," *The New Republic* (November 13, 1971), p. 15.

8

IMPACT OF UNDERDEVELOPMENT ON THIRD WORLD SOCIETIES

In Chapter One it was stated that real development must involve a structural transformation of the economy, society, polity and culture of the satellite country in order to allow the self-generating and self-perpetuating use and development of the people's potential. It was also stated that people of the satellite countries must become involved in a frontal attack on the oppression, exploitation, and poverty that they suffer at the hands of the dominant classes and their system. It was also stated that although a country may have been undeveloped, none was ever in an original state of underdevelopment. The process of development and underdevelopment came with the worldwide mercantilist and capitalist expansion of European nations. This process set in motion constellations of developing metropoles and underdeveloped satellites, connecting all parts of the global system from its metropolitan centre in Europe, and subsequently the U.S., to the farthest outpost in the African, Asian, and Latin American countryside.

The question we seek to answer here is what is underdevelopment and what is its impact on Third World countries? The definition of development given in this work emphasizes economic aspects. The reason is that the type of economy is itself an index of other social features; and we have emphasized *real* development as opposed to growth without development. Underdevelopment does not mean absence of development; it makes sense only as a means of comparing levels of development.

Thus, underdevelopment refers to the state of an economy of a satellite economy characterized by underemployment of human and material resources; such an economy is characterized by low real income per capita in comparison with those of North America and Western Europe; it is characterized by illiteracy, poverty, overpopulation, and diseases. Thus until the underdeveloped countries can make a break from the old aristocratic order and the colonial or neocolonial system they will never break out of their underdevelopment.

In his interesting work on *The Sociology of Survival*, Charles Anderson, the prolific American writer, notes:

> The condition of underdevelopment simply deepens the longer a country remains as a backward cog in the world capitalist system. The elite-mass cleavage widens. Rural-urban inequalities increase. City slums grow. Unemployment increases. Illiteracy abounds. Agricultural production stagnates. Malnutrition spreads. Diseases debilitate millions. Birth rates remain high. Death rates begin to rise in some areas. Imported luxuries drain foreign exchange. Foreign debt and balance of payments deficits mount. Inflation runs rampant. Military spending for army and police repression increases. Foreign corporations drain huge amounts of raw materials and profits from the country. Such are some of the hallmarks of an underdeveloped society. Economic growth in the underdeveloped society means unbalanced growth which neglects the most urgent social needs of the people while catering to the consumption whims of the national bourgeoisie and the tax and profit concerns of foreign investors.[1]

As we have emphasised in a previous chapter, the multinationals are the energizing force of world capitalism. They are an extension of some particular national economy and interests. As Christopher Tugedhat has stated:

A characteristic of multinational companies is that their subsidiaries operate under the discipline and framework of a common global strategy, and common global control. The head office is their brain and nerve centre. It evolves the corporate strategy, decides where new investment should be located, allocates export markets and research programms to the various subsidiaries, and determines the prices that should be charged in inter-affiliate exchanges.[2]

The multinationals are nothing but an extension of the competition between advanced capitalist countries for control of raw materials, labour, markets, prices and profits.

Simultaneously, as the advanced countries are creating the conditions for underdevelopment in Third World countries, "they are pushing each other toward further growth and expansion in an arena of international competition. The Third World is caught in a crunch between the growth drives of different advanced capitalist states and between those of different corporations from the same foreign power."[3] Underdevelopment may begin with colonialism; with foreign cultural, military, or economic intervention, and become neocolonialism. But regardless of the initial roots, "the impetus behind underdevelopment is the growth drive of the developed economies, their systematic pursuit of economic gain through control of raw materials, cheap labour, export markets, tax concessions, prices and a variety of financial gains."[4] In what follows, using various indicators, we demonstrate the impact of underdevelopment on Third World societies.

Gross National Product and Poverty

Underdevelopment has resulted in the low standard of living of Third World peoples. By standard of living I mean the material conditions under which Third World people live.

201

We can use the gross national product (GNP) to measure standards of living. GNP refers to the value to the final consumer of all goods and services consumed in a particular country in a given year. In table 8.1 it is clear that of the twelve African countries shown on the table only Nigeria came close in 1971 to having a GNP of ten billion. All others are very small. The white supremacist regime of South Africa which is not included in the Table in 1971 had an estimated GNP of $18.4 billion. On the other hand, the GNP for North American and Western European countries far outstrip those shown for African countries. This low GNP gives an indication of the standard of living in Third World countries.

In the work edited by Millikan and Blackmer, calculations of "real GNP" showed that in 1961, the developed countries of Western Europe, North America, and Oceana, as well as Japan and South Africa, accounted for 58.7 percent of the total world real gross national product, or some $1,029 billion.[5] The communist countries of the Soviet Union, Eastern Europe, China, North Korea, and South Vietnam accounted for 23.7 percent of the world's real GNP, or some $415 billion. On the other hand, the underdeveloped countries of Africa, Asia, Latin America, and the Middle East accounted for only 17.5 percent of the world's real GNP, or some $306 billion. In the same study it was shown that the U.S. alone accounted for 29.4 percent of the world's real GNP, and the Soviet Union for 12.1 percent.

Millikan and Blackmer also report that the countries with a per capita GNP of over $1,200 represented 6.8 percent of the world's population and 40 percent of the world's money GNP. Those countries with a per capita GNP of $100 and below had 50.1 percent of the world's population and accounted for a meagre 8.5 percent of the world's money GNP.[6] What is clear from this picture is that about one-half of the world's population dispose of less than $100 worth of goods and services per head per year.

TABLE 8.1

Gross National Product
(in millions of U.S. dollars)

Country	Year	GNP $
AFRICA		
Mali	1971	278 million
Morocco	1971	3.45 million
Cameroon	1971	1,060 million
Chad	1971	195.3 million
Sudan	1971	1.83 million
Tanzania	1971	1.3 billion
Uganda	1970	1.066 billion
Nigeria	1971	9.9 billion
Kenya	1971	1,650 million
Egypt	1971	6.91 billion
Zaire	1970	1.96 billion
Zambia	1971	1,500 million
WESTERN EUROPE AND NORTH AMERICA		
U.S.	1971	1,050 billion
U.K.	1971	130 billion
Canada	1972	102 billion
Belgium	1972	26 billion
Italy	1971	103.6 billion
Spain	1971	37.1 billion
France	1971	170 billion
West Germany	1971	210 billion
Portugal	1971	6.25 billion

Source: Compiled from *Associated Press Almanac*, 1973. All the figures on
this Table have been estimated.

While international comparisions of absolute levels of GNP is informative, per capita figures have much to say. In 1961 there were only two countries in the world that had a per capital GNP that exceeded $2,000; these were the U.S. with $2,790 and Canada with $2,080.[7] Western Europe (excluding Greece, Spain, Portugal, Italy, and Netherlands), New Zealand and Australia fell in the $1000 to $2000 bracket. The Soviet Union ($818), East Germany, and Czechoslovakia were the only three communist countries to fall within the $500-$1,000 range. From Latin America only Venezuela, Puerto Rico, and Argentina fell within this range but none of them exceeded $700. With the exception of Albania, other communist countries fell in the $250 to $500 range. Spain, Greece, Uruguay, Cuba, Chile, Mexico, Columbia, Panama, Costa Rica, Brazil, and the Dominian Republic were within the $250-$500 range. No Asian nation had a per capita GNP of more than $383 recorded by Japan; most of the Asian nations' per capita GNP ranged from $47 recorded by Nepal to $123 recorded by Ceylon. In the case of Africa only the then Rhodesia and Nyasaland recorded a per capita GNP of $161; most of the other African countries registered a per capita GNP of under $100. China and India recorded per capita GNP of $83 and $70 respectively.

Table 8.2 shows population and per capita GNP figures for 1970 for the world. From these figures it is evident that there has been some improvement in the per capita GNP of the underdeveloped countries but the imbalance between the "haves" and the "have nots" has persisted. It is sad to notice that as of 1970 there still existed African countries with per capita GNP of $60.

Previously the line between economically advanced and underdeveloped countries was set by the U.N. at $500-$ 600 of GNP per capita. Table 8.3 shows data on GNP per capita and annual growth rates for the 1963 to 1973 decade. The data were compiled by the U.S. Department of State in

TABLE 8.2

Population and per capita GNP figures for 1970

AFRICA

Country	Population (in millions)	P.C. GNP (in $)
Nigeria	55.0	120
Egypt	33.3	210
Ethiopia	24.6	80
South Africa	22.2	760
Zaire	18.8	90
Sudan	15.7	120
Morocco	15.5	230
Algeria	14.3	300
Tanzania	13.3	100
Kenya	11.2	150
Uganda	9.8	130
Ghana	8.6	310
Mozambique	7.7	240
Malagasy Republic	7.3	130
Cameroon	5.8	180
Angola	5.5	300
Upper Volta	5.3	60
Rhodesia	5.3	280
Tunisia	5.0	250
Mali	5.0	70
Ivory Coast	4.9	310
Malawi	4.4	80
Zambia	4.1	400
Niger	4.0	90
Guinea	3.9	120
Senegal	3.8	230
Chad	3.6	80
Rwanda	3.5	60
Burundi	3.5	60
Somalia	2.8	70
Dahomey	2.7	90
Sierra Leone	2.5	190
Togo	1.9	140
Libya, Arab Republic of	1.9	1,770
Central African Republic	1.5	140

Liberia	1.5	240
Mauritania	1.1	140
Lesotho	0.9	90
Congo, Peoples Republic of	0.9	300
Mauritius	0.8	240
Botswana	0.6	110
Portuguese Guinea	0.5	250
Reunion	0.4	800
Swaziland	0.4	180
Gabon	0.4	630
Gambia	0.3	120
Equatorial Guinea	0.2	210

ASIA

Country	Population (in millions)	P.C. GNP (in $)
China, Peoples Republic of	836.0	160
India	538.1	110
Pakistan and Bangladesh	130.1	100
Japan	103.3	1,920
Philippines	36.8	210
Thailand	36.2	200
Korea, Republic of	31.7	250
Iran	28.6	380
Burma	27.5	80
Vietnam (North)	21.1	100
Vietnam Republic of	18.3	200
Afghanistan	14.3	80
China, Republic of (Taiwan)	14.0	390
Korea (North)	13.8	330
Sri Lanka	12.5	110
Nepal	11.0	80
Malaysia	10.9	380
Iraq	9.6	320
Khmer Republic	7.5	130
Saudi Arabia	7.3	440
Syria, Arab Republic of	6.0	290
Yemen, Arab Republic of	5.7	80
Hong Kong	3.9	970
Laos	2.9	120
Israel	2.9	1,960

Lebanon	2.7	590
Jordan	2.3	250
Singapore	2.0	920
Mongolia	1.2	460
Yemen, Peoples Democratic Republic of	1.2	120
Ryukyu Island	0.9	1,050
Bhutan	0.9	70
Kuwait	0.7	3,760
Oman	0.6	350
Macao	0.3	150
United Arab Emirates	0.2	2,390
Bahrain	0.2	550
Sikkim	0.1	80
Brunel	0.1	1,220
Qatar	0.1	1,730
Maldive Islands	0.1	100

EUROPE

Country	Population (in millions)	P.C. GNP (in $)
U.S.S.R.	242.7	1,790
Germany, Federal Republic of	61.5	2,930
United Kingdom	55.7	2,270
Italy	53.7	1,760
France	50.7	3,100
Turkey	35.2	310
Spain	33.6	1,020
Poland	32.8	1,400
Yugoslavia	20.5	650
Romania	20.2	930
Germany (East)	17.2	2,490
Czechoslovakia	14.4	2,230
Netherlands	13.0	2,430
Hungary	10.3	1,600
Belgium	9.6	2,720
Portugal	9.6	660
Greece	8.8	1,090
Bulgaria	8.4	760
Sweden	8.0	4,040
Austria	7.3	2,010

207

Switzerland	6.2	3,320
Denmark	4.9	3,190
Finland	4.6	2,390
Norway	3.8	2,860
Ireland	2.9	1,360
Albania	2.1	600
Cyprus	0.6	950
Luxembourg	0.3	2,890
Malta	0.3	810
Iceland	0.2	2,170

NORTH AND CENTRAL AMERICA

Country	Population (in millions)	P.C. GNP (in $)
United States	204.80	4,760
Mexico	50.6	670
Canada	21.4	3,700
Cuba	8.3	530
Guatemala	5.1	360
Haiti	4.8	110
Dominican Republic	4.0	350
El Salvador	3.5	300
Puerto Rico	2.8	1,650
Honduras	2.5	280
Nicaragua	1.9	430
Jamaica	1.8	670
Costa Rica	1.7	560
Panama	1.4	730
Trinidad and Tobago	1.0	860
Martinique	0.3	910
Guadalupe	0.3	760
Barbados	0.2	570

SOUTH AMERICA

Country	Population (in millions)	P.C. GNP (in $)
Brazil	92.7	420
Argentina	23.2	1,160

Colombia	21.6	340
Peru	13.5	450
Venezuela	10.3	980
Chile	9.7	720
Ecuador	6.0	290
Bolivia	4.9	180
Uruguay	2.8	820
Paraguay	2.3	260
Guyana	0.7	370
Surinam	0.3	530

OCEANIA AND INDONESIA

Country	Population (in millions)	P.C. GNP (in $)
Indonesia	115.5	80
Australia	12.5	2,820
New Zealand	2.8	2,700
Papua New Guinea	2.4	300
Portuguese Timor	0.6	110
Fiji Islands	0.5	430

Source: International Bank for Reconstruction and Development, *World Bank Atlas of Population, Per Capita Product and Growth Rates* (Washington, D.C., © 1972).

1975. The separating point as of that year stood at roughly $1,500 (1972 dollars).

Table 8.3 shows a tremendous growth in world economy but the disappointing fact is that this growth has not been equally distributed, nor has it led to the closing of the gap between economically advanced and underdeveloped countries. Figures show that the average GNP per capita of the developed countries increased from 12.88 times that of underdeveloped countries to 14.13 times that amount in a decade. Average annual growth rate in developed countries during the same period was 3.9% as compared with 3.2% in underdeveloped nations. The figures for the underdeveloped

TABLE 8.3

Gross National Product Per Capita (in 1972 Dollars), 1963-73

Year	Developed Nations*	Underdeveloped Nations*	World
1963	2,381	185	821
1964	2,509	194	857
1965	2,619	202	887
1966	2,742	207	917
1967	2,832	208	934
1968	2,967	212	967
1969	3,074	223	996
1970	3,164	236	1,020
1971	3,256	244	1,043
1972	3,378	251	1,071
1973	3,561	252	1,112
Average annual growth	3.9	3.2	2.9

* "Developed nations" include: United States: Canada, all European NATO countries except Greece and Turkey; all Warsaw Pact countries except Bulgaria; and Austria, Finland Ireland, Sweden, Switzerland, Australia, New Zealand, Japan and South Africa. Twenty-eight countries were classified as developed. "Underdeveloped nations" include all those in Latin America; in the Near East including Egypt; in East Asia except Japan; in South Asia; in Africa except South Africa; and also Albania, Bulgaria, Greece, Malta Spain, Turkey, and Yugoslavia. One hundred eight countries were classified as underdeveloped.

Source: A. Portes, "On the Sociology of National Development. Theories and Issues," *American Journal* LXXXII/1 (July, 1976), p. 57.

countries are inflated by inclusion of the oil-producing countries, which had an exceptional growth during the period. The OPEC countries altogether had an estimated growth rate of 4.7% per year.

By cross-classifying individual countries by their 1963 per capita GNP and by average annual growth rates from 1963 to 1973, Portes' analysis reveals various trends. Table 8.4 shows

TABLE 8.4

Gross National Product Per Capita and Growth Rates, 1963-73

Average Annual Growth Rate 1963-73 (%)	GNP per capita 1963 (in 1972 Dollar Equivalents)							
	Less than 100	100-199	200-299	300-499	500-999	1,000-1,999	2,000-2,999	3,000 or More
Less than 1.00	Afghanistan, Burma, Chad, India, Nepal, Somalia, Upper Volta	Cambodia, Haiti, Niger, Sudan, North Vietnam, South Vietnam, Yemen	Egypt, Ghana, Jordan, Senegal	Zambia	Cuba, Lebanon, Mongolia, Uruguay			Kuwait
1.00-1.99	Burundi, Dahomey, Ethiopia, Mali, Rwanda	Central African Republic, Guinea, Malagasy Republic, Sierra Leone	El Salvador, Honduras, Morocco	Albania, Congo, Nicaragua, Peru		Venezuela	Iceland, Luxembourg, United Kingdom, New Zealand	Sweden, Switzerland, United States
2.00-2.99	Bolivia, Uganda	Ceylon	Colombia, Iraq, Paraguay, Philippines, Syria		South Africa			
3.00-3.99	Indonesia, Laos, Tanzania	Cameroon, China (People's Republic), Kenya, Liberia, Nigeria Togo, Zaire	Ecuador, Ivory Coast, North Korea, Tunisia	Algeria, Costa Rica, Dominican Republic, Guatemala, Malaysia	Argentina, Jamaica, Mexico, Trinidad-Tobago	German Democratic Republic, Ireland	Australia, Denmark, Norway	Canada, German Federal Republic
4.00-4.99	Mauritania, Pakistan	Thailand		Brazil, Turkey	Panama	Austria, Czechoslovakia, Finland, Italy, Hungary, Poland, Soviet Union	Belgium, France, Netherlands	
5.00-5.99					Spain, Yugoslavia,	Israel		
6.00 or more		South Korea	China (Taiwan), Iran	Gabon, Saudi Arabia	Bulgaria, Cyprus, Greece, Rumania, Lybia, Portugal	Japan		

Source: A. Portes, "On the Sociology of National Development: Theories and Issues, "*American Journal of Sociology,* LXXXII/1 (July, 1976). p. 57 © 1976 by the University of Chicago Press.

that all countries considered as developed grew at an annual rate of at least 2%. Among those with per capita GNP of below $300 in 1963 referred to as "least developed countries" nearly all failed to reach the 2% annual growth figure, and only 10% exceeded growth rates of 4%. In what Portes calls "the intermediate categories" (per capita GNP between $300 and $999 in 1963) a little more than one third of the countries had growth rates of 4% or higher: one third fell below the minimal criterion of 2% per year.

The per capita GNPs that we have been discussing are averages; the actual distribution of income within the underdeveloped world is just as lopsided as the distribution of income among nations where the total and per capita product appear relatively good, as in South Africa, the real situation is not satisfactory at all. The bulk of the product in some cases generate in one major industry (e.g., petroleum, gold, and diamond mining) and both totals and per capita figures seem to lose their meaning in a social and political context.[8]

As emphasized time and again in this work the persistent and extensive interventions (imperialism and exploitation) of the developed countries are the underlying reason for Third World underdevelopment, and the distorted and unbalanced growth in those countries. The distortion in the organization and utilization of a nation's human and natural resources makes it extremely difficult for such a country to make a transition to a balanced and self-sustaining growth. But this transition has to be made in order to cope successfully with the survival challanges. As Anderson has noted:

> The difference between balanced and umbalanced growth, between growth that equips people to meet their own urgent needs and growth that sinks them into deepening poverty, may be readily observed in the contrast between China and India, Cuba and Puerto Rico, Vietnam and Thailand. Real growth means

growth in nutritious diets for everyone, growth in
health services and medical care for everyone, growth
in health services and medical care for everyone,
growth in literacy and education for everyone, growth
in constructive employment and income for everyone,
growth in adequate clothing and housing for everyone,
and growth in community participation and decision-
making for everyone. Distorted growth means luxury
and power for the few at the expence of the many. It
means the best the Western world has to offer for a
miniscule elite and a deepening despair for the masses
of people. It means luxurious jetports, highrise office
buildings and hotels, new cars and expressways, exclusive villas and resort retreats to the national
bourgeoisie and foreign bigwigs and tourists... 'their
people wind up as bellhops and souvenir sellers, desk
clerks and entertainers, and their proudest traditions
soon degenerate into crude caricatures'. This is if they
are "lucky" enough to get such jobs. All too often
prostitution stands between someone's child and starvation in the 'growth' economies of the Third World.[9]

A symposium on the Third World held in 1972 noted
that "in many countries high growth rates have been accompanied by increasing unemployment, rising disparities in incomes both between groups and between regions, and deterioration of social and cultural conditions."[10] Among the
glaring illustrations of growth distortions or growth without
development are Brazil, Liberia, and Ivory Coast. Bourgeois
economists have described Brazil's "growth rate" of about 10
percent as phenomenal. But growth in Brazil, as growth in
other underdeveloped countries, is attributable not so much
to the indigenous development of Brazil as a sovereign state
as to the activities of foreign multinationals and financial
interests. The most lucrative enterprises are foreign-owned
and controlled, especially by Americans.[11]

Bill Warren has observed that since 1960 and the rapid
increase in foreign investment, per capita economic growth

213

in the underdeveloped world has been drastically reduced.[12] Even the growth paragon of Brazil sustained in 1970 a foreign debt of $5.2 billion, with debt interest payments alone eating away one-third of that country's foreign exchange earnings. This ugly international financial position of Brazil, as explained by Marcio Alues, is largely due to the fact that foreign capital controls three-quarters of Brazilian heavy industry and consumer durable production.[13] Other factors accounting for this foreign debt include Brazil's big military equipment import bill.

The drain of Latin American capital overall is such that about two-thirds of the continent's foreign exchange earnings have to be turned around for payment to foreigners for profit on investments, debt servicing, royalties and managerial fees, transportation and travel, and other financial demands. With little foreign exchange left to pay for goods imports, which the wealthy and powerful desire very much, the balance of payments situation worsens more and more and the debt accelerates even further. The financial noose with which the rich and powerful countries hold the poor and underdeveloped ones in abeyance can be again tightened. The national bourgeoisie become even more dependent and subservient to foreign financial and political power.[14] What happens in Latin America is equally true of Africa and Asia.

Using Brazil further for our illustration, growth in that country as it is in other countries of the underdeveloped world is geared to the power and privilege of the few. In 1970 the Ministry of Health of Brazil received only 1 percent of the government budget at a time when its rural inhabitants had one doctor for every 14,727 people while the rich and powerful men of Rio de Janeiro enjoyed one of the highest concentration of doctors anywhere in the world.[15] In the same budget the armed forces and international security police had a comparably large amount of money alloted to them. The consumer durable goods industry has been growing at the astronomical rate of 25 per cent.[16] This aspect of the Brazilian economy actually caters for the export market and the national bourgeoisie. On the other hand, the industry has been growing at the miserable rate of 1.8 percent and textiles 0.1 percent.[17] Landowners who used to grow black beans, eaten mostly by the poor of Brazil, have abandoned it for soya beans, used as feed for the rich people's livestock; these beans are for export. The result of this is that the price of black beans has gone up 400 percent and potatoes 300 percent.

In a 1973 article in which Brazil is characterized as another Japan emerging from the jungle, the *Economist* is however forced to admit that "as for public investment, the contrast between private affluence and public squalor in the industrial belt is unbelievable. The roads are full of flashy new cars, while most of the houses do not even have water supply or sewerage."[19] The *Economist* went on to add that "in Brazil's cities middle managers think nothing of pulling $40,000 a year, and even secretaries in Rio de Janeiro can command up to $15,000 a year. But on the fringe of the cities, the poor live in shanty towns of incredible squalor and count themselves lucky if they earn $10 a week."[20] The *Economist* having noted the extremes of wealth and poverty states, "it is an imbalance, which seems to be characteristic of other fast growing nations, like Japan."[21] Although Nigeria is not another Japan like Brazil in terms of phenomenal growth, the same imbalance is equally true here. A look at Lagos the capital city of Nigeria, reveals a similar situation.

In Brazil one-third of the population is entirely outside the money market economy; almost 30 percent is somewhat marginal to the market; and 40 percent are without minimum access to the possibilities provided by contemporary modern life in Latin America.[22] In this same country 3 percent of the population holds 33 percent of the wealth and the poorest 40 percent only 9 percent of the wealth. In the area of income distribution, the richest 5 percent enjoy

215

33 percent of the total and the top 20 percent receive 63 percent, as compared with 3 percent of the income for the lowest 20 percent and 13 percent for the poorest 50 percent. The critical case of poverty or inequality in the midst of growth in Brazil has led Alves to state that "even though the U.S. government presents Brazil as a symbol of triumph before the rest of the underdeveloped countries, a society in which the prosperity of a small minority is gained at the price of the growing misery of the majority does not offer a very seductive model for other Third World countries."[23] But the problem here is that those countries which may care to take the advice given by Alves are those likely to face "destabilization" programmes and other frustrations from the U.S. that headquarters most of the world's international conglomerates. Chile and Lumumba's Zaire quickly come to mind.

Finally in this section, it is important to mention that whether one looks at the GNP or Gross Domestic Product (GDP), the sectoral origin of the product of the developed and the underdeveloped countries will be different. Table 8.5 shows the sectoral origin of the product (GDP) of both the developed and underdeveloped countries. In the case of Nigeria, oil swells up column 2 of the Table. But generally, the greater part of the GDPs of the underdeveloped economies come from the agricultural sector. This sector is often characterized by "hidden unemployment or under-employment, low productivity, non viable distribution of the cultivable area, scarcity of capital and primitive techniques. The manufacturing sector in such cases plays a relatively minor role."[24]

What is apparent in Table 8.5 is that in the under-developed world, a small national product is produced mostly by agriculture. The implication here is that agriculture is not quite efficient. It is common knowledge that the exports of such countries are largely products of agriculture, and in many cases one product such as cotton, rubber, cof-

TABLE 8.5

Percentage Distribution of Sectoral Origin of GDP

Country	1 Agri- culture	2 Mining & Quarrying Electricity, Gas, Water	3 Manufac- turing	4 Con- struction	5 Trade	6 Trans- port	7 Other
France (1976)	5	3	27	8	12	5	31
West Germany (1976)	3	4	37	7	10	6	31
Portugal (1975)	14	3	30	6	13	6	19
Italy (1975)	9	33*	...	8	14	6	28
Spain (1975)	9	3	27	8	16	6	27
Belgium (1975)	3	3	28	7	12	8	32
Canada (1976)	4	6	19	7	11	7	35
U.S. (1976)	3	5	24	4	18	6	37
U.K. (1976)	3	5	25	6	9	8	33
Zaire (1975)	19	11	11	6	16	4	28
Zambia (1975)	13	12	18	10	14	5	25
Malawi (1973)	49	2	9	4	12	5	14
Morocco (1975)	24	9	15	9	24	19	
Liberia (1975)	21	27	4	3	6	5	12
Chad (1970)	50	1	7	1	16	4	13
Kenya (1976)	31	2	11	5	10	5	24
Sudan (1974)	39	2	9	4	16	6	18
Nigeria (1974)	24	45	6	4	8	2	2
Ethiopia (1975)	44	1	10	4	9	5	19
Uganda (1971)	53	2	8	2	9	3	17
Ghana (1974)	51	3	11	5	13	4	12

Source: Compiled from Table 189, *U.N. Statistical Yearbook.*

* Together with mining and quarrying, electricity, gas and water.

Note: The figures do not add up to 100 but this is the way they are in the
source.

fee, sugar or ground nuts will form the greater part of the exports. Heavy dependence on agriculture and on agricultural exports has often been a serious cause of instability for the economies of the underdeveloped countries. The great dependence of the underdeveloped countries on agricultural exports, especially the export of a single crop, makes the underdeveloped economies subject to the fluctuations of international commodity prices. Natural disasters such as flood and drought can do serious damage to the agricultural economies of the poor countries. But apart from such factors as stated above, the rich and powerful countries do go out of their way to destabilise the economies of those poor countries that are unwilling to dance to their tune.

A case in point is the Cuban situation. Because Cuba tried and apparently has succeeded in forcing out Yankee imperialism from her borders, the U.S. has been trying to disrupt that country's sugar trade. There had been attempts by the U.S. to purchase large amounts of sugar and then dump them in a certain foreign market so as to disrupt the market for Cuban sugar. As it happened "a more serious attack on Cuban sugar occurred in August 1962 when a British freighter under lease to the Soviets docked in Puerto Rico for repairs. The freighter, carrying Cuban sugar destined for the Soviet Union, was placed in a bonded warehouse while the ship was in dry dock. CIA agents broke into the warehouse and contaminated the sugar with a non-poisonous but unpalatable substance."[25] Apart from all this, the developed countries know that if the agricultural producing countries do not sell their products they will rot. That the developed countries capitalise on this fact cannot be disputed.

Apart from the above problems, "exhaustive theoretical and applied policy studies all conclude that the rate of increase in earning from the export of primary products cannot, for low income countries exporting primary products taken together, be expected to exceed 2 or 3 percent a year during the next two decades."[26] There are various reasons for this. First, the demand of the rich countries for most primary products do not increase at the same rate as per capita income. It does not follow when a family's income doubles, its members simultaneously double their consumption of sugar, or coffee, or tabacco. Second, as the industrialised countries move from the production of light manufactures, like textiles, to more complex products such as electronic equipment, the share of raw materials required in the total national product is reduced. Third, as the developed countries develop synthetics based on coal, oil and temperate softwoods, there is a relative reduction in the demand for many raw materials, such as cotton and rubber. Technological innovations, like the discovery of new tinplating methods, has also made possible radical economizing on raw material use.[27]

It is also an established fact that any economy that depends on raw material exports lacks the flexibility to adjust to new market situations. While the industrial countries can shift their exports from products for which demand is declining to those for which it is growing much more easily, those economies built around the export of one or two crops or minerals cannot. The drastic drop in the demand for oil has seriously affected Nigeria and other oil-producing countries. "The poor, single-crop economies, whether colonial or formally sovereign, tend to remain dependent on the same export regardless of changes in world market conditions."[28]

Export-oriented economies such as characterise Third World countries do not contribute to the technical knowledge, or to the training of skilled administrative managers, technicians and workers, crucially needed for rapid economic growth. Export-oriented economies perpetuate development of underdevelopment.

Furthermore, production of exports does not provide a focus around which an integrated national economy can develop.[29] The tendency for the slowly changing production pattern in the export economy is to "fossilize." Foreign investment tends to concentrate in the export sector and services connected with it. Because of lack of markets, technology and infrastructure, the tendency is for other sectors to appear less profitable in the short run.

Studies of African economies demonstrate a lack of adequate flow between the export-oriented sector and the remainder of the economy. The economy imports a large share of the goods consumed and invested in the relatively modern export sector and secondary industries related to it from overseas. It exports to overseas markets most of the goods produced by that sector. Even in the absence of declining terms of trade, such "fossilization" around the export sector would impede growth. With either stagnant or falling world demand for the economy's exports, it will lead to ... "immiserizing growth." Not only export earnings, but the entire national product which is heavily dependent on export earnings, will decline, unemployment will mount, and *per capita* income will fall or at best creep upward.[30]

Finally, the export-oriented economies created by the colonial imperialists "have developed patterns of income distribution and economic-political power that thwart modern industrial and agricultural growth."[31] In these economies foreign firms and personnel, whether in mining and plantations or commerce and trading, always receive huge shares of the national product — sometimes as large as half — in the form of profits, interests and high salaries. But very few indigenous large-scale African farmers and merchants receive relatively high incomes. In addition, the bulk of unskilled workers and peasant farmers receive incomes at or sometimes even below subsistence levels. In many African countries statutory marketing boards and high export duties have increased the share of the public sector and reduced the share exported by foreign firms and personnel. But the fact remains that the perpetuation in many African countries of the pattern of income distribution carried over from colonial rule limits the demand for domestically manufactured goods and modern services. This also fails to contribute to capital accumulation directed at industrial growth. At the same time the wealthy elite prefer to invest their money in commerce and speculative real estate, which does not call for new knowledge or skills and is highly lucrative, that is, brings in high profits, at least in the short run.[32]

Apart from the problems already mentioned, the export-oriented economies tend to perpetuate

> the community of interest initiated in colonial days between the large foreign firms, immigrant medium-scale business communities, African commercial inter-mediaries and lower-level foreign firm managers, and the African plantation or large farm owners. This community of interest seeks, as a rule, to block economic policies — high income taxes, high import duties, foreign exchange control, land reform — de-signed to make the wealth of higher income groups available for investment in economic growth so as to benefit the majority of people. Yet such policies are vital to economic development. To the extent that the export economy enhances the power of this political alliance, it becomes statically self-perpetuating, with results distinctly hostile to social and economic de-velopment, as may be seen in many Latin American and Middle Eastern nations.
>
> In short, the basic economic structure of most in-dividual African states is unsuitable for growth, not simply because existing ventures are small or existing marketing and production techniques so inadequate, but rather because the economies are biased towards sectors with a low growth in demand (nationally or internationally) low rates of increase in productivity, little contribution to the development of technology

and skills, small interrelation and impact between sectors, and an inhibiting pattern of income distribution and economic interest.[33]

The result of all these problems is low income levels for the masses of the population. And this in turn means low standard of living. With low income levels it is not possible to enjoy the kind of life chances that the rich and powerful do. A country like the U.S. really wastes a substantial portion of their food. Various television investigative reports, have demonstrated that at least a third of the food that Americans cook end up in the dustbins. By doing this they deprive other members of the world their due share of the cake.

Infant Mortality and Life Expectancy at Birth

With low levels of income come poverty and poverty connotes malnutrition, unbalanced and irregular diets, endemic disease, high infant mortality and low life expectancy rates. Tables 8.6 and 8.7 tell the story. In Table 8.6 Portugal is the Western country with the worst infant mortality rate. But this is still much better than Zambia whose rate is about 4.4 times that of Portugal.

In Table 8.7 we have no difficulty in concluding that life expectancy in the underdeveloped countries is deplorable. A Nigerian child born between 1965 and 1966 could expect to live up to 37 years if male and approximately the same 37 years if female. Or a child born in Ethiopia between 1970 and 1975 expects to live for 37 years if male and 40 years if female. By contrast, Portugal with the worst figures in Western Europe is much better than Nigeria or Ethiopia. A child born in Portugal in 1974 expects to live for 65 years if male and 72 years if female. Sure enough there has been some improvement in the Nigerian life expectancy since 1965-66 but it is not up to 60 years for either males or females.

TABLE 8.6

Infant Mortality: Western Europe, North America, and Africa

Country	Infant Mortality per 1,000 Births
WESTERN EUROPE & NORTH AMERICA	
France	16.4
West Germany	23.3
Portugal	59.2
Italy	30.3
Spain	40.0
Belgium	21.7
Canada	19.3
U.S.	19.8
U.K.	18.5
AFRICA	
Zaire	104
Zambia	259
Mali	120
Morocco	149
Cameroon	137
Chad	160
Nigeria	68
Kenya	48.9
Egypt	117
Sudan	94
Tanzania	163
Uganda	160

Source: Compiled from *Associated Press Almanac*, 1973.

TABLE 8.7

Expectation of Life at Birth

Country	Date	Male	Female
	AFRICA		
Nigeria	1965-1966	37.2	36.7
Ghana	1970-1975	41.9	45.1
Egypt	1960	51.6	53.8
Sudan	1970-1975	47.3	49.9
Uganda	1970-1975	48.3	51.7
Kenya	1969	46.9	51.2
Zambia	1970-1975	42.9	46.1
Morocco	1970-1975	51.4	54.5
Mali	1970-1975	36.5	39.6
Zaire	1970-1975	41.9	45.1
Cameroon	1970-1975	40.9	44.1
Chad	1963-1964	29.0	35.0
Malawi	1970-1972	40.9	44.2
Ethiopia	1970-1975	36.5	39.6
	WESTERN EUROPE AND NORTH AMERICA		
Italy	1970-1972	68.97	74.88
Spain	1970	69.69	74.96
Canada	1970-1972	69.34	76.36
Belgium	1968-1972	67.79	74.21
U.S.	1974	68.2	75.9
England and Wales	1970-1972	68.9	75.1
West Germany	1972-1974	67.87	74.36
Portugal	1974	65.29	72.03
France	1972	68.6	74.4

Source: Table 19 of *U.N. Statistical Year Book*, 1976 (Adaptation).

Malnutrition

The factors that contribute to poor life expectancy are many and varied. They include malnutrition, general neglect, over-crowding, and the lack of public health and medical services. According to *War on Hunger,* a publication of the U.S. Agency for International Development (AID) of August, 1975:

> Hunger is one of the most critical problems confronting a troubled world. It is especially serious in the developing countries where:
>
> Between 300 million and 500 million people do not get enough food. Up to 800 million are poorly nourished.
>
> One of every five children dies before the age of five; at least half of these deaths are malnutrition related.
>
> Malnutrition of pregnant women, nursing mothers, and infants affects the mental development of surviving children.
>
> Consumption is generally below minimum standards and large areas now suffer from widespread and severe food shortages.
>
> Food output has increased 3 percent annually since 1955, but, because of the uncontrolled population growth, per capita food production has increased only slightly.
>
> Due to inflation of food prices, people now must spend between 70 and 80 percent of their income on food.
>
> If the world is to meet the challenge of hunger, food supplies must double by the year 2000.

At the World Food Conference held in Rome in November, 1974, U.S. Secretary of State Henry Kissinger said: "The profound promise of our era is that for the first time we may have technical capacity to free mankind from the scourge of hunger. Therefore ... we ... proclaim a bold objective — that within a decade no child will go to bed hungry, that no family will fear for its next day's bread, and that no human being's future and capacities will be stunted by malnutrition."[34] This statement, like many other international statements, has to date remained rhetoric.

Table 8.8 shows the range in average daily caloric intake for the nations within three selected regions. The range is very wide for the African region, however, because few countries (e.g., South Africa and Rhodesia) may have unusually high average caloric supplies. It is evident that most of the underdeveloped countries of Africa are not supplying their teeming populations with adequate calories.

Generally, the food supply is often discussed in terms of a caloric measure, but the difference between sickness and health is determined by quality and not by the amount of intake. Thus whereas malnutrition is the result of a lack of quality in their food, undernutrition results from an insufficient quantity of food. Malnutrition is more prevalent than undernourishment but malnutrition is also rampant among populations who also suffer undernourishment. The average Nigerian diet consists primarily of starchy tubers such as yans and cassava, with some beans and nuts, a little fish (usually smoked) and quite often no meat or eggs. One may therefore suspect a high rate of malnutrition among the population. On the other hand, the average North American or Western European eats in a day enough meat or fish or both, eggs, bread, fruit, vegetables, and drinks enough milk to give him more than an adequate amount of daily caloric intake.

Public health in the underdeveloped world remains an acute problem. Tables 8.9, 8.10, and 8.11 reveal the problem. Table 8.9 merely tells us the number of inhabitants per physician but says nothing about the amount of availability of equipment and drugs to the physicians. One who has been reading the Nigerian dailies must be disturbed about

TABLE 8.8

The Range and Median of National Estimate within Regions: Calorie and Protein Content of Average per Capita Food

| Regions | Average No. of Calories per Person per Day | | | Average Grams of Protein per Person per Day | | | |
| | | | | Total | | Animal | |
	Date	Range	Median	Range	Median	Range	Median
Western Europe	1966-67	2860-3400	2900	75-100	86.4	29.8-61.0	49.4
North America	1967-68	3180-3200	3200	95.4-95.6	95.6	64.1-68.6	68.6
Africa	1962-63	1800-2820	2120	35.9-80.2	52.3	3.1-31.5	10.3

Source: Adapted from Shirley F. Hartley, *Population: Quantity vs. Quality* (Englewood Cliffs, N.J.: Prentice-Hall, 1972), Table 5.3. See also U.N. Food and Agriculture Organization, *The State of Food and Agriculture 1969* (Rome: FAO, 1969).

TABLE 8.9

Health Personnel

Country	Year	Physicians	Population per Physician
AFRICA			
Nigeria	1973	2,343	25,463
Mali	1972	135	38,963
Zaire	1973	818	28,802
Cameroon	1973	21	13,810
Chad	1974	89	44,382
Morocco	1974	1,223	13,802
Sudan	1974	1,400	12,371
Uganda	1974	540	20,685
Kenya	1973	766	16,292
Egypt	1974	7,495	-
Zambia	1971	527	8,159
Ghana	1974	856	11,227
WESTERN EUROPE / NORTH AMERICA			
Italy	1973	109,166	502
Spain	1973	51,743	673
Canada	1974	37,277	603
Belgium	1974	17,272	566
U.S.	1973	338,111	622
West Germany	1974	120,260	516
Portugal	1974	10,312	851
France	1974	77,143	681

Source: Compiled from *U.N. Statistical Year Book, 1976*, Table 206.

TABLE 8.10

Health Personnel

	Year	Dentists	Pharmacists	Nursing Personnel	Midwifery Personnel
AFRICA					
Nigeria	1973	103	499	9,567	4,063
Ghana	1974	44	444	11,011	4,168
Egypt	1974	2,083	2,627	8,241	7,414
Sudan	1974	149	312	11,160	6,684
Uganda	1974	19	28	1,627	1,977
Kenya	1973	65	163	3,711	1,350
Zambia	1971	35	81	1,762	733
Morocco	1974	114	364	-	55
Mali	1972	7	14	1,526	168
Zaire	1973	22	131	9,285	1,235
Cameroon	1973	3	3	148	20
Chad	1974	2	5	565	77
Malawi	1969	10	17	484	201
WESTERN EUROPE / NORTH AMERICA					
Italy	1973	-	37,689	-	18,375
Spain	1973	3,613	17,498	-	4,088
Canada	1974	8,487	13,267	-	-
Belgium	1974	2,153	6,614	-	3,422
U.S.	1973	107,320	132,899	134,900	-
U.K.	1973-4	16,384	17,574	214,633	22,953
West Germany	1974	31,613	24,787	222,932	5,958
Portugal	1974	-	-	10,749	646
France	1974	25,069	30,059	281,531	8,803

Source: Compiled from *U.N. Statistical Year Book 1976*, Table 206.

TABLE 8.11

Hospital Establishments

Country	Year	Total	Beds	Population per Bed
AFRICA				
Nigeria	1972	-	42,101	1,378
Kenya	1972	-	15,904	759
Egypt	1973	1,444	76,611	464
Sudan	1974	137	15,792	1,097
Tanzania	1970	-	16,640	775
Zanzibar	1967	15	875	400
Uganda	1974	241	15,723	710
Mali	1971	54	3,718	1,382
Morocco	1974	144	23,056	732
Cameroon	1972	30	612	458
Chad	1974	45	3,464	1,140
Zaire	1973	-	72,090	327
Zambia	1969	540	13,242	313
WESTERN EUROPE / NORTH AMERICA				
France	1973	-	534,023	98
West Germany	1974	3,483	716,530	87
Portugal	1974	581	53,454	163
Italy	1972	2,189	575,162	95
Spain	1973	1,285	180,547	193
Belgium	1974	479	87,164	112
Canada	1973	1,386	207,699	106
U.S.	1974	7,370	1,418,939	149

Source: Compiled from *UN Statistical Year Book, 1976*, Table 206.

the constant reports of acute shortage of drugs. Added to this problem is the fact that Nigeria, like other Third World countries, continues to be a theatre for experimental drugs. Yes, Nigeria continues to be a dumping ground for experimental drugs because of the naira-hungry leaders who approve the importation of such drugs. In other words, Nigerians are bribed to allow foreign countries to have their newly invented drugs tested in the country. Nigerians of the 1970s continue to serve as guinea pigs for Western drugs because of some faceless, naira-monger leaders. This is true of other underdeveloped countries.

As Atwater, Forster, and Prybyla have noted, "the big killers in almost every underdeveloped country are the very diseases that have been brought under control by modern medical science elsewhere. Pneumonia, typhus, tuberculosis, smallpox, measles, and other infective and parasitic diseases lead the way, with anaemias, senility, and diseases peculiar to early infancy as close seconds."[35] Many parts of Central and South America are plagued with yellow fever. In most parts of Africa diseases caused by worms in blood are prevalent, whereas in India cholera, smallpox, and yellow fever are endemic. Given in a decending order, the main causes of death in the advanced countries are arteriosclerotic and degenerative heart disease, malignant enoplasms (cancer), and vascular lesions affecting the central nervous system. These diseases are relatively few in the economically retarded areas of the world.

Illiteracy

Substandard education and illiteracy cannot be disassociated from poverty. Education is the handmaiden of development. Table 8.12 tells the story of it. This is the direct result of colonial imperialism which carefully made it difficult for Africans to acquire education; this was discussed in an

TABLE 8.12

Illiteracy for Western Europe, North America, and Africa

Country	Illiteracy Rate
WESTERN EUROPE AND NORTH AMERICA	
Italy	7%
Spain	3%
U.K.	Negligible
U.S.	1%
Canada	0-3%
Belgium	0-3%
West Germany	0-1%
Portugal	35-40%
France	0-3%
AFRICA	
Nigeria	75%
Kenya	75-80%
Egypt	70%
Sudan	85-90%
Tanzania	80-85%
Uganda	80%
Cameroon	85%
Chad	90%
Mali	95%
Morocco	86%
Zaire	60%
Zambia	80-85%

Source: Compiled from *Associated Press Almanac, 1973*

earlier chapter. No nation can make much headway by way of development with the bulk of its population remaining stark illiterates. The underdeveloped countries are aware of this but lacking the necessary funds to translate their dreams into practical reality there is not much being done.

Capital Endowment

An important factor in Third World underdevelopment is inadequate capital; they have very little machinery and other equipment to work with. Much of the equipment used in the underdeveloped world is simple and out of date.

A Texas farmer, for example, has on the average 1.1 tractors, 0.2 combines, 0.07 hay balers, 0.05 corn pickers, 0.8 tricks, and 0.9 automobiles. His home is equipped with 0.6 telephones and 0.6 food freezers. He applies to the soil about 3 tons of commercial fertilizers a year. The Soviet farmer has, on the average, 0.4 tractors, 0.2 grain combines, and 0.03 motor trucks. He applies to the land 0.1 tons of commercial fertilizer a year. An Average farmer in Communist China has 0.001 tractors, 0.0001 combines, and uses 0.005 tons of commercial economy, production in the underdeveloped countries is highly labor-intensive and physically demanding.[36]

Table 8.13 shows the consumption of chemical fertilizers in a selected number of countries in Africa and Europe. The Table shows how far behind Africa is to Europe and North America in consumption of chemical fertilizers.

Almost every underdeveloped country suffers from the lack of adequate equipment in industry and transportation. (Ref. Table 8.14) One notices the relatively high number of passenger automobiles in such countries as Morocco, Kenya, and Nigeria. Though small in comparison with the number of passenger automobiles one finds in the developed coun-

TABLE 8.13

Consumption of Chemical Fertilizer, 1975/76

Country	Phosphate	Nitrogenous	Potash
(Thousand metric Tons)			
AFRICA			
Nigeria	16.1	30.2	6.0
Kenya	21.3	20.5	2.7
Egypt	83.0	415.0	3.2
Sudan	0.1	95.0	-
Uganda	3.3	1.4	0.5
Swaziland	1.5	5.5	2.4
Ghana	8.9	14.2	4.6
Zambia	24.7	41.3	12.0
Morocco	64.5	63.2	35.3
Mali	0.4	1.6	
Zaire	0.6	2.6	1.9
Ethiopia	20.0	13.1	-
Chad	5.6	2.2	1.3
Malawi	0.6	9.0	1.5
WESTERN EUROPE AND NORTH AMERICA			
Italy	489.6	724.3	275.6
Spain	422.2	763.2	257.5
Canada	526.0	562.0	215.0
Belgium-Luxembourg	133.5	182.0	148.5
U.S.	4731.2	9384.7	4724.2
U.K.	391.0	1045.0	399.0
West Germany	779.7	1228.1	1099.0
Portugal	73.7	141.0	30.0
France	1618.3	1707.8	1314.0

Source: Compiled from Tables 174, 175, and 176 of *U.N. Statistical Year Book, 1976.*

234

TABLE 8.14
Capital Endowment, 1976

Country	1 Electric Energy (Installed Capacity) Thous. Kw.	2 Kilometres Railways (Millions) Passengers	3 Kilometres Railways (Millions) Net Tom	4 Motor vehicles (Passenger) Thousand Units	5 Commercial vehicles Thousand Units	6 Merchant Ships Thousand GRT* (1977)
France	50,266	51,168	68,508	15,900.0	2,410.0	11,614
West Germany	81,631	36,451	59,219	18,919.7	1,353.9	9,592
Portugal	3,588	5,235	854	1,034.0	288.0	1,281
Italy	44,831	39,118	16,376	15,925.3	1,682.0	11,111
Spain	26,591	16,686	9,842	5,351.4	1,091.6	7,186
Belgium	10,942	8,191	6,637	2,738.0	293.6	1,595
Canada	65,566	3,090	195,642	8,870.3 (1975)	2,157.8 (1975)	2,823
U.S.	550,369	15,688	1,146,492	109,003.0	26,152.0	15,300
U. K.	78,597	.....	20,400	14,235.8	1,855.9	31,646
Zaire	1,217	447 (1973)	3,017 (1973)	84.8 (1974)	76.4 (1974)	110
Zambia	1,261	.....	.....	85.8 (1974)	62.0 (1974)	.....
Mali	39	121	148	11.1 (1974)	7.0 (1974)	.....
Morocco	980	828	3143	347.4	145.7	270
Liberia	300	.....	.....	12.1 (1974)	10.0 (1975)	983
Chad	23	.....	.....	5.8 (1973)	6.3 (1973)	.....
Kenya	284	.....	.....	98.3 (1975)	69.2 (1975)	.....
Sudan	210	.....	2,288 (1973)	29.2 (1972)	21.2 (1972)	43
Nigeria	960	785 (1974)	972 (1974)	150.0 (1973)	82.0 (1973)	336
Ethiopia	320	132	260	52.5	13.1	.....
Uganda	163	.....	.....	27.0 (1974)	8.9 (1974)	.....
Ghana	900	431 (1972)	305 (1972)	64.0	46.0	183

* Gross Registered Tons.
Source: Compiled from U.N. *Statistical Year Book*, 1977, Tables 143, 157, 159 and 160.

tries, it warrants mention in view of the retarded state of highways in the underdeveloped countries. It would not be wrong to assume that these represent town passenger traffic by a small portion of the population (including government officials) given to at least some appearance of what sociologists call conspicuous consumption.

Table 8.15 shows an annual rate of population increase for 1970-1975. It is clear that here again the underdeveloped countries contrast sharply with the developed world. Latin America has an average increase rate of 2.7 percent to lead the underdeveloped continents while Africa and Asia score 2.6 percent and 2.1 percent respectively. What Table 8.15 shows us is that from the standpoint of sheer numbers, the underdeveloped countries are expanding faster than those which are economically advanced. What is apparent in the Table is that in some countries the rate of population growth exceeds by a substantial margin the rate of growth in GNP. In other words, any gains in material welfare stemming from growth is bound to be wiped out by population increases which are faster than total output.

What we have discussed in this chapter together form the symptoms of what economists refer to as the "low level equilibrium trap" or the "vicious circle of poverty." The sermon always given to the underdeveloped societies is that they must accumulate capital if they must get out of the morass and stagnation of underdevelopment. Capital formation depends on the willingness and ability of the people to save resources from present income. But the fact of the matter is that there is little capital, productivity is low and as a consequence real income is equally low. Since real income is low the capacity to save must be small, and this in turn means little accumulation of capital. On the demand side, capital formation is a function of the inducement to invest, but this may fall below in view of the small purchasing power of the people. "Small purchasing power is due to the people's real income, which is due to low productivity which is the result of too little capital, which in turn, is due to the small inducement to invest."[37] In order for the underdeveloped world to break out of the low level equilibrium trap, they are asked to: (1) adopt appropriate growth mentality, that is, a willingness and determination to break the circle of poverty; (2) there must be a method or strategy which would translate the growth impulses into economically sound action; and (3) there must be an organization or the institutional arrangements of which enhance rather than hinder such action. These three things are often reduced to the problem of motivation, method, and system.[38] But as has been apparent in previous chapters, Africa's underdevelopment is not the result of lack of motivation, the problem of method or system. The primary answer lies in the reordering of the international economic system so that Third World countries can get out of the role which has been theirs for several centuries, the role which has enriched the now developed countries while dialectically impoverishing the underdeveloped ones.

By way of recapitulation, the greater part of the world and over two-thirds of the globe's people are languishing under the grips of abject penury. In most of these countries their GNP is quite small and its distribution is lopsided both as regards the sectors of origin and those of final use. In Third World countries about 90 percent of the population is engaged in agriculture. Needless to say this agriculture is primitive, capital-deficient, and highly labour-intensive. There would be nothing wrong here since this takes care of the superfluity of labour. But the problem lies in that people are underemployed and because the farms in the villages almost always lack social amenities, the tendency is for the young school leavers to flee the farms and cause overpopulation in the towns and cities. A further consequence is that relatively old people are left to toil on the farms.

Furthermore in the underdeveloped world less than 5 percent of the GNP is saved, and investments tend to be

TABLE 8.15
Annual Rate of Population Increase, 1970-75
(percent), Surface Area and Population Density 1975
(per sq. kilometer of surface area)

Macro Regions and Regions	Population Increase Rate (%)		Surface Area	Density
	1965-75	1970-75	1975	1975
WORLD	1.9	1.9	135,830	29
AFRICA	2.7	2.6	30,319	13
West Africa	2.5	2.6	6,142	19
Eastern Africa	2.7	2.7	6,338	18
Northern Africa	2.8	2.7	8,525	11
Middle Africa	2.4	2.3	6,613	7
Southern Africa	2.9	2.7	2,701	10
AMERICA	2.0	2.0	42,082	13
Northern America	1.0	0.9	21,515	11
Latin America	2.7	2.7	20,566	16
Tropical South America	3.0	2.9	14,106	13
Middle America	3.2	3.2	2,496	32
Temperate South America	1.5	1.4	3,726	10
Caribbean	1.9	1.9	238	113
ASIA	2.1	2.1	27,580	82
East Asia	1.6	1.7	11,756	86
China	1.7	1.7	9,597	87
Japan	1.2	1.3	372	298
Other East Asia	2.2	2.2	1,786	31
South Asia	2.6	2.5	15,825	79
Middle South Asia	2.5	2.4	6,785	123
Eastern South Asia	2.7	2.7	4,498	72
Western South Asia	2.8	2.8	4,542	19
EUROPE	0.6	0.6	4,937	96
Western Europe	0.7	0.6	995	154
Southern Europe	0.7	0.7	1,315	100
Eastern Europe	0.6	0.6	990	107
Northern Europe	0.4	0.4	1,636	50
OCEANIA	2.0	2.0	8,510	3
Australia and New Zealand	1.9	1.8	7,956	2
Melansia	2.4	2.4	524	6
Polynesia and Micronesia	2.6	2.6	30	43
USSR	1.0	1.0	22,402	11

Source: Compiled from *U.N. Statistical Year Book, 1976*, p. 8.

dissipated in acquisitions of land and real estate. The inducement to save tends to be low whereas the inducement to repatriate whatever capital may be available tends to be high. Not less than 8% of the people in the underdeveloped world are illiterate and subject to endemic disease resulting from malnutrition and neglect or nonexistence or paucity of public health services. Mortality rates are quite high and life expectancy rates low, very low in some countries. In the 1970's there are still countries with per capita income of well below $100. Not very much has been done to explore natural resources or to provide the people with social overheads, such as roads and railroads. Instead they embark on prestige projects such as gigantic airports. Technical skills have not been well developed. The national bourgeoisie remain phantom bourgeoisie, lacking in capital to be able to behave like their counterparts in Europe. The result is that whatever industry there is tends to be owned and operated by foreigners.

Thus, decisions affecting vital national interests are made in New York, London, Paris and Bonn, headquarters of most of the world's global giants. Monoculture and great dependence on the export of a single crop or mineral are perennial. This sort of dependence and imperialist manipulations contribute to instability and great impediment to sustained growth.

As a way of escape from this despicable condition, the underdeveloped world must be able to accumulate capital. They must be able to generate domestic savings from their meagre incomes and invest those savings in growth-producing projects. But the unfortunate thing is that saving and investment are prohibitively difficult under conditions of material penury because of the low marginal propensity to save and similar low inducement to invest. As already stated above, for the underdeveloped world to break out of its low equilibrium trap, the international economic order must be reordered. This forms the subject of our concluding chapter.

REFERENCES

[1] Charles H. Anderson, *The Sociology of Survival* (Homewood, Ill.: The Dorsey Press, 1976), p. 253.
[2] Christopher Tugedhat, *The Multinationals* (London: Eyre and Spottiswoode, 1971), p. 95. Also cited by *ibid.*
[3] Anderson, *The Sociology of Survival*, p. 255.
[4] *Ibid.*, p. 254.
[5] Marx F. Millikan and Donald L. M. Blackmer, eds., *The Emerging Nations; Their Growth and United States Policy* (Boston: Little, Brown and Company, 1961).
[6] *Ibid.*
[7] P. N. Rosentein-Rodan, "International Aid for Underdeveloped Countries," *Review of Economics and Statistics,* Vol. XLIII (1961), pp. 107-133.
[8] Elton Atwater, Kent Forster, and Jan Prybyla, *World Tensions: Conflict and Accommodation* (New York: Appleton-Century-Crofts, 1967), p. 193.
[9] Anderson, *The Sociology of Survival*, pp. 34-35.
[10] Quoted by *ibid.*
[11] *Ibid.*
[12] Bill Warren, "Imperialism and Capitalist Industrialization," *New Left Review*, Vol. 81 (September-October, 1973), pp. 3644.
[13] Marcio Moreira Alves, "The Political Economy of the Brazilian Technocracy," *Berkeley Journal of Sociology*, Vol. 9 (1974-75), p. 113.
[14] Anderson, *The Sociology of Survival*, p. 257.
[15] Alves, "The Political Economy," p. 118.
[16] Anderson, *The Sociology of Survival*, pp. 35-36.
[17] *Ibid.*, p. 35.
[18] *Ibid.*, p. 36.
[19] Quoted by *ibid.*
[20] *Ibid.*, p. 36.
[21] *Ibid.*
[22] Andre Gunder Frank, cited by *ibid.*
[23] Alves, "The Political Economy," p. 123.
[24] Atwater, Forster, and Prybyla, *World Tension*, pp. 193-94.
[25] Marchetti and Marks, *The CIA and the Cult of Intelligence*, p. 53.
[26] Green and Seidman, *Unity or Poverty?*, p. 45.
[27] *Ibid.*
[28] *Ibid.*, p. 47.
[29] *Ibid.*, p. 49.
[30] *Ibid.*
[31] *Ibid.*
[32] *Ibid.*, p. 50.
[33] *Ibid.*
[34] *War on Hunger* (August, 1975).
[35] Atwater, Forster, and Prybyla, *World Tensions*, p. 199.
[36] *Ibid.*, p. 202.
[37] *Ibid.*, p. 209.
[38] *Ibid.*, p. 210.

9

TOWARD A NEW INTERNATIONAL ECONOMIC ORDER

It has been our contention that the modernisation theories of development propounded by bourgeois social scientists headquartered in the U.S. and Western Europe do not explain African underdevelopment. The rapid spread of new production methods from a few centres radiating technological innovations resulted in a process tending to create a world-wide economic system. It follows that underdevelopment is a consequence of the technical processes and the international division of labour commanded by the few societies that espoused the Industrial Revolution of the 19th century. The emergent relations between these societies and the underdeveloped world involve forms of dependence that can hardly be overcome.

> The dependence was initially based on an international division of labour in which the dominant centers reserved for themselves the economic activities that concentrated technological progress. In the following phase, the dependence was maintained by controlling the assimilation of new technological processes through the installation of productive activities within the dependent economies all under the control of groups, integrated into the dominant economies.[1]

Thus it is inferred that underdevelopment cannot be studied as a "phase" of the development process since such a "phase" would not have arisen if certain factors had come into play simultaneously. From our analysis it is quite clear that we consider the underdeveloped economies as contemporaries of and in one way or another dependent on their developed counterparts. Thus, development and underdevelopment should be viewed as two aspects of the same historical process involving the creation and the spread of contemporary technology. The underdeveloped societies remain so today because they were forcefully brought into the international economic system at a very immature stage, and also because the dominant-dominated relationship continues.

In his marathon speech at the seventh special Economic Session of the U.N. General Assembly in September, 1975, U.S. Secretary of State Henry Kissinger said, "Exports of primary products — raw materials and other commodities — are crucial to the incomes of developing countries. These earnings can lift living standards above bare subsistence; generate profits to support the first steps of industrialisation; and provide tax revenues for education, health, and other social programs for development."[2] In other words, the honourable Secretary wants the underdeveloped countries to continue with their international role in the global economic system, namely, the production of raw materials for exports.

Constraints of Primary Producer Countries

Underdeveloped primary-producer countries operate under constraints that are colossal and defeating in nature; even when productivity has increased rather dramatically the situation has not changed in any appreciable way. The so called "scissors" phenomenon continues to be a detriment to the underdeveloped countries that rely heavily on the production of raw materials. They have increased production of these raw materials while their earnings from these increased exports have been decimated by falls in world prices. That of Ghana is a case in point.

In his *Neo-colonialism*, Nkrumah complained about the falling earnings of cocoa despite the doubling of production. Nkrumah, like any progressive leader anywhere in the Third World, had incurred the emnity of the U.S. and its NATO allies. So when they finally succeeded in removing him from office they naturally had to embark on malicious propaganda to justify his overthrow. They talked and wrote about "the shortcomings and extravagencies of investment-policy, particularly the dissipation of sterling reserves, accumulated from cocoa sales, on irrational schemes, on 'prestige projects' and simply into private pockets."[3]

Nothing was ever said about the intrigues of the U.S. aid programmes and of U.S. corporations, as detailed by Green and Seidman in their *Unity or Poverty*[4] let alone mentioning the fact that under Nkrumah production of cocoa had doubled and that the reward for this doubling of production was a decline in the price paid for cocoa on the world market. Table 9.1 tells the story.

> Farm-income can often be cushioned against fluctuations for a short time, but not on this scale over such a long period. More commonly, swings in world prices are felt very directly and immediately by the peasant producer, who never knows what he is to expect. What happens on the New York and other commodity exchanges is directly experienced by plantation-workers and by every small farmer involved in the money economy in remote African and Asian villages. World economic fluctuations of this kind thus directly touch the lives of millions who have been hoping for, even expecting, improvement in their lives. The peasant who has doubled his acreage finds himself where he started. Running in order to keep in the same spot may be funny in *Alice in Wonderland*, but not when it means foregoing the food, shirts, education, paraffin lamps, and bicycles one has looked forward to. Then it is likely to produce blind protest, despair, bafflement, or even, eventually, revolution.[5]

TABLE 9.1

Ghana Cocoa Bean Production and Income, 1956-65

Year		Spot Price of Cocoa Beans in U.S. cents/1b.	Ghana's Production in metric tons	Adjusted Revenue in U.S. $
1956		27.3		
1957		30.6		
1958		44.3	209,000	$204,471,080
1959		36.6	259,500	
1960		28.4	321,900	
1961		22.6	439,000	
1962		21.0	416,000	
1963		25.3	428,400	
1964		23.4	427,700	$220,157,960
1965	Feb.	20.6		
	June	13.8		
	Aug.	14.0		

Source: Cocoa Statistics, January 1, 1966, a publication of the U.N. Food and Agriculture Organization.

The deterioration of prices of raw materials, in the face of rising costs of finished products from the industrial societies is not a question of business cycle. It is a matter of progressive, secular deterioration. Fluctuation has serious repercussions on long-term planning. Large projects are stopped and started with "serious waste of resources and dislocation of organisation, since inter-related parts and phases of large-scale plans each depend upon the other."[6]

This situation has been blamed on the inelasticity of world demand. In other words, cocoa production has been increasing while world demand does not expand. The result is that the importing countries determine how much they pay for these raw materials. These very raw materials are processed in the industrialised countries and are then shipped back for sale at exorbitant prices to the underdeveloped countries. The fall in world coffee prices resulted in the fall in the standard of living of the Brazilians, and culminated in a political disorder and military take-over. Tanzania suffered severely when the world price of sisal fell sharply. In addition, the industrial nations have come up with a new chemical substitute. Sudan which depends on the export of cotton for a significant portion of its GNP has to compete with the man-made fibres.

The purpose of this discussion is to bring about an international action to alter the relationship between prices for primary products and prices for manufactured goods. Despite the cry for a new international economic order by the underdeveloped countries and the platitudes and rhetorics by the rich and powerful nations, nothing has really changed and is not likely to change in the foreseeable future. The Soviet Union has always contended that the responsibility for correcting the imbalance lies with the U.S. and its Western allies.[7]

Despite the much discussed closing of the gap between the rich and poor countries, nothing practical is being done to achieve this goal. Asymmetrical terms of trade, and the divisions within Africa and the Third World countries have further enhanced their exploitation by the rich and powerful countries. The NATO is united not to fight the Soviet Union and its allies but to facilitate the domination and exploitation of the underdeveloped countries.

There was a time when poor countries hoped that foreign aid would help solve their problems. Their hopes were utopian. The amount of aid however was not as massive as during the Marshall Plan aimed at the economic recovery of Western Germany after the Second World War.

> Never very remarkable, the volume of aid has stayed at a rather uninspired level for several years. Nothing is more full of pitfalls for the statistics commonly fail to distinguish the aid component proper from general capital flow; do not always separate private investment from governmental grants and loans; and achieve the astounding vanishing trick by which military aid is made to disappear, or is re-titled 'support.' Nor, if we do distinguish, say a food program as 'non-military' aid does this epithet mean very much when that food is going to South Viet Nam?[8]

Aid, as we have noted in an earlier chapter, goes mostly to those countries that comply with the politico-military and economic strategies of the rich countries. Aid, in the U.S. context, is tied to a country's vote at the U.N. Those countries that vote along with the U.S. in the U.N. are rewarded with aid. In black Africa, Zaire, Kenya and Ivory Coast are among the most favoured countries. Both the U.S. and the Soviet Union are guided primarily by considerations of world-power in their aid policies. So in the final analysis, we are back where we started: the problem of underdevelopment is not about to be solved, because the rich countries have a great interest in the status quo.

Disunity Among Third-World Countries

A change in the status quo will come about only when the underdeveloped countries come together to take a common stand against their exploiters. But as of now the underdeveloped countries are balkanized and the divide and rule policy of the rich and powerful nations is very successful. This situation further complicates the problems encountered by the underdeveloped countries in overcoming their micronational limitations, creating regional groups, replacing the built-in orientations of trade towards single metropolitan centres, overcoming the entrenched interests of the bourgeois leaders, and the different ideological orientations of the leaderships of neighbouring states. These are a tremendous set of tasks. All these problems make it virtually impossible to coordinate progressive and rational economic policies. In West Africa, for example, economic cooperation between the Francophone territories and their Anglophone neighbours has been very difficult to achieve. It is too soon to speculate on the success of the Economic Community of West African States (ECOWAS). Rather than organise their own economic unions Africans prefer to be tied to the apron strings of the developed countries by way of subordinate association.

> The situation in East Africa is not at all encouraging. Existing channels of economic and infrastructural coordination and communication have broken down in the face of new competitions and conflict between a Kenyan policy oriented towards private investment from the "West" and a Tanzanian policy aiming at her own variant of socialism open both to the traditional "Western" connection and Eastern Europe and China. New banks and currency, new customs barriers, and competing investment in the same fields (such as the cotton industry) signify not so much the failure to move towards federation, but the dismantling of what little serious institutionalized cooperation exists.[9]

The idea of a continental economic common market in Africa is a remote idea because no regional common market has yet been successful. And yet such a continental market could presumably deal more effectively with the European Economic Common Market than individual Africans states. But a word of caution. The Economic Commission for Africa has divided Africa into four zones: West Africa, East Africa, North Africa and Central Africa. The industrially advanced countries have always welcomed the idea of

247

economic groups in the underdeveloped countries. The reason is that a common market in an underdeveloped region starts off with the notion that the greatest obstacle to development is lack of capital. It then tries to expand the market in order to attract foreign capital. The tendency among common market participants is to compromise their differing political and ideological principles in order to accommodate one another. Thus, they are likely to be less radical or progressive in order to attract foreign capital. "The moderating instability will not often be enough to rock the boat. In some ways, in fact, the West views a common market in Africa as an insurance against communism and exportation."[10]

Although an African economic market is a desirable adventure, one must be aware of the possibility of its serving the interests of our economic and political enemies instead of ours. This situation would be greatly enhanced by the existence of the Mobutus and Houphouet-Boignys. Even if there were no willing collaborators the NATO allies would bribe their way through or use some kind of force to break their unity. One needs to recall that the U.S. even threatened to use its military might to take over the oil fields of the oil producing countries if the U.S. considered itself threatened. The U.S. threatened "denial to the principal OPEC gougers, notably Iran and Saudi Arabia, of the American weaponry technology, training and other goods and services that they want and gladly pay high prices for."[11] Secretary of the Treasury, William Simon applied "a hard-nosed policy" against OPEC countries. Excepting only projects that had been in the works a long time, "with guarantees of U.S. financing," Simon required "the Export-Import Bank, over which the Treasury has policy control, to deny new loans and underwriting to OPEC governments and to prospective American suppliers of those governments." Simon also successfully "advocated a similar policy of denial at the World Bank and such regional institutions as the Inter-American and Asian Development Banks. This approach pleases fellow toughies in the government..."[12] Today OPEC is "more divided than the Athenians," to quote Machiavelli. This needs a little elaboration.

Since the formation of OPEC and especially since the 1973-74 Arab oil embargo, the U.S. had sought to balkanize it. Their efforts were excessive in trying to curtail the control of power and shift in world wealth to the oil-producing countries. The formation of the International Energy Agency by the U.S. and its allies offered them a forum to discuss and plan strategies concerning how to break the unity of the OPEC countries. Not only this, the U.S. and its allies have been able to persuade some Third World countries not to join OPEC. In addition to the existence of these non-OPEC oil exporting countries — Brazil, Mexico, Zaire, Trinidad and Tobago, Angola, Bahrein, Bolivia, Brunel, Congo, Egypt, Malaysia, Oman, Syria and Tunisia — plus the availability of the Alaskan and North Sea oil, the Saudis have been able to persuade Iran, Kuwait and the United Arab Emirate to adopt their often antagonistic position toward the organization. All these have not been helpful to OPEC. What we see here is the most powerful nation on earth using its influence to create schisms in the organisation and the greatest beneficiaries are the multinationals that actually exploit the oil fields profits.

One would have expected that the poverty of the underdeveloped countries would bring them solidly together to seek ways and means to ameliorate their condition. But the fact so far is that "apart from declaratory statements at UNCTAD and in other organs of the U.N., the actual tendency amongst Third World states has been towards bilateral bargains with whatever developed countries were prepared to conclude them."[13] The implication from international activities is that the economic gap between the rich and the poor countries will be narrowed or obliterated by political action by the Western countries. This is errant nonsense because only the boldest sacrifice on the part of the underdeveloped world could bring about any uniform change in their living standards, and nothing can be done that is not "difficult, prolonged, and chancy."

Closing the Gap between the Rich and Poor

It seems clear that, other things being equal, a per capita GNP ratio of 4,760:60 can become an important international source of tensions. This was actually an issue as the former colonies of Western Europe were emerging out of the shackles of colonial imperialism as independent nations. Thus, in 1964 the UNCTAD was founded as a forum to enable the poor countries to assert their rights before the developed governments. As Calvez has noted, "the dignity of the world's poor could never be secured without concessions from the rich — on trade arrangements, commodity agreements, technical cooperations, etc."[14] The formation of UNCTAD represented a significant shift in the consciousness of the international community.

In both the 1964 and 1968 sessions the rich nations agreed to make some concessions. The real debate that went on in Santiago, Chile, in 1972, was the power of the underdeveloped countries to determine their fate relative to the controlling interests of the rich and powerful countries of the world. As pointed out earlier the rich nations became very evasive and defensive to the demands of the poor countries.

Rather than consider the UNCTAD as a decision-making body, the industrialised nations consider it to be a forum for an exchange of opinions and intent on matters of rich-poor relations. The rich nations often prefer to discuss policy matters on forums which they control. The poor nations pressed hard at the 1972 UNCTAD meeting to upgrade the status of the body in order to get it to take up certain policy-making functions, and to also reform certain international institutions, e.g. IMF.

One of the resolutions taken at UNCTAD 3 was the enlargement of the governing committee to include underdeveloped countries. This resolution has been partially implemented. The UNCTAD 3 representatives also agreed on a code of 13 principles to govern international trade relations and trade policies conducive to development. Some of these principles included the recognition of the sovereign right of every nation to freely dispose of its natural resources in the interest of economic development and the well-being of its inhabitants, as well as reaffirmation of the desirability to extend trade concessions to the underdeveloped countries.

The conference also adopted a resolution specifying measures to be employed internationally for the benefit of the "least developed" among the underdeveloped nations. The conference also put together a list of 25 countries identified as "hard core" least developed among the underdeveloped countries. Matters of controls on restrictive business practices in the developing world to regional integration to commodity agreements to a Generalised System of Preferences were among those discussed and eventually referred to the UNCTAD Secretariat for further exploration. Issues such as terms of developing financing, debt service, foreign private investment and the transfer of technology were also discussed.

Prior to the UNCTAD conference in Nairobi, Kenya, in 1976, there was a U.N. Seventh Special Economic Session of the General Assembly in September, 1975. As usual, various resolutions were passed. These included measures concerning international trade, transfer of resources for development and monetary reform, science and technology, industrialisation, food and agriculture, cooperation among underdeveloped countries and restructuring of economical and social sectors of the U.N. system.

251

In 1976, the fourth UNCTAD meeting was held in Kenya and various resolutions were taken. Earlier in March, 1975, President Gerald R. Ford speaking at the University of Notre Dame, had said, "People throughout America realize that no structure of world peace can endure unless the poverty question is answered. There is no safety for any nation in a hungry, ill-educated and desperate world."[15] Two months later, Secretary of State Henry Kissinger, speaking at Kansas City International Relations Council, said:

> We export 23 percent of our farm output and 8 percent of our manufactures. We import far more raw materials than we export; oil from abroad is critical to our welfare. American enterprise overseas constitutes an economy the size of Japan's. America's prosperity could not continue in a chaotic world economy...
>
> A serious concern must be the needs of the poorest... Their fate affects us morally as well as materially. Their prosperity would contribute to ours. And their participation in the global economy is required so that all nations, and not only the richest, have the stake in the world which we are building...
>
> If we respond to the challenge with the visition and determination that the world has come to expect from America, our children will look upon this period as the beginning of America's greatest triumphs.[16]

Interestingly enough, these statements were made for the consumption of the Congress. The purpose was to get that body to agree to a 3/100th percent increase of aid over that of 1974. The State Department then listed some facts about American economy. (1) Almost 40 per cent come from the underdeveloped societies. (2) Nearly 33 percent of U.S. exports go to the underdeveloped world. These markets help create jobs for American workers. (3) Twenty-five percent of U.S. investment in 1973 went into underdevelopment countries. (4) The poor countries need American skills and

capital resources to feed their people; develop their resources and assure their people an equitable participation in
the benefits of growth; exploit their natural resources in en-
vironmentally sound ways; and strengthen their cooperation
in building a peaceful, stable world community.[17]

These statements, like UNCTAD resolutions, are lofty
ideals, non-binding resolutions, which cannot be considered
authentic progress until policy implementation results. The
UNCTAD is a mere advisory body and the implication here
is that matters of the economic and therefore political independence of the underdeveloped countries will continue to
be determined by benevolence of the world's rich and powerful nations alone.

Table 9.2 shows the performance of the 17 Develop-

TABLE 9.2

Comparative Aid Performance:
Official Development Assistance as
Percent of GNP (1975)

Donor Country	Percent of GNP
Sweden	.82
Netherlands	.75
Norway	.66
France	.63
Australia	.61
Belgium	.59
Denmark	.58
Canada	.57
New Zealand	.52
Germany	.40
U.K.	.38
U.S.	.27
Japan	.24
Switzerland	.19
Finland	.18
Austria	.17
Italy	.11

Average: All DAC donor countries = .36%
Source: *War on Hunger,* September, 1975.

ment Assistance Committee (DAC) members. Aid provided by the 17 DAC countries rose from $ 11.3 billion in 1974 to $13.6 billion in 1975. The proportion of GNP of all 17 countries designated for aid rose from .33 percent in 1974 to .36 percent in 1975. This is still less than the .42 percent recorded in 1965-67. But the 1975 figure remains well below the DAC target of .7 percent.

The U.S. total of slightly more than $4 billion was the highest since 1965, representing .27 percent of the U.S. GNP, an increase of 3/100th percent over the 1974 figure. In 1965-67 the aid GNP ratio was .45 percent. It hit its lowest point in 1973 with a .23 percent figure. The U.S. ranked 12th in aid/GNP ratio in 1975 among the 17 nations, up one notch from 1974. Sweden as Table 9.2 shows, led with .82 percent, and the Netherlands followed with .75 percent. They were the only countries to exceed the .7 percent DAC target.

The DAC is sometimes referred to as "the conscience of the rich nations" and is an arm of the organisation for Economic Cooperation and Development (OECD). It acts as a catalyst for foreign aid initiatives and a forum where development programmes could be analysed. Besides the 17 nations listed in Table 9.2, the Commission of the European Economic Communities (EEC) is a member. The World Bank and IMF are both observers. The DAC defines official "aid" or "assistance" as "government grants or concessional loans that are development motivated and have a grant element of 25 percent or more. Technical cooperation also is included. The official Development Assistance furnished by the United States includes AID loans and grants, Food for Peace sales and donations, and Peace Corps programs."[18]

In addition to official Development Assistance, grants from private sources and non-concessional flows from all DAC nations rose during the year by 39 percent. The total flow of $38.8 billion in 1975 was 1.02 percent of the DAC members' combined GNP, compared to .81 percent in 1974.

This was the first time that the GNP target of 1 percent for total flows had been reached. But these funds are hopelessly insufficient for the demands of the poor countries. The U.S. which always makes the most flamboyant speech in UN-CTAD conferences and to which other nations look up for leadership does not seem to be doing very much. It thus goes a long way to confirm what Henry Kissinger had said during the Seventh Special Session of the U.N. General Assembly, September 1, 1975, namely that "developing countries themselves will have to provide most of the effort..."

Nationalisation/Indigenisation

One of the fundamental ways that the underdeveloped countries try to introduce a new international economic order is to endeavour to get the indigenes of those countries to determine their own economic fortune, by using equity ownership as a stepping stone into the board room where policies and programmes are discussed and determined, and into management where they are implemented. The method they adopt is indigenisation or nationalisation. Various countries in Africa such as Nigeria, Zaire, Ghana, Kenya, Mauritania, Sierra Leone, Senegal, Togo, Zambia, Tanzania, Uganda, Ethiopia, Somalia, Congo, Benin, Mali, Malagasy, and Guinea have either indigenised or nationalised. Because of our familiarity with Nigeria we use this as our case study. Furthermore, we shall touch briefly on Cuba.

Indigenisation: The Case of Nigeria

Foreign ownership has been common in the commerce and industry of almost all of the underdeveloped countries. In Africa, however, this has had complete dominance. This situation resulted from the fact that Africa was forced into the international economic system at a time when it was not ready. In the course of this master-slave relationship, the possibility for her generating locally-owned enterprises was very slim, in fact, non-existent since the colonial policy was to stifle any domestic economic initiative that stood in the way of the metropoles. In the early part of the twentieth century large foreign trading companies spread their tentacles all over the continent to buy raw materials and to sell consumer goods. Subsequently these trading companies and the European settlers (in the case of East Africa) established small manufacturing plants to process domestic products and make simple articles. At the same time various other foreigners — such as Indians, Syrians, Pakistanis and Lebanese — came into the continent to begin small trade and, occasionally, small manufacturing.

The large global giants in this century have become involved in establishing plantations, digging mines and, in recent times, drilling oil wells. They have also established plants to serve the African market. Foreign banks, insurance companies, public utilities, and service companies have been coming into the continent. These companies have not come to Africa because they love Africans or have any genuine interests in developing Africa. In fact they have a keen interest in African underdevelopment. They are here because African countries offer them excellent investment terms, which include cheap labour and agreement to allow them to export profits.

At the achievement of independence in the 1960s, "the economy of the typical black African state consisted of three levels: Europeans and Americans at the top holding the large industries, Asians in the middle doing much of the wholesale and retail trading, and Africans at the bottom continuing in farming, market-trading, and rudimentary services. Foreign domination of African economies, as already discussed, has contributed in no small measure to underdevelopment and growth without development. In an attempt to correct these anomalies African countries have resorted to nationalisation and indigenisation. Nationalisation refers to the taking over of foreign-owned companies by a government. It is a kind of social and economic reform for the betterment of the citizens. Indigenisation on the other hand refers to a situation in which a government restricts participation in particular industries to indigenes of the country thus forcing alien business owners to sell them. This usually affects small and medium-sized enterprises which Africans can handle.

Africanisation, on the other hand, involves replacing non-African employees with Africans. Every African government requires foreign industries to limit the employment of foreigners to those positions the duties of which cannot be performed by Africans. Needless to say foreign companies either ignore this or find some ways to circumvent the law in order to perpetuate their exploitation and underdevelopment. According to Habibu Sani:

> Those ... countries striving to free themselves from the sprawling hands of the super-powers, often embark on the promotion of their own indigenous enterprises — a policy measure popularly known as indigenisation by the citizens of the host country. Chile under Salvador Allende, Nigeria under military rule, Uganda under Field Marshall Idi Amin, Ghana under Nkrumah, Senegal under Leopold Senghor, Tanzania under Julius Nyerere, Cuba under Fidel Castro, Guinea under Sekou Toure, Cambodia under Prince Norodom Silhanouk, and Sri Lanka under Mrs. Bandaranaike, to mention only the most prominent ones, all had their own brands of nationalization and indigenisation policies aimed at wrenching the national economy from the hands of neocolonialist powers and their trading agents like the multinationals.
>
> There is one common denominator which relates to the experiences of these countries in their struggles

to be economically independent. They suffer from the deliberate manoeuvres which the multinationals and their imperialist matters place in their ways in order to sabotage their indigenisation policies.[20]

The following section discusses a few basic things about the Nigerian indigenisation programme and in the light of the above charge by Sani, it is possible to draw judgment on whether or not foreigners have tried to sabotage the programme.

As already discussed, political independence has refused to usher in economic independence. It has been impossible to undo in less than two decades what took several centuries to accomplish. The path out of underdevelopment which began about four centuries ago has been long and arduous and to many African countries, indigenisation seems to be the way out. Rood has argued that African countries have resorted to indigenization or nationalisation because of their lack of respect for international law. He writes:

> There was... an absence of legal inhibitions within the African cultures: the sanctity of contract, the law of the responsibility of states for their actions, and the whole system of international law which had grown up in the West were not a part of the African heritage. They have been thinly grafted onto the African system, and without much thought or consent by the local people. *Rather than holding these legal concepts sacred, as do Westerners,* Africans are more likely to regard them as the means by which the outsiders maintained injustice for centuries.[21] (Italics mine)

Not surprisingly, Rood is not able to overcome his *bias* (polite term for racism) which generally characterises white analysis of blacks the world over. It is ridiculous that Rood does not know that Westerners do not hold "legal concepts sacred" at least as far as peoples of colour are concerned.

Britain, U.S., West Germany, France and Belgium have been busting U.N. sanctions against Zimbabwe and South Africa. As far as international law is concerned the U.S. is the greatest outlaw, an international bandit. She pays lip service to international law and creates a monster, the CIA, and licenses it to move about like a rouge elephant committing all sorts of crimes against people whose only crime is refusal to be stooges or protégés of the U.S. — by adopting policies that are opposed to the business and political interests of the U.S. They jubilated over the overthrow of President Nkrumah and at the assassination of Lt. General Murtala Muhammed who not only initiated progressive policies in Nigeria but also was largely responsible for the defeat of U.S. policy in Angola. Even within the U.S., it is suprising that Rood is not aware of the CIA revelations which have to do with the violations of laws against innocent U.S. citizens.

Nationalisation and indigenisation far from being the result of lack of respect for the sanctity of law, have resulted from the genuine belief of the exploited peoples of the Third World that the way out of their present underdevelopment consists of their exerting a significant control in their economic lives. Unlike the now famous Byrd Amendment in which all racist Congressmen banded together to circumvent U.N. sanctions against Zimbabwe in order to help their fellow racists in that country, the Nigerian Enterprises Promotion Decree No. 4/1972 — otherwise known as the Indigenisation Decree — was initiated with the following aims:

(1) to create more opportunities for Nigerian indigenous businessmen;

(2) to maximise local retention of profits; and

(3) to raise the level of intermediate and capital goods production

In practical terms, the Decree aimed:

(1) to domesticate all profits in Schedule 1 and about
    40% of the profits accruing from Schedule II en-
    terprises;

(2) to use these profits to mobilise more resources
    thereby enhancing the GNP to the benefit of the
    country; and

(3) to divert foreign investment into areas requiring
    large capital and specialist skills.

Finally, the decree enabled the Federal Military Government to acquire 40% shares in major commercial banks
and also obtained majority interests in the major oil-producing companies.

The Decree categorized certain selected areas of the
economy into Schedule I while others were labeled Schedule
II. Those in Schedule I were to be taken over by Nigerians
from April 1, 1974, while for Schedule II enterprises, it was
mandatory to have, by the effective date of the Decree, a
paid-up capital of over ₦400,000 or an annual turn-over of
1 million with 40% equity participation by Nigerian citizens
or associates.

As contained in the Federal *Gazette*, 1972 (Supplement)
"... as from the appointed day, no person, other than a
Nigerian citizen or association, shall be the owner or part
owner of any such enterprise in Nigeria; and ... no alien
enterprise on or after the date of commencement of this
Decree shall be established in Nigeria." Schedule I was designed to give protection to existing indigenous businesses in
areas where there had been intensive local investment, and
to also offer them additional opportunities in areas which
were up till then dominated by foreigners. Such areas included advertising agencies and public relations business,
blending and bottling of alcoholic drinks, blocks, bricks and
ordinary tiles manufacture for building and construction
works, bread and cake making, candle manufacture, casinos
and gaming centres, cinemas and other places of entertain-

ment, hairdressing, manufacture of jewellery and related articles, newspaper publishing and printing, municipal bus services, taxis, radio and television broadcasting, rice milling, singlet manufacture, and tyre retreading.

Schedule II was designed to enable Nigerians to acquire equity participation in service industries and commercial companies and industrial ventures such as beer brewing, boat building, bicycle and motor-cycle type manufacture, bottling soft drinks, coastal and inland waterways shipping, construction industries, cosmetic and perfumery manufacture, departmental stores and supermarkets, estate agency, furniture making, manufacture of bicycles, manufacture of cement, manufacture of matches, manufacture of metal containers, paper conversion industries, poultry farming, printing of books, shipping, travel agencies, wholesale distribution. All these constituted what is known as indigenisation Phase I.

Indigenisation Phase II was put into effect on April 1, 1977. In Phase II enterprises were categorized into three instead of two. Schedule I remained as in phase I but the new Schedule II involved industries and activities which must have a minimum Nigerian equity participation of 60%. Schedule III with 40% Nigerian participation consisted of enterprises in which Nigerians are sufficiently experienced to have controlling interest. The "policy of indigenisation." as stated by Dr. Adebayo Adeji, former Federal Commissioner for Economic Development and Reconstruction, "would optimise interests of foreign investors as well as those of the government and people of Nigeria ... our policy of indigenisation simply means local participation through negotiation and the payment of equitable prices for the equity shares of those foreign businesses covered by that policy."[22] Foreign investors were given a three-year period during which they were to effect orderly transfer of their business to Nigerians willing and able to buy them. And to ensure equity in such transactions the FMG set up a national enterprise promotion board as an overseer.

The FMG foresaw two problems: (1) money to buy over alien businesses, and (2) lack of managerial skill and know how among the Nigerian businessmen. One of the solutions was establishing the Nigerian Enterprises Promotion Board and the Council for Management Education and Training. This Board has launched a country-wide scheme of management training for local businessmen. The government established a liberal lending programme to help domestic businessmen. It also established the small-scale credit scheme (SCCS) to give loans to small-scale industrialists in order to set up viable manufacturing, processing or service industries in the small-scale sector. It also established Industrial Development Centres (IDCs) to provide free consultative and extension services as well as managerial and skill training for staff of small-scale enterprises.

It is one thing to promulgate a decree but another to implement it. How successful has been the indigenisation programme? Officially the indigenisation has been a success.[23] But it may not be as succesful as might have been expected. We proceed to summarize the report of the annual survey of foreign private investment in Nigeria, 1974.[24]

Table 9.3 shows that the inflow of private investments in 1974 was ₦507.1 million — that is, 12.2% lower than that of the preceding year. This contrasts with outflow increase by 19.1 percent from the 1973 level to ₦458.8 million in 1974. The result was that the net inflow was just ₦48.3 million in 1974 as against ₦192.6 in 1973.

For companies of United Kingdom origin, their total capital inflow was ₦119.7 million, a decline of 55.0% 1973. Their capital declined by 15.3% to ₦147.8 million, so that for that period, they registered a net outflow of ₦28.1 million.

Companies of U.S. origin registered a 13.3% decrease in investment inflow which was ₦151,1 million in 1954. But their total outflow increased by 3.9% to ₦159 million, thus resulting in a net outflow of ₦7.9 million for the year. The

TABLE 9.3

*Flow of Foreign Private Capital by Country
or Region of Origin*
(millions of ₦)

Country/Region of Origin	Inflow* (1)	Outflow (2)	Net flow (inflow minus outflow) i.e. (1) minus (2)
United Kingdom			
1969	36.2	46.0	- 9.8
1970	94.6	47.2	+ 47.4
1971	207.2	59.6	+147.6
1972	236.0	58.3	+177.7
1973	265.8	174.6	+ 91.2
1974	119.7	147.8	- 28.1
United States of America			
1969	56.2	54.2	+ 2.0
1970	74.6	48.2	+ 26.4
1971	151.4	44.0	+107.4
1972	17.1	67.8	- 50.7
1973	174.3	153.0	+ 21.3
1974	151.1	159.0	- 7.9
Western Europe			
1969	39.4	14.8	+ 24.6
1970	58.0	28.4	+ 29.6
1971	92.6	56.4	+ 36.2
1972	150.9	44.9	+106.0
1973	91.7	43.5	+ 48.2
1974	172.6	128.0	+ 44.6
Others Unspecified			
1969	18.8	4.0	+ 14.8
1970	23.8	5.6	+ 18.2
1971	38.4	10.0	+ 28.4
1972	28.8	13.5	+ 15.3
1973	46.0	14.1	+ 31.9
1974	63.7	24.0	+ 39.7
TOTAL			
1969	150.6	119.0	+ 31.6
1970	251.0	129.4	+121.6
1971	489.6	170.0	+319.6
1972	432.8	184.5	+248.3
1973	577.8	385.2	+192.6
1974	507.1	458.8	+ 48.3

* Excludes undistributed profits of oil prospecting companies.
Source: Central Bank of Nigeria, *Economic and Financial Review* Vol. 15 (June, 1977), p. 30.

net inflow in 1973 was ₦21.3 million.

For companies of West European origin their levels of inflow and outflow increased tremendously. Their inflow increased by 88.2% from the level in 1973 to ₦172.6 million in 1974. Their outflow increased by 194.3% from 1973 level to reach ₦128 million in 1974. Thus, a net inflow of ₦44.6 million was registered in 1974 as against ₦48.2 million in 1973.

There was an increase in inflow and outflow of investment for companies owned by nationals of "other" unspecified countries. Their inflow and outflow increased by 38.5% and 70.2% from their respective levels in 1973 to ₦63.7 million, respectively in 1947. The result was an overall net inflow of ₦39.7 million in 1974.

Table 9.4 shows the components of net capital flow, analysed by region or country of origin. According to the report "The large overall net outflow of ₦39.3 million reflected the impact of the Nigerian Enterprises Promotion Decree which required indigenous participation of at least 40 percent in the equity capital of foreign-owned companies. The increased inflow to companies of 'other' unspecified countries indicated expansion of their investment activities, into new areas in that year."[25]

Table 9.5 shows data for commulative foreign private investment analysed by country or region of origin. The figure of ₦1,812.1 million in 1974 shows that foreign private investment was 2.7% higher than the level attained in 1973. The rise in foreign private investment was due mainly to "the rapid increase in the equity of foreign-owned companies. Equity capital including reserves accounted for 44.6 percent in 1974 compared with 43.1 per cent in 1973."[26]

Table 9.6 furnishes data on cumulative foreign private investment analysed by type of economic activities. Cumulative investment in the mining and quarrying sector totaled ₦818.1 million, a decrease of 11.6% in the level attained in 1973. The manufacturing and processing sector showed cum-

Components of Net Capital Flow by Origin
(₦ million)

Component	United Kingdom	United States	Western Europe (Excluding U.K.)	Others (Unspecified)	Total
Unremitted Profits*					
1969	+ 11.0	+ 2.0	+ 7.0	+ 5.0	+ 25.0
1970	+ 14.2	+ 6.6	+ 8.0	+ 8.8	+ 37.6
1971	+ 27.6	+ 9.2	+ 12.6	+ 10.2	+ 59.6
1972	+ 34.5	+ 6.6	+ 17.5	+ 9.6	+ 68.2
1973	+ 41.6	+ 9.5	+ 18.8	+ 13.6	+ 83.5
1974	+ 33.5	+ 10.0	+ 23.4	+ 19.0	+ 85.9
Changes in Foreign Share Capital (Net)					
1969	− 0.4	+ 1.4	+ 7.2	+ 5.8	+ 11.2
1970	+ 2.6	+ 0.6	+ 5.6	+ 6.2	+ 9.8
1971	+ 12.4	+ 5.2	+ 1.8	+ 9.0	+ 28.4
1972	+ 5.9	+ 4.4	+ 1.3	+ 4.7	+ 16.3
1973	+ 20.3	+ 4.0	+ 6.1	+ 6.3	+ 36.7
1974	− 43.1	+ 0.7	− 8.8	+ 11.9	− 39.3
Trade and Suppliers Credits (Net)					
1969	+ 9.2	+ 22.0	+ 15.4	+ 4.8	+ 51.4
1970	+ 16.0	+ 28.6	+ 12.6	+ 5.2	+ 62.4
1971	+ 25.6	+ 33.0	+ 7.4	+ 1.4	+ 67.4
1972	+ 15.9	+ 12.9	+ 22.0	+ 1.4	+ 26.4
1973	+ 99.2	+ 53.9	+ 24.9	+ 5.9	+ 183.9
1974	+ 18.5	− 29.9	+ 84.1	+ 8.9	+ 81.6
Other Foreign Liabilities (Net)					
1969	− 25.4	+ 29.0	− 4.4	+ 1.8	+ 1.0
1970	+ 26.2	+ 25.0	− 3.8	+ 1.0	+ 3.6
1971	− 25.2	+ 23.8	− 35.4	+ 7.8	− 29.0
1972	− 18.2	− 28.2	+ 2.7	+ 1.7	− 42.0
1973	+ 62.0	− 145.2	+ 1.8	+ 3.1	− 208.5
1974	+ 12.1	− 74.7	+ 3.2	+ 4.4	− 63.8
Liabilities to Head Office (Net)					
1969	− 4.2	− 49.6	− 0.6	− 2.6	− 57.0
1970	+ 6.4	+ 15.6	+ 7.2	− 1.0	+ 15.4
1971	+107.2	− 36.2	+ 49.8	...	+193.2
1972	+139.6	+ 20.6	+ 62.5	− 2.1	+179.4
1973	− 7.9	+ 99.1	+ 3.4	+ 9.2	+ 97.0
1974	+ 49.1	+ 85.9	− 57.3	+ 4.4	− 16.1
TOTAL					
1969	+ 9.8	− 2.0	+ 24.6	+ 14.8	+ 31.6
1970	+ 47.4	+ 26.4	+ 29.6	+ 18.2	+121.6
1971	+147.6	+107.4	+ 36.2	+ 28.4	+319.6
1972	+177.7	− 50.7	+106.0	+ 15.3	+248.3
1973	+ 91.2	+ 21.3	+ 48.2	+ 31.9	+192.6
1974	− 28.1	+ 8.0	+ 44.6	+ 39.8	+ 48.3

ulative investment of ₦520.4 million in 1974, an increase of 12.7% over the level in 1973. In 1973 investment in this sector accounted for 23.2% but in 1974 this was 28.7%. Changes will also be observed with respect to transport and communications; agriculture, fishing and forestry; building and construction; and trading and business services sectors.

Table 9.7 shows the short and long-term components of the "other liabilities" in the last two tables being further disaggregated. Here again, various changes are observed. For example, the "other liabilities" component of investment in 1974 was slightly higher than the level in 1973; there was a further decline in the long-term liabilities component of investment in the mining and quarrying area.

Table 9.8 shows the analysis by type of industry of cumulative investment in the manufacturing and processing sector, and data on the level of investment in fixed assets at cost and book value. Investment in 1974 in the manufacturing and processing sector was ₦287.1 million, a decline of 29.8% from the 1973 level. The decline affected most of the industrial sub-sectors but was more severe in food, beverages, furniture and fixtures, paper and paper products, rubber products and transport equipment industries. "The increase in the value of fixed assets while there was a general decline in investment in the manufacturing and processing sector, suggests that there was some re-valuation of the assets by foreign-owned companies."[27]

Table 9.9 shows a detailed breakdown of investment in fixed assests at cost and book value and the analysis by economic activities of the size of reserves provided for each type of asset. The value of fixed assets owned by foreign-owned businesses in 1974 was ₦2,615 million, an increase of 29.4% over 1973.

Table 9.10 shows the owernship of capital by type of economic activities. There are changes here, too. In the quarrying sector, the proportion of equity owned by foreigners fell to a "record low" of 41.3%. The equity of own-

Cumulative Foreign Private Investment in Nigeria by Country
or Region of Origin
(₦ million)

Country of Origin	Paid-up Capital + Reserves* (1)	Other** Liabilities (2)	Total (1)+(2) (3)	% Distribution of Total (4)	Investment* in Fixed Assets+ (5)	Distribution of Total (6)
United Kingdom						
1969	261.0	136.0	397.0	45.0	476.5	56.2
1970	272.6	171.8	444.4	44.0	234.2	32.1
1971	312.6	279.4	592.0	44.8	239.1	30.6
1972	352.9	416.8	769.7	49.0	553.0	40.1
1973	414.8	446.1	860.9	48.8	581.8	44.2
1974	405.2	427.6	832.8	45.9	671.7	39.8
United States						
1969	19.0	184.6	203.6	23.1	168.2	19.9
1970	26.2	203.8	230.0	22.9	289.4	39.6
1971	40.6	296.8	337.4	25.5	341.4	43.6
1972	51.6	235.0	286.6	18.2	337.4	24.5
1973	65.2	242.8	308.0	17.5	383.5	29.2
1974	75.9	224.1	300.0	16.6	506.2	30.0
Western Europe (Excluding U.K.)						
1969	89.8	105.4	195.2	22.2	160.4	18.9
1970	103.4	121.4	224.8	22.4	139.1	18.8
1971	117.8	143.2	261.0	19.7	151.1	19.3
1972	136.5	230.5	367.0	23.4	425.8	30.9
1973	161.4	253.8	415.2	23.5	257.7	19.6
1974	175.9	283.9	459.8	25.4	342.7	20.3
Others (Unspecified)						
1969	51.2	34.6	85.8	9.7	42.5	5.0
1970	66.0	38.0	104.0	10.4	69.2	9.5
1971	85.2	47.2	132.4	10.0	50.9	6.5
1972	99.5	48.3	147.8	9.4	61.8	4.5
1973	119.3	60.3	179.6	10.2	91.9	7.0
1974	150.3	69.2	219.5	12.1	166.4	9.9
TOTAL						
1969	421.0	460.6	881.6	100.0	847.6	100.0
1970	468.2	535.0	1,003.2	100.0	729.9	100.0
1971	556.2	766.6	1,322.8	100.0	782.5	100.0
1972	640.5	930.6	1,571.1	100.0	1,378.0	100.0
1973	760.7	1,003.0	1,763.7	100.0	1,314.9	100.0
1974	807.3	1,004.8	1,812.1	100.0	1,687.0	100.0

* Excludes unremitted profit of oil prospecting companies.
** Other liabilities include trade and suppliers credit, other foreign liabilities and liabilities to head office.
(3) This represents the book value of fixed assets at cost less cumulative depreciation.
Source: Central Bank of Nigeria, *Economic and Financial Review*, Vol. 15 (June, 1977), p. 32.

267

TABLE 9.6

Cumulative Foreign Private Investment in Nigeria Analysed by Type of Activity
(₦ million)

Type of Activity	Paid-Up Capital including Reserves 1	Other Liabilities 2	Total (1)+(2) 3	Percentage distribution of Total 4	Investment in Fixed Assets at Book Value	
					Actual 5	% of Total 6
Mining and Quarrying						
1969	155.0	234.6	389.6	44.2	510.4	60.2
1970	173.0	342.4	515.4	51.4	304.8	41.8
1971	125.0	569.0	694.0	52.5	483.2	61.8
1972	171.9	687.8	859.7	54.7	830.1	60.2
1973	248.9	676.4	925.3	52.5	822.5	62.5
1974	130.3	687.8	818.1	45.3	865.7	51.3
Manufacturing & Processing						
1969	119.4	76.6	196.0	22.2	228.8	27.0
1970	132.8	92.0	224.8	22.4	287.5	39.3
1971	277.0	101.8	378.8	28.6	201.8	25.8
1972	241.9	114.7	356.6	22.7	344.9	25.0
1973	275.6	133.4	409.0	23.2	330.1	25.2
1974	376.3	144.1	520.4	28.7	559.7	33.2
Agriculture Forestry & Fishing						
1969	7.2	3.8	11.0	1.3	6.6	0.8
1970	8.0	3.2	11.2	1.1	17.4	2.4
1971	13.0	2.4	15.4	1.2	12.5	1.6
1972	9.1	0.3	9.4	0.6	9.4	0.7
1973	6.4	1.5	7.9	0.4	10.6	0.8
1974	14.8	5.9	20.7	1.1	18.1	1.1

Transport and Communications						
1969	8.4	3.0	11.4	1.3	7.8	0.9
1970	9.2	4.6	13.8	1.4	6.4	0.9
1971	8.2	3.8	12.0	0.9	6.4	0.8
1972	8.8	3.4	12.2	0.8	19.2	1.4
1973	6.3	5.3	11.6	0.6	9.4	0.7
1974	13.9	8.0	21.9	1.2	21.1	1.2
Building and Construction						
1969	8.2	14.0	22.2	2.5	5.8	0.7
1970	9.0	4.8	13.8	1.4	12.3	1.7
1971	8.2	7.2	15.4	1.2	8.7	1.1
1972	21.7	12.6	34.3	2.2	22.1	1.6
1973	28.8	16.2	45.0	2.6	32.4	2.5
1974	44.3	19.9	64.2	3.5	85.6	5.1
Trading and Business Services						
1969	114.2	116.8	231.0	26.2	76.4	9.0
1970	127.0	79.6	206.6	20.6	75.2	10.3
1971	113.6	73.6	187.2	14.1	56.6	7.2
1972	142.4	100.3	242.7	15.4	108.7	7.8
1973	139.5	155.2	294.7	16.7	93.6	7.1
1974	193.0	128.3	321.3	17.7	122.0	7.2
Miscellaneous						
1969	8.6	11.8	20.4	2.3	11.8	1.4
1970	9.2	8.4	17.6	1.7	26.3	3.6
1971	11.2	8.8	20.0	1.5	13.3	1.7
1972	44.7	11.5	56.2	3.6	43.5	3.3
1973	55.2	15.0	70.2	4.0	16.3	1.2
1974	34.7	10.8	45.5	2.5	14.8	0.9
TOTAL						
1969	421.0	460.6	881.6	100.0	847.6	100.0
1970	468.2	535.0	1,003.2	100.0	729.9	100.0
1971	556.2	766.6	1,322.8	100.0	782.5	100.0
1972	640.5	930.6	1,571.1	100.0	1,378.0	100.0
1973	760.7	1,003.0	1,763.7	100.0	1,314.9	100.0
1974	807.3	1,004.8	1,812.1	100.0	1,687.0	100.0

* Excludes unremitted profits of oil prospecting companies.

Source: Central Bank of Nigeria, *Economic and Financial Review*, Vol. 15 (June, 1977), p. 34.

TABLE 9.7

Foreign Liabilities (excluding paid-up capital and reserves) Current and Long-Term by Type of Economic Activity and Country or Region of Origin (₦ '000)

Type of Activity		United Kingdom				United States				
		Current Liability (1)	Long-Term Liability (2)	Total Liability (1 + 2)	Current as % of Total	Current Liability (3)	Long-term Liability (4)	Total Liability (3 + 4)	Current as % of Total	Current Liability (5)
Mining and Quarries	1969	7,000	23,810	30,810	22.7	48,080	99,404	147,484	32.6	7,060
	1970	912	108,696	109,608	0.8	13,650	151,876	165,526	8.2	9,414
	1971	702	193,416	194,118	0.4	9,504	264,982	274,486	3.5	11,998
	1972	846	313,616	314,462	0.3	5,766	204,114	210,880	2.7	9,756
	1973	175	325,048	325,223	0.1	45,129	177,229	222,358	20.3	21,400
	1974	170	293,279	293,449	0.1	30,587	160,985	191,572	16.0	51,915
Manufacturing and Processing	1969	29,174	29,084	58,258	50.1	1,362	1,230	2,592	52.5	2,050
	1970	12,758	6,808	19,566	65.2	6,474	7,172	13,646	47.4	10,600
	1971	25,224	17,208	42,432	59.4	4,184	4,944	9,128	45.8	5,564
	1972	27,080	21,008	48,088	56.3	4,020	4,430	8,450	47.6	5,126
	1973	23,806	16,392	40,198	59.2	2,819	1,032	3,851	73.2	26,725
	1974	28,305	15,500	43,805	64.6	4,431	6,495	10,926	40.6	26,574
Agriculture, Forestry and Fishing	1969	100	2,970	3,070	3.2	—	—	—	—	158
	1970	1,616	290	1,906	84.5	160	—	160	100.0	6
	1971	596	560	1,156	51.6	640	166	806	79.4	—
	1972	22	98	120	18.3	—	—	—	—	—
	1973	1,227	306	1,533	80.0	—	—	—	—	—
	1974	4,960	597	5,557	89.3	—	—	—	—	—
Transportation and Communication	1969	1,338	—	1,338	100.0	402	392	794	50.6	20
	1970	636	—	636	100.0	1,946	—	1,946	100.0	1,056
	1971	1,670	518	2,188	76.3	500	184	684··	73.1	144
	1972	658	—	658	100.0	492	102	594	82.8	392
	1973	1,308	21	1,329	98.4	242	743	985	24.6	647
	1974	5,329	—	5,329	100.0	469	—	469	100.0	577
Building and Construction	1969	2,608	4,184	6,792	38.4	—	1,170	1,170	—	3,628
	1970	—	56	56	—	—	—	—	—	3,320
	1971	678	3,686	4,364	15.5	—	—	—	—	688
	1972	274	1,456	1,730	15.8	588	3,576	4,164	14.1	3,946
	1973	1,417	5,095	6,512	21.8	214	363	577	37.1	4,715
	1974	2,100	5,138	7,238	29.0	—	—	—	—	8,831
Trading and Business Services	1969	28,360	15,842	44,202	64.2	10,598	15,788	26,386	40.2	17,224
	1970	4,898	13,894	18,792	26.1	7,826	—	7,826	100.0	29,316
	1971	21,058	10,950	32,008	65.8	7,124	2,356	9,480	75.1	13,504
	1972	39,154	7,110	46,264	84.6	6,852	1,624	8,476	80.8	32,586
	1973	64,664	4,104	68,768	94.0	6,195	2,158	8,353	74.2	42,430
	1974	44,667	24,790	69,457	64.3	11,336	4,014	15,350	73.9	21,834
Miscellaneous Activities	1969	844	824	1,668	50.7	1,232	3,970	5,202	23.7	476
	1970	266	1,826	2,092	12.7	3,116	1,836	4,952	62.9	—
	1971	606	2,528	3,134	19.3	484	1,732	2,216	21.8	—
	1972	1,308	4,164	5,472	23.9	2,114	334	2,448	86.4	514
	1973	694	1,874	2,568	27.0	377	6,283	6,660	94.2	942
	1974	1,867	875	2,742	68.1	1,200	4,586	5,786	19.4	225
TOTAL	1969	69,442	76,714	146,156	47.5	61,674	121,954	183,628	33.4	30,616
	1970	21,086	131,570	152,656	13.8	33,172	160,884	194,056	17.1	53,712
	1971	50,534	228,866	279,400	18.1	22,436	274,364	296,800	7.6	31,898
	1972	69,342	347,452	416,794	16.6	19,832	215,180	235,012	8.4	52,320
	1973	93,291	352,840	446,131	20.9	54,976	187,808	242,784	20.1	96,859
	1974	87,398	340,179	427,577	20.4	48,023	176,080	224,103	21.4	109,956

Source: Central Bank of Nigeria, *Economic and Financial Review*, Vol. 15 (June 1977), p. 35.

	Western Europe			Others			Total for all Countries			
Long-term Liability (6)	Total Liability (5 + 6)	Current as % of Total	Current Liability (7)	Long-term Liability (8)	Total Liability (7 + 8)	Current as % of Total	Current Liability (9)(10)	Long-term Liability (9 + 10)	Total Liability Total	Current as % of
49,112	56,172	12.6	—	—	—	—	62,140	172,326	234,466	26.5
57,918	67,332	13,9	—	—	—	—	23,976	318,490	342,466	7.0
88,492	100,490	11.9	—	—	—	—	22,204	546,890	569,094	3.9
152,694	162,450	6.0	—	—	—	—	16,368	671,424	687,792	2.4
106,724	128,124	16.7	13	671	684	1.9	66,717	609,672	676,389	9.9
150,212	202,127	25.7	83	631	714	11.6	82,755	605,107	687,862	12.0
2,884	4,934	41.5	4,520	6,392	10,912	41.5	37,106	39,590	76,696	48.4
14,226	24,826	42.7	19,606	14,410	34,016	57.6	49,438	42,616	92,054	53.7
15,614	21,178	26.3	17,708	11,364	29,072	60.9	52,680	49,130	101,810	51.7
11,860	16,986	30.2	21,424	19,748	41,172	52.0	57,650	57,046	114,696	50.3
22,605	49,330	54.2	21,906	18,166	40,074	54.7	75,256	58,197	133,453	56.4
7,162	33,736	78.8	43,002	12,684	55,686	77.2	102,312	41,841	144,153	71.0
—	158	100.0	538	—	538	100.0	796	2,970	3,766	21.1
22	28	21.4	1,160	—	1,160	100.0	2,942	312	3,254	90.4
—	—	—	304	—	304	100.0	1,540	726	2,260	68.0
—	—	—	66	104	170	38.8	88	202	290	30.3
—	—	—	—	—	—	—	1,227	306	1,533	80.3
—	—	—	26	307	333	7.8	4,986	904	5,890	84.7
586	606	3.3	246	—	246	100.0	2,006	578	2,584	67.2
916	1,972	53.5	—	—	—	—	3,638	916	4,554	79.9
752	896	16.1	—	—	—	—	2,314	1,454	3,768	61.4
546	934	41.8	258	922	1,180	21.9	1,800	1,570	3,370	53.4
2,334	2,981	21,7	—	—	—	—	2,197	3,098	5,285	41.5
1,646	2,223	26.0	—	—	—	—	6,375	1,646	8,021	79.5
2,390	6,018	60.3	—	—	—	—	6,236	7,744	13,980	44.6
1,318	4,638	28.4	14	212	226	12.4	3,334	1,586	4,920	67.8
72	760	90.5	48	2,046	2,094	2.3	1,414	5,804	7,218	19.6
618	4,564	86.4	1,426	738	2,164	65.9	6,234	6,388	12,622	49.4
4,288	9,003	52.4	23	42	65	35.4	6,367	9,788	16,157	39.4
2,040	10,871	81.2	604	1,175	1,779	34.0	11,535	8,353	19,888	58.0
13,810	31,034	55.5	14,538	700	15,238	95.4	70,738	46,140	116,878	60.5
12,720	42,036	69.6	9,302	1,574	10,876	85.5	51,342	28,188	79,530	64.6
6,022	19,526	69.2	12,318	358	12,676	97.2	54,004	19,686	73,690	73.3
10,162	42,748	76.2	2,526	264	2,790	90.5	81,118	19,160	100,278	80.9
16,850	59,280	71.6	15,270	3,511	18,781	81.3	128,559	26,623	155,182	82.8
11,821	33,655	64.9	4,222	5,452	9,674	43.6	82,059	46,077	128,136	64.0
194	670	71.0	3,208	1,124	4,332	74.1	5,760	6,112	11,872	48.5
70	70	—		1,014	1,014	—	3,382	4,746	8,128	41.6
350	350	—	546	2,508	3,054	17.9	1,636	7,118	8,754	18.7
2,308	2,822	18.2	800	-	800	100.0	4,736	6,806	11,542	41.0
4,124	5,066	18.6	397	317	714	55.6	2,410	12,598	15,008	16.1
1,039	1,264	17.8	486	479	965	50.4	3,778	6,979	10,757	35.1
68,976	99,592	31.1	23,050	8,216	61,266	75.1	184,782	275,860	460,642	40.1
87,090	140,902	17.1	30,082	17,210	47,292	46.1	138,052	396,854	534,906	25.8
111,302	143,200	22.3	30,924	16,276	47,200	65.6	135,792	630,808	766,600	17.7
178,188	230,508	22.7	26,500	21,776	48,276	54.9	167,994	762,596	930,590	18.1
156,925	253,784	38.2	37,609	22,709	60,318	62.4	282,735	720,282	1,003,017	28.2
173,920	283,876	38.7	48,423	20,728	69,151	70.0	293,800	710,907	1,004,707	29.2

TABLE 9.8

Foreign Private Investment (Cumulative) in the Manufacturing Sector Analysed by Type of Industry

(₦ thousand)

Type of Activity	1969 Paid-up Capital (1)	1969 Other Liabilities (2)	1969 Total (1)+(2)	1970 Paid-up Capital (3)	1970 Other Liabilities (4)	1970 Total (3)+(4)	1971 Paid-up Capital (5)	1971 Other Liabilities (6)	1971 Total (5)+(6)	1972 Paid-up Capital (7)	1972 Other Liabilities (8)	1972 Total (7)+(8)
Food	14,640	9,902	22,542	12,930	6,352	19,282	36,432	7,242	43,674	32,502	10,969	43,198
Beverages	9,194	7,726	16,920	10,382	9,098	19,480	17,246	12,220	29,466	11,718	13,218	24,936
Tobacco	17,364	5,898	23,262	20,348	8,302	28,650	31,206	8,118	39,324	11,334	2,684	14,018
Textiles	16,486	8,766	25,252	20,912	19,035	39,948	50,326	13,746	64,072	49,198	17,900	67,098
Footwear & Wearing Apparels, etc.	1,066	678	1,744	1,030	960	1,990	1,840	692	2,532	3,908	1,238	5,146
Wood and Cork	336	178	514	234	138	372	1,098	116	1,214	1,146	440	1,586
Furniture and Fixtures	1,468	818	2,286	1,638	1,304	2,942	6,404	1,916	8,320	12,058	1,444	13,502
Paper and Paper Products	2,408	1,430	3,838	5,768	5,354	11,122	12,120	5,130	17,250	6,796	3,746	10,542
Printing and Publishing	2,032	1,428	3,460	948	678	1,626	782	8	790	3,928	1,838	5,766
Leather and Leather Products	242	144	386	990	608	1,598	1,442	614	2,056	1,920	582	2,502
Rubber Products	3,932	2,798	6,730	2,688	1,388	4,076	9,988	3,450	13,438	11,058	5,084	16,142
Chemicals	12,866	11,436	24,302	9,114	8,896	18,010	20,246	7,472	27,718	20,098	8,214	28,312
Products of Petroleum & Coal	12,876	5,118	17,994	12,278	5,952	18,230	14,080	6,210	20,290	6,185	3,910	10,428
Non-Metalic Mineral Products	10,250	10,742	20,992	13,990	6,404	20,394	41,108	3,378	44,486	27,496	7,386	34,882
Basic Metal (Iron & Steel)	1,968	1,434	3,402	1,724	1,956	3,680	8,552	6,308	14,860	6,606	1,526	8,132
Metal Products	6,490	6,360	12,850	4,886	4,270	9,156	7,018	3,356	10,374	10,718	3,944	14,662
Machinery (Except Electrical)	118	194	312	342	574	916	1,708	3,710	5,418	802	564	1,366
Electrical Machinery	1,124	622	1,746	806	714	1,520	1,330	1,000	2,330	98	1,200	1,298
Transport Equipment	3,122	2,620	5,742	4,920	4,132	9,052	4,254	7,360	11,614	17,988	17,792	35,780
Miscellaneous	1,364	404	1,768	6,906	5,938	12,844	9,892	9,764	19,656	5,988	11,290	17,278
Total	119,346	76,696	196,042	132,834	92,054	224,888	277,072	101,810	378,882	241,878	114,696	356,574

TABLE 9.8 (continued)

Foreign Private Investment (Cumulative) in the Manufacturing Sector Analysed by Type of Industry

(₦ thousand)

Type of Activity	1973 Paid-up Capital (9)	1973 Other Liabilities (10)	1973 Total (9)+(10)	1974 Paid-up Capital (11)	1974 Other Liabilities (12)	1974 Total (11)+(12)	Fixed Assets 1969 (13)	Fixed Assets 1970 (14)	Fixed Assets 1971 (15)	Fixed Assets 1972 (16)	Fixed Assets 1973 (17)	Fixed Assets 1974 (18)
Food	36,970	11,520	48,490	13,758	11,398	25,156	32,568	39,054	33,706	55,630	43,343	64,528
Beverages	19,340	13,478	32,818	7,432	10,963	18,395	25,098	32,072	18,522	28,610	37,448	54,539
Tobacco	22,581	4,033	26,614	19,390	7,552	26,942	15,423	14,980	9,538	4,600	15,302	63,368
Textiles	51,773	16,731	68,504	28,509	29,790	58,299	42,403	54,572	46,742	72,764	70,532	130,900
Footwear & Wearing Apparels, etc.	4,066	2,989	7,055	7,529	6,135	13,664	2,850	4,874	2,728	4,818	9,364	22,993
Wood and Cork	1,483	543	2,026	367	209	576	336	338	240	1,234	311	5,104
Furniture and Fixtures	13,055	1,660	14,715	3,889	2,073	5,962	1,790	3,604	3,876	8,962	8,753	15,863
Paper and Paper Products	11,586	4,854	16,440	1,236	605	1,841	4,770	17,708	13,558	19,718	20,501	6,613
Printing and Publishing	4,803	1,960	6,763	3,582	750	4,332	5,009	2,178	44	5,318	1,019	2,060
Leather and Leather Products	2,129	538	2,667	2,688	1,419	4,107	331	950	564	1,590	2,070	5,618
Rubber Products	12,087	7,997	20,084	3,129	4,673	7,802	10,615	8,092	4,402	17,500	10,519	21,173
Chemicals	25,252	10,832	36,084	13,804	20,522	34,326	16,509	18,902	8,868	9,796	35,811	52,101
Products of Petroleum & Coal	7,412	6,767	14,179	2,265	3,110	5,375	21,682	17,694	7,902	7,426	5,896	7,451
Non-Metalic Mineral Products	30,279	8,485	38,764	11,673	11,441	23,114	29,198	38,436	33,414	66,998	37,892	55,009
Basic Metal (Iron & Steel)	8,067	4,977	13,044	4,224	9,725	13,949	4,071	2,528	4,530	5,082	4,486	5,272
Metal Products	6,008	4,621	10,629	2,409	9,307	11,716	7,662	8,814	1,886	3,688	7,720	721
Machinery (Except Electrical)	1,052	3,184	4,236	4,556	7,482	12,038	205	302	502	376	4,699	7,524
Electrical Machinery	1,600	1,293	2,893	552	421	973	1,111	1,008	1,024	1,060	234	73
Transport Equipment	8,717	13,944	22,661	3,274	2,195	5,469	6,612	6,098	1,188	10,704	685	14,118
Miscellaneous	7,337	13,048	20,385	8,706	4,383	13,089	605	9,228	8,602	19,066	13,462	24,669
Total	275,597	133,454	409,051	142,153	144,153	287,125	228,848	281,512	201,836	344,940	330,097	559,697

This represents the book value of fixed assets, i.e., fixed assets value at cost less cumulative depreciation. Fixed assets are not disaggregated into foreign and Nigerian components while paid-up capital and other liabilities are exclusively foreign.

Source: Central Bank of Nigeria, *Economic and Financial Review,* Vol. 15 (June, 1977), p. 37.

274

TABLE 9.9

Reserves for Depreciation
(N thousand)

Type of Activity	Fixed Assets (At Cost) (1)					Cumulative Reserves for Depreciation (2)				
	R/E	M/E	F/F	M/V	Total	R/E	M/E	F/F	M/V	Total
Mining and Quarrying										
1969	429,006	164,928	1,624	3,514	599,072	52,414	33,552	646	1,968	88,580
1970	97,548	413,390	2,868	14,524	528,330	11,460	199,942	1,982	10,140	233,524
1971	111,106	433,134	3,970	14,826	563,036	18,234	53,070	1,250	7,290	79,844
1972	245,578	755,354	6,294	18,714	1,025,940	10,134	175,772	1,606	8,294	195,806
1973	510,703	637,244	24,666	61,498	1,234,111	167,140	220,578	4,309	19,617	411,644
1974	537,445	739,516	15,946	23,704	1,316,611	168,391	249,123	12,992	20,422	478,081
Manufacturing and Processing										
1969	107,694	165,880	12,502	9,264	295,340	18,916	37,224	4,860	5,492	66,492
1970	147,318	236,686	10,172	11,388	405,564	24,932	84,230	3,526	5,364	118,052
1971	111,898	154,380	14,428	10,580	291,286	16,980	61,256	4,282	6,932	89,450
1972	191,352	290,722	14,894	17,748	514,716	29,544	113,000	11,396	15,836	169,776
1973	163,214	276,651	40,759	22,044	502,668	33,953	110,879	14,866	12,873	172,571
1974	266,421	476,250	43,123	29,620	815,414	62,655	166,703	11,853	14,506	255,717
Agric. Forestry & Fishing										
1969	5,228	5,538	2,576	2,078	15,420	3,482	1,350	2,306	1,722	8,860
1970	13,050	6,506	7,948	1,838	29,342	7,686	3,204	140	974	1,200
1971	11,534	2,556	5,236	1,450	20,776	5,822	2,113	94	1,015	8,244
1972	8,116	6,830	1,568	4,642	21,156	3,768	3,202	230	4,518	11,718
1973	843	5,876	3,082	1,579	11,380	60	308	335	60	763
1974	23,204	21,768	280	1,339	46,591	14,607	12,773	158	916	28,454
Transport and Communications										
1969	6,370	4,918	708	188	12,184	1,228	2,486	402	124	4,240
1970	4,382	4,726	704	654	10466	472	2,824	464	280	4,040
1971	5,234	4,964	882	1,194	12,274	778	3,510	522	1,050	5,860

Year										
1972	13,048	12,754	1,762	4,570	32,134	1,118	8,248	1,308	2,280	12,954
1973	5,172	6,162	1,815	4,066	17,215	1,590	3,330	651	2,284	7,855
1974	14,432	15,069	1,525	10,343	41,369	11,895	4,902	384	3,130	20,311

Building & Construction

Year										
1969	3,848	10,742	774	3,188	18,552	1,888	7,774	562	2,700	12,924
1970	5,972	18,370	1,176	5,702	31,220	2,558	11,182	792	4,360	18,892
1971	4,760	9,750	702	3,074	18,286	1,050	5,130	542	2,684	9,586
1972	10,418	25,188	3,058	7,020	45,684	3,120	13,508	2,470	4,510	23,608
1973	10,123	32,145	2,449	14,119	58,836	4,063	18,133	1,355	2,864	26,415
1974	32,189	64,554	3,531	24,647	124,921	2,307	24,692	2,057	10,286	39,342

Trade and Business Services

Year										
1969	83,884	37,800	13,956	12,282	147,922	30,638	28,084	7,896	4,934	71,552
1970	83,712	43,822	17,132	12,162	156,828	31,836	37,246	5,704	6,636	81,622
1971	61,416	29,498	10,894	9,730	111,538	22,316	20,064	3,298	9,294	54,972
1972	99,808	67,086	19,932	13,718	200,544	31,150	41,462	7,504	11,712	91,828
1973	96,143	24,309	24,519	18,593	164,564	39,855	13,448	8,632	8,985	70,920
1974	117,226	80,699	28,153	12,929	239,007	67,385	34,519	6,456	8,616	116,976

Miscellaneous Activities

Year										
1969	6,700	11,616	1,634	1,564	21,514	1,472	6,416	1,292	496	9,676
1970	18,184	17,198	1,272	1,200	37,854	3,512	10,152	726	720	11,524
1971	9,492	8,122	794	1,034	19,442	1,968	4,034	-37	211	6,176
1972	34,056	19,558	6,076	6,662	66,352	5,002	12,126	3,705	2,024	22,856
1973	8,081	8,352	10,920	4,904	32,257	4,149	3,961	7,081	739	15,930
1974	15,325	10,765	3,278	1,761	31,129	5,026	7,990	2,429	906	16,351

Total

Year										
1969	642,730	401,422	33,774	32,078	1,110,004	110,038	116,886	17,964	17,436	262,324
1970	370,166	740,698	41,272	47,468	1,199,604	82,456	348,980	13,334	18,476	469,658
1971	315,440	642,404	36,906	41,888	1,036,638	66,348	149,357	9,951	34,888	244,132
1972	602,376	1,177,492	53,584	73,074	1,906,526	83,836	367,318	28,218	49,174	528,546
1973	794,279	991,739	108,210	126,803	2,021,031	250,810	370,637	37,229	47,422	706,098
1974	1,006,242	1,408,621	95,836	104,343	2,615,042	332,266	527,855	36,329	58,782	955,232

Note: Data on fixed assets have not been disaggregated into foreign and Nigerian components.

R/E = Freehold and leasehold real estates; M/E = Machinery and equipment; F/F = Furniture and Fixtures; M/V = Motor Vehicles.

TABLE 9.9 (continued)
Reserves for Depreciation
(₦ thousand)

Book Value of Assets (fixed Assets at Cost Less Cumulative Depreciation) (3)					Reserves for Depreciation During Reporting Period (4)					Percentage of Current Reserves to Fixed Assets at Cost (5)				
R/E	M/E	F/F	M/V	Total	R/E	M/E	F/F	M/V	Total	R/E	M/E	F/F	M/V	Total
376,592	131,376	978	1,546	510,492	13,050	15,054	168	940	29,212	3.0	9.1	10.3	26.3	4.9
86,088	213,448	886	4,384	304,806	1,314	27,986	1,144	1,436	31,880	1.3	6.8	39.9	9.9	16.0
92,872	380,064	2,720	7,536	483,192	4,042	19,500	366	4,958	28,866	3.6	4.5	9.2	33.4	5.1
235,444	579,582	4,688	10,420	830,134	872	58,046	316	7,510	66,744	0.4	7.7	5.0	10.1	6.5
343,563	416,666	20,357	41,881	822,467	46,209	77,677	1,048	2,825	127,759	9.0	12.2	4.2	4.6	10.4
359,054	490,393	2,954	3,282	865,683	42,749	73,674	657	1,941	19,021	8.0	10.0	4.1	8.2	9.0
88,778	128,656	7,642	3,772	228,848	3,690	12,100	1,256	1,238	18,254	3.4	7.3	10.1	13.4	6.2
122,386	152,456	6,646	6,024	281,512	3,792	17,204	1,990	1,806	24,792	2.6	7.3	19.6	15.9	5.1
94,918	93,124	10,146	3,648	201,836	2,788	11,782	812	1,652	17,034	2.5	7.6	5.6	15.6	5.9
161,808	177,722	3,498	1,912	344,940	5,234	20,194	2,408	5,196	33,032	2.7	6.9	16.2	29.3	6.4
129,261	165,772	25,893	9,111	330,097	6,909	21,035	4,764	4,572	37,280	4.2	7.6	11.7	20.7	7.4
203,766	309,547	31,270	15,114	559,697	10,872	29,033	2,394	4,642	46,941	4.0	6.1	5.6	15.7	5.8
1,746	4,188	270	356	6,560	172	64	94	74	404	3.3	1.2	3.6	3.6	2.6
5,364	3,302	7,808	864	17,338	518	818	20	106	1,662	4.0	12.6	0.3	16.6	5.7
6,512	443	5,142	435	12,532	206	260	12	72	550	1.8	10.2	0.2	5.0	2.6
4,348	3,628	1,338	124	9,438	112	246	72	358	788	1.4	3.6	4.6	7.7	3.7
783	5,568	2,747	1,519	10,617	25	462	92	19	598	3.0	7.1	3.0	1.2	5.3
8,597	8,995	122	423	18,137	1,399	576	31	133	2,139	6.0	2.6	11.1	9.9	4.6

6.0	12.8	3.1	10.1	3.0	732	24	22	498	188	7,944	64	306	2,432	5,142
5.8	15.0	7.9	8.1	1.6	608	98	56	382	72	6,426	374	240	1,902	3,910
6.2	18.4	10.2	7.1	1.8	758	220	90	354	94	6,414	144	360	1,454	4,456
6.1	7.6	29.2	7.8	0.7	1,946	350	514	992	90	19,180	2,290	454	4,506	11,930
8.1	11.7	13.0	8.1	3.7	1,401	476	237	497	191	9,360	1,782	1,164	2,832	3,582
7.8	9.0	10.8	5.8	8.6	3,216	926	164	881	1,245	21,058	7,213	1,141	10,167	2,537
8.6	13.0	13.4	8.2	5.1	1,594	416	104	878	196	5,628	488	212	2,968	1,960
7.9	11.7	8.8	8.0	3.7	2,470	668	104	1,474	224	12,328	1,342	384	7,188	3,414
8.4	20.1	10.5	7.5	2.4	1,536	618	74	730	114	8,700	390	160	4,440	3,710
8.8	12.3	11.2	9.1	5.0	4,026	866	344	2,298	518	22,076	2,510	588	11,680	7,298
9.7	10.9	10.7	10.7	5.0	5,750	1,540	263	3,445	502	32,421	11,255	1,094	14,012	6,060
8.0	11.3	10.7	9.5	2.3	9,978	2,781	378	6,117	702	85,579	14,361	1,474	39,862	29,882
4.0	6.0	5.3	4.5	3.3	5,922	740	734	1,700	2,748	76,370	7,348	6,060	9,716	53,246
5.3	11.8	4.2	8.1	3.2	8,372	1,436	718	3,534	2,684	75,206	5,526	11,428	6,376	51,876
5.9	23.4	4.6	7.5	2.7	6,636	2,272	502	2,202	1,660	56,566	436	7,596	9,434	39,100
5.9	24.9	6.1	6.4	3.0	11,930	3,424	1,218	4,302	2,986	108,716	2,006	12,428	25,624	68,658
10.4	22.7	15.2	20.8	4.0	17,062	4,227	3,728	5,269	3,838	93,644	9,608	15,887	11,861	56,288
7.4	24.0	4.8	7.1	6.3	17,589	3,103	1,364	5,700	7,422	122,031	4,313	21,697	46,180	49,841
6.1	8.4	4.5	8.1	2.3	1,302	132	74	942	154	11,838	1,068	342	5,200	5,228
5.9	13.9	2.4	7.7	2.5	2,254	168	300	1,330	456	15,206	480	-504	7,046	14,672
7.0	15.5	39.5	8.5	2.1	1,368	160	314	692	202	13,266	823	831	4,088	7,524
5.4	9.6	7.7	10.2	1.6	3,622	640	466	1,986	530	43,496	4,638	2,372	7,432	29,054
9.8	10.4	4.3	14.4	11.9	3,150	512	471	1,202	965	16,327	4,165	3,839	4,391	3,932
9.0	35.8	16.7	10.1	3.4	2,789	631	547	1,089	522	14,778	855	849	2,775	10,299
5.2	11.2	7.2	7.8	3.1	57,420	3,564	2,452	31,236	20,168	847,680	14,642	15,810	284,536	532,692
6.0	12.5	10.5	7.1	2.4	72,038	5,918	4,332	52,728	9,060	729,946	22,580	27,938	391,718	287,710
5.5	23.8	5.9	5.5	2.9	56,748	9,952	2,170	35,520	9,106	782,506	13,412	26,955	493,047	249,092
6.4	10.8	10.0	7.5	1.7	122,088	18,344	5,338	88,064	10,342	377,980	23,900	75,366	810,184	518,540
9.5	11.2	9.8	11.0	7.4	193,000	14,171	10,603	109,587	58,639	1,314,933	79,381	70,981	621,102	543,469
7.7	13.6	5.8	8.3	6.5	201,673	14,157	5,535	117,070	64,911	1,686,963	45,561	59,507	907,919	673,976

TABLE 9.10

Components of Capital Analysed by Type of Economic Activities
(N thousand)

Type of Economic Activities	Year	Common Stock Held Overseas			Preferred Stock Held Overseas			Capital (1) + (2) Held Overseas			Grand Total Nigerian/Foreign	Foreign Capital as % of Total	Non-Residents as % of Total Overseas
		By Nigerians	Affiliate Parent (1)	Non-Residents	By Nigerians	Affiliate Parent (2)	Non-Residents	By Nigerians	Affiliate Parent	Non-Residents			
Mining and Quarrying	1969	-	101,110	1,900	-	-	-	-	101,118	1,900	103,018	100.0	1.8
	1970	-	108,444	172	-	-	-	-	108,444	172	108,616	100.0	0.2
	1971	-	107,040	-	-	800	-	-	107,840	-	107,840	100.0	-
	1972	1,934	109,892	-	-	834	-	1,934	110,726	-	112,660	98.3	-
	1973	43,979	80,755	98	-	920	-	43,979	81,675	98	125,752	65.0	0.1
	1974	77,819	53,619	382	-	761	-	77,819	54,378	382	132,579	41.3	0.3
Manufacturing and Processing	1969	42,204	49,452	21,140	10,382	1,902	4,096	52,586	51,354	25,236	129,176	59.3	32.9
	1970	43,734	52,020	12,956	6,208	1,302	638	49,942	53,322	13,594	116,858	57.3	20.3
	1971	43,334	73,092	16,542	4,376	818	862	47,710	73,910	17,404	139,024	65.7	19.1
	1972	68,498	78,908	17,742	5,874	956	888	74,372	79,864	18,630	172,866	57.0	18.9
	1973	69,856	81,099	19,676	2,474	463	96	72,330	81,562	19,772	173,664	58.4	19.5
	1974	84,920	115,982	17,268	9,460	1,450	1,186	94,380	117,432	18,449	250,261	59.0	8.0
Agriculture Forestry and Fishing	1969	1,324	4,358	28	-	-	-	1,324	4,358	28	5,710	76.8	0.6
	1970	2,514	4,070	166	898	168	198	3,412	4,238	364	8,014	57.4	7.9
	1971	1,320	6,552	-	196	172	-	1,516	6,724	-	8,240	81.6	-
	1972	1,168	6,732	-	270	178	-	1,438	6,910	-	8,348	82.8	-
	1973	1,841	7,031	1,210	-	-	-	1,841	7,310	1,210	10,082	81.7	14.7
	1974	5,514	4,303	2,136	-	-	-	5,514	4,303	2,136	11,953	53.9	17.9
Transport and Communication	1969	2,110	1,782	70	72	-	-	2,182	1,782	70	4,034	45.9	3.8
	1970	1,360	1,372	-	-	-	-	1,360	1,372	-	2,732	50.2	-
	1971	1,518	2,646	266	232	-	844	1,750	2,646	1,110	5,506	68.2	29.6

Category	Year	(1)	(2)	(3)	(4)	(5)	(6)	(7)	(8)	(9)	(10)	(11)	(12)
	1972	1,486	2,766	290	-	-	1,006	1,486	2,766	1,296	5,548	73.2	31.9
	1973	1,929	2,403	270	-	-	-	1,929	2,403	270	4,602	58.1	10.1
	1974	6,458	4,621	832	-	-	-	6,458	4,621	832	11,911	45.8	7.0
Building and Construction	1969	294	3,106	1,454	-	96	-	294	3,202	1,454	4,950	94.1	31.2
	1970	356	3,586	1,732	-	100	-	356	2,668	1,732	4,756	92.5	39.4
	1971	218	3,868	850	-	100	-	218	3,968	850	5,036	95.7	17.6
	1972	506	4,230	1,098	-	-	-	506	4,230	1,098	5,834	91.3	20.6
	1973	3,792	6,161	1,643	-	689	713	3,792	6,850	2,356	12,998	70.8	25.6
	1974	5,645	8,669	1,060	-	-	-	5,645	8,869	1,060	15,374	63.3	7.0
Trading and Business Service	1969	2,220	45,512	6,330	84	2,954	12	2,304	48,466	6,342	57,112	96.0	11.6
	1970	3,782	66,706	2,366	480	578	26	4,262	67,284	2,392	73,938	94.2	3.4
	1971	5,868	61,824	2,180	354	1,698	72	6,222	63,522	2,252	71,996	91.4	3.4
	1972	6,410	64,982	3,248	238	1,784	118	6,648	66,766	3,366	76,780	91.3	4.8
	1973	14,411	82,124	6,359	580	925	2,389	14,991	83,049	8,748	106,788	86.0	9.5
	1974	28,664	69,783	6,797	380	998	453	29,044	70,781	7,250	107,075	72.9	7.8
Miscellaneous Activities	1969	456	3,912	688	-	28	-	456	3,940	688	5,084	91.0	14.9
	1970	776	3,400	532	-	222	-	776	3,622	532	4,930	84.3	12.8
	1971	10	4,506	516	-	2,684	-	10	7,190	516	7,716	99.9	6.7
	1972	12,284	5,232	542	-	2,832	-	12,284	8,064	542	20,890	41.2	6.3
	1973	17,514	15,041	30,067	-	307	-	17,514	15,348	30,087	62,949	72.2	66.2
	1974	715	6,078	1,683	1,026	3,041	-	1,741	9,119	1,683	12,543	86.1	13.4
Total	1969	48,608	209,240	31,610	10,538	4,980	4,108	59,146	214,220	35,718	309,084	80.9	14.3
	1970	52,522	238,580	17,924	7,586	2,370	862	60,108	240,950	18,786	319,844	81.2	7.2
	1971	52,268	259,528	20,354	5,158	6,272	1,778	57,426	265,800	22,132	345,358	83.4	7.7
	1972	92,286	272,742	22,920	6,382	6,584	2,012	98,688	279,326	24,432	402,926	75.5	8.2
	1973	153,322	274,614	59,343	3,054	3,304	3,198	156,376	277,918	62,541	496,835	68.5	18.4
	1974	209,735	263,053	30,158	10,866	6,250	1,634	220,601	269,303	31,792	521,696	57.7	6.1

(1) This represents paid-up capital excluding reserves in all foreign owned (wholly and jointly) companies in Nigeria. Figure negligible.

(2) The 1974 figures revised to exclude debentures which are loan capital and reserves.

Source: Central Bank of Nigeria, *Economic and Financial Review*, Vol. 15 (June, 1977), p. 40.

ership by foreigners in the transport and communication sector fell from 58.1% in 1973 to 45.8% in 1974; in the building and construction sector it fell from 70.8% in 1973 to 63.3% in 1974; in the trading and business services sector, it fell from 86% in 1973 to 72.9% in 1974. In conclusion the report noted:

> As expected equity participation in foreign-owned companies by Nigerians increased in 1974. This was in line with the objectives of the Nigerian Enterprises Promotion Decree which came into effect on the 1st of April 1974. The level of indigenous participation in some companies in the trading and business services as well as in miscellaneous activities sector, however, appeared to be lower than was expected.[28]

Is this increase in equity real or is it only on paper? In other words, can we sincerely say that foreign nationals have not been using Nigerians to sabotage or circumvent the Decree? The Federal Military Government knew that foreign nationals would use willing and unpatriotic Nigerians to evade the law and that was why the Federal *Gazette* 1972 (Supplement) carried this clause:

> Any person, who:
>   (a) acts as a front or purports for the purpose of defeating or in a manner likely to defeat the object of this Decree, to be the owner of any enterprise; or
>   (b) operates any enterprise for or on behalf of any alien who is under this Decree:
>   (i) not permitted to operate the enterprise or
>   (ii) disqualified from operating the enterprise; or
>   (iii) not permitted to own or be part owner of such enterprise, shall be guilty of an offence under this section, and shall be liable on conviction to a fine of ₦ 7,500 or to imprisonment for a term of 5 years or to both such fine and imprisonment.

> It shall not be lawful of any Nigerian citizen or association to employ whether on full time or part time basis, any alien for the operation of any enterprise previously owned wholly or partly by that alien which the alien has disposed of pursuant to the provisions of this Decree, except with the written prior approval of the Federal Commissioner for Internal Affairs.[29]

In his 1979-80 budget speech, the Head of State, Lt. General Olusegun Obasanjo said that at independence in 1960, the modern sector of the Nigerian economy was almost the exclusive preserve of British companies and operators. In trading and manufacturing activities, firms such as the UAC, John Holt, G.B. Ollivant, Rovintry Bry and Cadbury, Lever Brothers, Nigerian Breweries, Barclays Bank and British Bank of West Africa, among others, were dominant. Companies from other countries came in at independence to dilute British colonial dominance "while at the same time increasing the totality of foreign control of the economy." Of crucial importance is the fact that these companies were often fully-owned subsidiaries of multinational companies with their headquarters in Europe, North America, or Japan "where the policies governing their operations in Nigeria were discussed, determined and handed down." At the same time participation by Nigerians either in the equity capital or the management of these companies was minimal. Thus, the indigenisation policy articulated and adopted during the second National Development Plan, 1970-74 was in reaction to the above situation.

General Obasanjo then claimed that significant progress had been made in transferring equity ownership to Nigerians under Phases I and II of the Indigenisation Programme. Since 1972, the Head of State claimed, about 500 million shares, valued at ₦472 million, had been transferred to Nigerians from foreign shareholders. He further stated that some 1,858 companies had been affected and that their op-

281

erations cover the entire range of economic activities.

Furthermore, the Head of State did not see the indigenisation programme just as a means of transferring shares and earning of dividends. The basis for indigenisation was political. It aimed at "getting Nigerians themselves to determine their own economic fortune by using equity ownership as the springboard into the board room where policies and programmes are discussed and determined, and into management where they are implemented."

The Head of State further stated that some companies with what he called "the right perception" had already begun to implement this aspect of the indigenisation decree "by reflecting in the composition of their boards, the new equity structure which has emerged after indigenisation. They have also embarked on placing Nigerians in chief executive and management positions."

But in the same speech the Head of State acknowledged that there were companies that were slow in implementing that aspect of the decree. He said that the Federal Military Government had already begun to make contacts with their top officers. This was a mild admission that all was not going well with the programme and that he might have exaggerated the success of the indigenisation programme.[30]

There are good reasons to believe that Nigerians have become willing stooges for imperialist exploitation. There is good reason to believe that Nigerians have been used by the expatriate companies to subvert the Decree. The following statement by a former Federal Commissioner for Industries seems to spell out the plight that the government is facing. "Nigerian businessmen should not allow themselves to be used as fronts by foreigners to defeat the aims of the Federal Government's indigenisation decree. The government will be quite firm and every appointment will be examined on its own merit, so that nobody frustrates the government's efforts to make Nigerians have a say in the development of the country's economy."[31]

Furthermore the Director-General of Nigeria Stock Exchange, Mr. H. I. Alile, expressed the fear that foreign companies were making cosmetic changes such as appointing some well-known Nigerian public figures to boards as chairmen and directors while leaving management in the hands of foreign partners. "Nigerians do not chair or direct anything; they are only interested in the money that they receive by being unpatriotic."[32] In June, 1978 the chairman of the Nigerian Enterprises Promotion Board, Malam Ali Al Hakim revealed that 700 alien firms had refused to send their compliance proposals to the board and the Capital Issues Commission.[33] What all these suggest is that all is not going well with the indigenisation programme.

It is, however virtually impossible to find reliable documentation to support categorical statements about such matters. One reason is that the Indigenisation Decree establishes a penalty for any Nigerian who allows himself to be used as a front by any foreign concern. No Nigerian or any foreign businessman is going to agree that he is violating a Nigerian law, because he knows the consequences attending such an act.

Secondly, it would be a herculean task to try to verify whether Nigerians are acting as fronts because Nigerians and their accomplices are extremely clever in what they do. They manipulate their accounts and other records to make it virtually impossible to know what is going on. There have been instances in which the government threatened to take drastic action against certain foreign enterprises which did not comply with the Decree but within a few days Nigerians emerged with millions of naira to buy up the company and then retained all the expatriates as their employees. There also have been instances in which the government wanted to sell shares to private citizens in order to embark on a new industry. Quite often Nigerians have emerged with fantastic sums of money. There was a particular instance in which a state government wanted to build a certain industry and it encouraged citizens to buy shares. Suddenly a person who had never been heard of in the world of finance as a heavy weight came up with ₦1.4 million to buy 30% of the shares. All that he said was that he had worked abroad for a foreign company and accumulated that much money and that the government of that country had been so magnaminous as to allow him to transfer the money to Nigeria.[34]

Finally it has not been possible to document that Nigerians are being used as fronts because the government is very cautious in the matter knowing fully well that these foreign concerns can always invest their money in some other countries where they will not worry about indigenisation.

Cuban Nationalization

Prior to the Cuban Revolution of 1958, the government of that country shouldered the responsibility of protecting the interests of U.S. corporations through tax privileges, favourable tariff controls, cheap labour, and the general political climate. Cuba, as Anderson has referred to it, "served as an off-shore United States corporate plantation and mine, and whorehouse, casino, and luxury hotel for the vacationing rich."[35] The rural proletariat toiled on plantations for the profits of export agrobusinesses, while at the same time being subjected to food shortage themselves. Miners toiled for U.S. nickel, copper, and aluminuim concerns, while they themselves remained technologically backward. Urban factory workers assembled processed products for export to the U.S., while they were too poor to purchase or have any use for them themselves. The unemployed population in the cities and rural slums looked on from their shattered homes as the rich and powerful lavishly squandered their portion of the spoils at luxury resorts. The rich Cubans spent their money on imported goods thus consuming what domestic wealth might be available for investment and imports for the mass needs. "Isolated enclaves of industrial development were matched by a sea of backwardness surrounding them. Unemployment was so extensive that less than two-fifths of the labour force was employed all year. Fully 51 percent held jobs for less than ten weeks! A U.S. supported dictatorship maintained police surveillance. All of the trappings of underdevelopment were present including racism."[36]

After Fidel Castro took over the reigns of power in 1958, he set out to restructure the economy of Cuba. Trying to undo underdevelopment was not easy, and this situation was made worse by the fact that restructuring the Cuban economy was bound to adversely affect U.S. corporations' interest. The U.S. had earlier vowed to crush national reform movements in the Third World as their success would be tantamount to the triumph of communism. The U.S. assembled disgruntled Cubans, trained them militarily, supplied them with military hardware and the result was the now famous Bay of Pigs invasion.[37] Failing this, the U.S. embarked on an economic warfare against Cuba. But thanks to the Soviet Union and other East European countries that came to the aid of Cuba, Cuba nationalised U.S. concerns and embarked on a socialist path of development.

Today, Cuba has made significant advances in the areas of health care, education, employment, housing, nutrition, and recreation. In general:

> The Cuban people have obtained a new lease on life with the Revolution. Daily survival is no longer the pressing concern for the masses it had previously been. Living standards have been continually improved. A level of economic security is afforded everyone and the real promise of a better future is available to all. With today's high level of literacy, and the presence of medical clinics throughout the countryside, the Cuban

birth rate has declined to among the lowest in all of Latin America, significantly below its Caribbean and Central American neighbors. Thus, there are strong indications that there is a gradual alleviation of demographic pressures taking place within Cuba as well.[38]

To further improve their lot the underdeveloped countries have made agreements between importing countries and themselves in an attempt to stabilize the prices of certain primary products — cocoa, olive oil, wheat, tin, sugar and coffee. The primary commodities producing countries would like to see these agreements extended to include many more products but they have been very difficult to administer. In 1969 the U.S. and the European Community nations refused to sign the sugar agreement; they are in fact giving export subsidies to their exporters to dump their expensive beet sugar on the world market.[39]

In an attempt to compensate for their dependence on unstable international markets for products, the underdeveloped nations try to diversify their exports by way of developing processed primary products, such as canned foods and cotton textiles and some other relatively unsophisticated manufactured products. This then goes a long way to bear out Galtung's contention discussed in Chapter Three, namely, that the kind of processed goods that the underdeveloped countries can export to the industrialised countries are "predominantly goods produced in the early period of industrial development."[40] Most of the manufactured goods in the Third World go to industrialised countries. But the fact of the matter is that 80 poor countries put together account for only 5 percent of the world's total exports of manufactured and semi-manufactured goods; and about one-half of this comes from Hong Kong, India, Yugoslavia, Mexico, and Taiwan.[41]

These efforts notwithstanding, the poor countries have great obstacles on their way to development. The rich and powerful countries constitute a formidable impediment, the nemesis to Third World development. But if the Third World must get out of its present condition the rich nations must cooperate.

Controlling the Multinationals

The role of the multinationals in the development of underdevelopment has already been discussed. Not that they are incapable of contributing to development but that their malpractices wipe away any contributions that they can make.[42] The U.N. has been concerned about the role of the multinationals in the development of the underdeveloped countries. In its reports, the Commission on Transnational Corporations stressed the importance of fundamental recommendations "on non-interference in the internal affairs of states and the necessity for adopting strict sanctions against encroachment upon the national sovereignty of legitimate Governments."[43] The following year it was the view of the delegations that

> transnational corporations, because of their enormous economic power, had also been able to wield political power and indeed had on occasion, interfered in the internal affairs of sovereign host countries, and that such actions were a denial of national sovereignty and independence in the host countries and affected negatively the control of developing countries over their natural resources and economic development... the role of transnational corporations in supporting colonialist, racist and *apartheid* policies of certain countries, constituted a threat to peace, security and detente.... that the transnational corporations obstructed the full exercise of trade union rights.[44]

In the March 1976 report, many delegations reportedly "condemned corrupt practices of transnational corporations and called for immediate action to put an end to such practices.[45] The Group of 77 submitted a note in which they spelt out areas of concern regarding the operations and activities of transnational corporations. The list is a long one: (1) the transnational corporations or multinationals demand preferential treatment in relation to national enterprises; (2) the refusal by the multinationals to adjust "to the legislation of the host countries in the matters, *inter alia* of foreign investment and policies concerning credits exchange, fiscal matters, prices and commercial matters, industrial property and labour policies; (3) the non-positive attitude of the multinationals to renegotiate original concessions if such existed and if this should be considered necessary by the government of the host country; (4) their refusal to "accept exclusive jurisdiction of domestic law in cases of litigation"; (5) direct and indirect involvement in the domestic affairs of host countries by the multinationals; (6) requests by multinationals to the country of origin to intercede with the host government, with actions of a political or economic nature in support of the private interests of the multinationals; (7) the refusal of the multinationals to accept exclusive jurisdiction of domestic law in matters of compensation on nationalization; (8) extension by the multinationals of laws and regulations of the country of origin to the host country; (9) the activities of multinationals as "instruments of foreign policy, including for intelligence purposes, contrary to the interests of the country"; (10) the practice of multinationals to contribute "in the maintenance of racist and colonial regimes and support of policies of apartheid and foreign occupation"; (11) the role of multinationals in the illegal traffic of arms; (12) obstruction by multinationals of the efforts of the host country to assume its rightful responsibility and exercise control over the development and management of its resources, in contravention of the accepted principal of permanent sovereignty of countries over their natural resources"; (13) the tendency of multinationals not to comply with national policies, objectives and priorities for development established by the government of host countries; (14) withholding of information of their activities by multinationals, thereby making it difficult for host countries to carry out effective supervision and regulation of those activities; (15) excessive repatriation of financial resources from host countries and "failure to generate expected foreign exchange earnings in the host country"; (16) acquisition and control by multinationals "of national, locally capitalized enterprises through controlled provision of technology among other means"; (17) "superimposition of imported technology without any adaption to local conditions, creating various types of distortions"; (18) failure by multinationals to promote research and development in host countries; (19) obstruction or limitation by multinationals of access by host countries to world technology; (20) "imposition of restrictive business practices, *inter alia,* on affiliates in developing countries as a price for technical know-how"; (21) "lack of respect of the socio-cultural identity of host countries."[46]

Interestingly enough, the delegations of France, the Federal Republic of Germany, Italy, the United Kingdom of Great Britain and Northern Ireland and the United States of America submitted a note on areas of concern which relate to relations between transnational corporations and governments. Not surprising however, their positions were designed to counter each of the points raised by the Group of 77. Their concern centered around "prompt, adequate and effective compensation" in cases of expropriation of properties; "recourse to international arbitration, including that provided by the International Centre for Settlement of Investment Disputes, or other dispute settlement organizations or procedures" in cases of disputes arising out of the activities of multinationals. The implication here is that the NATO allies do not have confidence in the ability of the host countries to judiciously handle cases involving the multinationals.

As a long-term solution, the poor countries will have to completely revamp their economic structures through a programme of complete indigenisation. This would mean taking over the control of their economy from foreigners who have no genuine commitment to national economic development. But as a short-term solution the underdeveloped countries must devise means by which the multinationals can serve at least a minimum of their interests, that is, interests, of the host countries.

There should be an international code of conduct to be observed by multinationals.[47] The first of such a code of conduct should be that multinationals shall subject themselves to the laws and regulations of the host country and, in case of litigation, they would have to be subject to the exclusive jurisdiction of the courts of the country in which they operate. This would negate the claim of these corporations to a status, or to be beneficiaries of a privileged treatment, in the host country. The validation of this claim would mean exempting them from internal juridical order and this in turn would be injurious to the fundamental basis upon which the sovereignty of the state resides, which implies full competence over the territoriality in which the power of the State is exercised. In fact the multinationals should adjust their activities to the legislation of the host country, particularly in matters having to do with foreign investment, credit, exchange and fiscal policies, prices and commerce, industrial property, and labour policies. There should be no private, written or implied, agreement that should allow the courts of the country of origin of the multinational or a third state, or international arbitration body to intervene in case of litigation.

The multinationals should be compelled to stay away from all interference in the domestic affairs of the states where they operate. As we have already demonstrated there is a preponderance of evidence of interference by private multinational agents in political questions of the host country. There is much evidence to the effect that the multinationals have become involved in illegitimate political intervention in the internal affairs of the host countries, which has resulted in grave consequences in the case of developing countries. Multinationals and their agents are known to have exerted pressure in support of or against the governments of the host countries, according to whether or not they receive especially favourable treatment. There should be proscribed, in no uncertain terms, the use on the part of the transnational corporations of practices or procedures that involve an action, pressures, coercion, or any political interference in the domestic affairs of the host country.

The multinationals should be made to abstain from interference in relations between the government of a host country and other States and from troubling those relations. There is evidence to the effect that these corporations have perturbed relations between countries and have provoked confrontations between those states. There are instances in which the multinationals have requested their home government to intercede before the host government with actions of a political and economic nature in support of their private interests. It should be made illegal for the multinationals to exert pressure on governments of the countries of origin for the adoption of restrictive measures that may affect the interests of the host countries.

The most common cause of confrontation between countries of origin and host countries is nationalisation of properties of a foreign enterprise and the enterprise asks for the protection of its government of origin. Quite often the source of the controversy arises from the fact that the multinationals question the validity of the nationalisation itself or demand prompt, adequate and effective indemnity. The amount of the indemnity that should be paid and the manner in which this amount should be determined should be guided by the charter of Economic Rights and Duties of States. Any question arising from compensation should be resolved in conformity with the legislation and the courts of the state that nationalizes, unless that state should choose to bring in any other state or third party.

There should be a law banning the multinationals from serving as agents of the foreign policy of another State or as means of carrying to the host country provisions of the juridical order of the country of origin. There are instances in which exports to certain countries have been affected by the extraterritorial application, by the country of origin, of legislation that prohibits trading with certain states. It is a fact that the movement of capital to enterprises that operate in foreign countries and directives concerning the recovery of financial assets for the purpose of improving the balance of payments of the country of origin have been restricted. There are laws in the countries of origin that have an extraterritorial effect and that affect at least indirectly the capacity of the branches in foreign countries to comply to the policies of the host Government. The multinationals should not allow themselves to be used as instruments of foreign policy and of gathering intelligence.

The multinationals should be made to subject themselves to the exercise by the host country of its permanent sovereignty over all its wealth, natural resources and economic activities. It must be recognized that the natural resources of a country make up the national heritage of that country and of its people. The multinationals should be made to realize that every country has the inalienable right to exercise its sovereignty over its natural resources and, that it has a sacrosanct right to ownership and effective control of those resources. The activities of the multinationals should be carried out in a manner consistent with the priorities and developmental needs of the host country. They should also be made to operate in a manner that will enable the indigenes of the host country to participate meaningfully at all levels, and this includes that of decision making.

The multinationals should be made to operate in such a

way that they are subject to the national policies, objectives and priorities for development of the host country, and should make positive contributions to carrying them out. This enactment should make multinationals adjust their activities to fall in line with economic and social policy established by the government of the host country.

The multinationals should be made to furnish to the government of the host country pertinent information relating to their activities in order to ensure that these activities are in accord with the national policies, objectives and priorities of development of the host country. This will enable the governments of the host countries to be able to have sufficient information at their disposal in order to adequately supervise and regulate the activities of global giants.

The global giants should be made to conduct their operations in a way and manner that "results in a net receipt of financial resources for the host country." What this seeks to achieve is to make the multinationals contribute not only a net initial transfer but a continuing transfer of resources. It is common knowledge that the accounting practices of the corporations fail to reflect the real flow of the investment of the multinationals into the economy and that scarce domestic resources are as a matter of policy used to finance multinationals' activities. An example of this is the over-evaluation of imported capital goods or the overstatement of liabilities owed abroad. Multinationals should be made to generate foreign exchange by means of exportation of part of the goods and services produced or contribute to the savings of foreign exchange through the substitution of imports. They should be made to pay competitive international, market-based prices for financial services and technology, not applying transfer prices unless so authorized by the government of the host country. Also they should learn to respect the regulations of the host country regarding repatriation of capital and remittance of profits.

The multinationals should be made to contribute to the development of the scientific and technological capacity of the host country. In order for this to happen, the subsidiaries of the multinational should have the facilities and their own budget for research and development, promoting the use of the technologies that take into account the factors of production with which each country is endowed. But as it now stands, investigation is carried out in the host country even though the subsidiaries contribute to the research budget.

The multinationals should be made to refrain from "restrictive business practices." These companies limit the activities of their subsidiaries to their "respective domestic markets, through restriction of exports, control of the means of distribution, supply and external finance." Multinationals should engage in commercial practices which involve agreements with competitors for a division of market or of fixing prices which are detrimental to the receiving country.

The Latin American position paper identified twenty-one restrictive practices:

1. Full or partial export restrictions;
2. Compulsory purchase of products, machinery and equipment from either the suppliers or firms indicated by them;
3. Obligation of entering into a remunerated contract of "transfer of technology in order to obtain the possibility of acquiring products, machinery and equipment abroad;
4. Imposition of contractual secrecy in an abusive manner, tending to transform a technology not patented in the requiring country, into an industrial property right;
5. Collection of "royalties" on patents which have entered into the public domain or which have not been patented in the demand country;
6. Compulsory transfer of improvement and invention rights to the grants of technology when the improvements have been made by

the recipient;

7. Imposition of the use of a foreign trade mark for the acquisition or transfer of the technology;

8. The establishment of sales prices, including export prices;

9. Compulsory export through the technology supplier;

10. Total or partial limitation of production during and/or after the effective period of the technology contract;

11. Maintenance of a contractual vehicle, with or without remuneration, even property privileges;

12. Imposition of participation in the capital of the firm requiring the technology;

13. Limitation to the research policies of the firm requiring the technology;

14. Obligation of purchasing labour from the supplier;

15. Prevention of contesting the industrial property rights alleged or secured by the technology supplier;

16. Restrictions to obtaining technology from other suppliers;

17. Practices that make it compulsory for the firm requiring the technology to accept additional remunerated technology either not desired or not needed by it;

18. Practices by the supplier which apply quality control of production standards as a means to impose upon the acquirer of technology unjustified requirements;

19. Practices requiring higher payments for technology on goods produced for export *vis-a-vis* goods for the domestic market;

20. Submission to foreign courts of information or judgements in law-suits regarding the interpretation or fulfilment of contracts;

21. Mandatory provisions to be held beyond the life of the contract.[48]

The multinationals should be compelled to accord respect to the socio-cultural identity of the host country. The multinationals should not seek to transplant to the host country, their own models of social development that are known to significantly differ from the cultural identity and social structure of the host country. Importing culture peculiar to the industrialized nation to the developing ones tends to distort the local social and cultural character. The multinationals should conform to both formal and legal prescriptions as well as to "the political features, uses and customs observed by the host country."[49]

We already said something about the corrupt practices of the multinationals. The U.N. recognizes the corrupt practices of multinationals and had in 1975 passed a resolution condemning them. In its resolution the General Assembly said that the U.N.:

> 1. *Condemns* all corrupt practices including bribery, by transnational and other corporations, their intermediaries and others involved, in violation of the laws and regulation of the host countries;
>
> 2. *Reaffirms* the right of any State to adopt legislation and to investigate and take appropriate legal action, in accordance with its national laws and regulations, against transnational and other corporations, their intermediaries and others involved for such corrupt practices...[50]

It is extremely difficult to monitor corruption since it is not done in the open. But each country should make use of its intelligence apparatus and try to identify the culprits, both domestic and foreign. Implementing all of the above recommendations would be a herculean task but as long as we of the Third World are going to have the multinationals in our midst for many, many years to come, it is necessary that we begin to try to look for ways to control these monsters.

The way out of our present underdevelopment is not dependence on the multinationals and foreign aid, for the multinationals with their present practices will perpetuate our underdevelopment and growth without development and foreign aid will never be enough to meet our needs. Furthermore, the conditions attached to them will never enhance our development. The way out of our present economic dilemma is not Tubman's or Houphouet-Boigny's or Kenyatta's open door policies designed to attract foreign companies and capitals at all costs. Our salvation lies in our taking over the control of our economy from foreigners. This should be gradual by way of indigenisation and greater government direct participation. This will also aid us in increasing our foreign exchange earnings.

Africans, indeed all underdeveloped countries, must come together to form a solidarity group, both political and economic. Africans, for example, should eliminate the existence of separate monetary zones and artificial exchange rates. There are about 32 different African currencies. They should learn to trade among themselves and think in terms of continental economic as opposed to extraterritorial unions which, unfortunately, is the order of the day. They should stop thinking in terms of pro-West, pro-East, pro-North, or pro-South. They should be pro-Africa.

But while Africans try to reorder their economic house they should, along with the rest of the underdeveloped world, insist on a new International Economic Order. They should not be asking the rich nations for handouts or indemnities. They should insist on rectifying situations in which the doubling of production brings no tangible gains. As at present, the U.S. and its NATO allies seem to be saying that the Third World countries are greedy and that they want to gobble them. Despite the balloon of rhetoric about neocolonialism, the rich nations should realise that the power of the great multinational corporations is often too great for comfort especially in small countries that characterise Africa that may depend on a single one of them for nearly all of its wealth. They should recognise that commodity prices have been subject to ludicrous fluctuation to the non-industrial countries, and that international trade and finance in general have worked more often than not in favour of the rich and against the poor of the world. If the rich nations look at the present conflict in this perspective they will appreciate the need for revamping the international economic system.

President Allende of Chile said in his opening address to the UNCTAD delegates in 1972:

> The people of the world will not allow poverty and wealth to exist side by side indefinitely! They will not accept an international world order which will perpetuate their underdevelopment. They will seek and will obtain economic independence, and will overcome underdevelopment. Nothing can prevent it: neither threats, nor corruption, nor force.
>
> It depends upon the urgently necessary transformation of the world's economic structure, upon the conscience of countries, whether the progress and liberation of the vast underdeveloped world will be able to choose the path of cooperation — based on solidarity, justice, and respect for human rights — or whether, on the contrary they will be forced to take the path of conflict, violence and pains, precisely in order to apply the principles of the United Nations Charter.

Will this admonition prompt the rich nations to do something about the poverty of the underdeveloped countries? Time and history will tell.

298

REFERENCES

[1] Celso Furtado, *Obstacles to Development in Latin America* (Garden City, N.Y.: Doubleday and Company, 1970), p. xvi.

[2] *War on Hunger*, p. 3.

[3] Peter Worsley, *The Third World* (Chicago: The University of Chicago Press, 1967), p. 291.

[4] Reginald Green and Ann Seidman, *Unity or Poverty?* (Baltimore: Penguin Books, 1968).

[5] Worsley, *The Third World,* pp. 291-92.

[6] *Ibid.,* p. 292.

[7] Read, for example, speeches made at UNCTAD meetings.

[8] Worsley, *The Third World,* p. 295.

[9] *Ibid.,* pp. 294-95.

[10] C. C. Onyemelukwe, *Economic Underdevelopment: An Inside View* (London: Longmans, 1974), p. 94.

[11] *The New Republic* (July, 1975), p. 13.

[12] *Ibid.,* p. 14.

[13] J. D. B. Miller, *The Politics of the Third World* (New York: Oxford University Press, 1967), p. 124.

[14] Jean-Yves Calvez, *Politics and Society in the Third World,* translated by M. J. O'Connell (Maryknoll, N.Y.: Orbis Books, 1973), p. 319.

[15] *War on Hunger,* Special Fiscal 1976 issue, p. 1.

[16] *Ibid.,* p. 3.

[17] *Ibid.,* p. 2.

[18] *Ibid.* (September, 1976), p. 15.

[19] Leslie L. Rood "Nationalisation and Indigenisation in Africa," *The Journal of Modern African Studies* (1976), p. 428.

[20] *The Sunday Times* (April 16, 1978).

[21] Leslie L. Rood, "Nationalisation and Indigenisation in Africa," p. 429.

[22] *Nigeria: News from Nigerian Consulate-General* (New York) Vol. 4, No 12, 1973.

[23] *Nigeria Handbook,* 1977.

[24] *Economic and Financial Review* XV/1 (June 1977).

[25] *Ibid.,* p. 31.

[26] *Ibid.,* p. 33.

[27] *Ibid.,* p. 36.

[28] *Ibid.,* p. 40.

[29] Federal *Gazette* 1972 (Supplement), p. 116.

[30] The *Nigerian Chronicle* (April 4, 1979).

[31] Quoted by Habibu Sani, "The Invisible Governments," *The Sunday Times* (Lagos) (April 16, 1978).

[32] *Daily Times* (Lagos) (July 24, 1978).

[33] *Ibid.*

[34] *The Sunday Times* (April 22, 1979).

[35] Anderson, *The Sociology of Survival,* p. 263.

[36] Ibid.

[37] For details of this operation and U.S's silent war on Cuba, read Marchetti and Marks, *The CIA and the Cult of Intelligence.*

[38] Anderson, *The Sociology of Survival,* p. 267.

[39] Waterlow, *Superpowers*, p. 102.

[40] Galtung, *The European Community,* p. 71.

[41] Waterlow, *Superpowers,* p. 102.

[42] Olu Akinmoladun, "Dilemma of Oil Exporting Nations," *Daily Times* (July, 1978).

[43] *Commission on Transnational Corporations*, (17-28 March, 1976), p. 7.

[44] *Commission on Transnational Corporations* (1-12 March, 1976), p. 10.

[45] *Ibid.,* p. 15.

[46] *Ibid.,* pp. 21-22.

[47] In the discussion that follows I draw from the paper submitted to the U.N. Commission on Transnational Corporations in 1976 by Argentina, Barbados, Brazil, Columbia, Ecuador, Jamaica, Mexico, Peru, Trinidad and Tobago and Venezuela.

[48] *Commission on Transnational Corporations,* pp. 32, 33.

[49] *Ibid.,* p. 34.

[50] General Assembly Resolution 3514 (XXX) of 15th December, 1975. See also Commission on Transnational Corporations, p. 35.

INDEX

301